STRATEGY FOR ECONOMIC DEVELOPMENT OF BACKWARD REGIONS

STRATEGY FOR ECONOMIC DEVELOPMENT OF BACKWARD REGIONS

ABHIMANYU SINGH

ANMOL PUBLICATIONS PVT. LTD.
NEW DELHI-110 002 (INDIA)

ANMOL PUBLICATIONS PVT. LTD.
4374/4B, Ansari Road, Daryaganj
New Delhi-110 002

Strategy for Economic Development of Backward Regions

First Edition 1997

ISBN 81-7488-579-X

ICSSR Consultant: Dr. K. N. Kabra

[The publication of this book is financially supported by the Indian Council of Social Science Research (ICSSR). Responsibility for the facts stated, opinions expressed and conclusions reached is entirely that of the author. The Council bears no responsibility for them.]

PRINTED IN INDIA

Published by J. L. Kumar for Anmol Publications Pvt. Ltd., New Delhi-110 002 and Printed at Mehra Offset Press, Delhi.

This book is dedicated to the memory of

MY LATE PARENTS

whose moral values, love for excellence and fortitude served as inspiration for me.

Contents

Preface

Development of Backward Regions will be our main concern in future. Thus Bihar's backwardness in spite of its rich potential is paradoxical and naturally baffling. I was directly involved with implementation of different development schemes in the State for over two decades. As a keen student of economic development, this practical experience was invaluable to me. The problems we faced in this daunting task and the analyses of the events and the introspection have resulted in the present exposition. By concentrating on Bihar's experience, it has been possible to achieve sharper focus on issues relating to backwardness.

Several studies have tried to explain the sluggish rate of development by propounding the so-called 'neglect' theory, low per capita investment and Central apathy. If Congress rule was exploitative and corrupt; recent experience with opposition in power, espousing the cause of the poor, has been no different. States similarly placed, Uttar Pradesh and Madhya Pradesh, have shown higher growth rates than Bihar, and Orissa promises to have a bright future.

We have approached the subject of development with much diffidence and ignored disruptive 'factionalism' that has been debilitating the population, and 'corruption' that has negated investments. The non-economic forces are prevailing over economic factors. To put the economy on rails, we have to improve financial and economic discipline. We have to adopt the right development objectives, correctly lay down the priorities, and pursue the development goals honestly and stead-fastly. The political leaders are not serving the people, by distracting attention and confusing the issues, their parochial outlook and inability to look ahead, due to which they are unable to decide the priorities rightly; and their reluctance to accept efficiency criteria to govern investment decisions has resulted in the present fiasco.

The present study analyses in depth the reasons for under-development of the critical sectors contributing to development; and suggests action plan for overcoming the problems holding back development. The nexus between over population, tiny holdings, poor infrastructure support, especially power, low productivity, illiteracy, poverty and unemployment is close and interdependent. More than lack of investible funds, it is our failure to organise and execute development activities efficiently and support rational institutions conducive to development, which has resulted in stagnation. It is due to inability of the people to make the best use of available opportunities and lack of faith and confidence in them to achieve the development goals. Rational decisions based on consideration of 'efficiency' have a catalytic role in development and overcoming irrational forces, because of vested interests, is very difficult. The book prescribes norms and proposes courses of action for leading the economy on the path of development. The views expressed in the book are not to be mistaken in any way as expressing official view of the Government, they are entirely my own views.

Abhimanyu Singh

Acknowledgements

The present book is the result of nearly 30 years of practical experience of administering development programmes in the State of Bihar, one of the most backward regions in the country. During this period I was closely associated with Land Reforms, Public Works, Rural and Urban Development, Tourism, Irrigation and power development programmes. I had the good fortune of interacting with fellow administrators (Messrs Ranchor Prasad, N. Nagmani, Shankar Saran, S.N. Patanker, A.R. Bandhopadhyay and R.N. Dash) and benefiting from their invaluable experience. There were others, too, who took keen interest in my studies and helped me in analysing the issues more clearly. Mr. R.B. Singh of Planning Board; K.N. Tiwari, Ex. Director of Statistics; Dr. S.P. Singh, Ex. Joint Secretary, Ministry of Agriculture, P.N. Ramamurthy of Banking Division, Ministry of Finance; Messrs D.D. Guru, M.P. Pandey and A.N. Sharma of A.N. Sinha Institute of Social Studies, Sri Razi Ahmed of Gandhi Sangrahalaya, Dr. Ugra Mohan Jha of Bhagalpur University, Dr. S.S. Tulsyan of Patna University, Dr. Amrita Rangaswami of Centre for Relief Administration and my wife Dr. Usha Singh, Reader in Economics deserve special mention. Mr. Vincent Davies, I.C.S. (Retd.), Dr Sujay Guha of I.I.T., Delhi, Sarvashri D.P. Yadav, Kapildeo Singh and Rajendra Prasad Singh, Ex-Ministers offered me useful comments on the subject. I received much support from the Regional Office of the International Development Research Center (Canada), New Delhi.

Limitation of space does not permit met to thank all the persons individually for their valuable assistance in completing this book. Members of my staff who helped me in compiling the tables, typing and other miscellaneous work deserve special thanks for their ungrudging support.

The book draws on my doctoral dissertation presented to Patna

University in1993. It also draws on my earlier book, 'Planning for Developing a Backward Economy' 1988. I owe my inspiration to undertake the study of backwardness to my stint at London School of Economics in 1979-80, where the two renowned Development Economists—Professors P.T. Bauer and Hla Myint happened to be my tutors.

I am grateful to the Indian Council of Social Science Research for granting me financial assistance to publish the book under their aegis. The consultant, Prof. K.N. Kabra of I.I.P.A. provided me useful tips and helped me to recast the book and present the propositions coherently.

Abhimanyu Singh

Acknowledgements

The present book is the result of nearly 30 years of practical experience of administering development programmes in the State of Bihar, one of the most backward regions in the country. During this period I was closely associated with Land Reforms, Public Works, Rural and Urban Development, Tourism, Irrigation and power development programmes. I had the good fortune of interacting with fellow administrators (Messrs Ranchor Prasad, N. Nagmani, Shankar Saran, S.N. Patanker, A.R. Bandhopadhyay and R.N. Dash) and benefiting from their invaluable experience. There were others, too, who took keen interest in my studies and helped me in analysing the issues more clearly. Mr. R.B. Singh of Planning Board; K.N. Tiwari, Ex. Director of Statistics; Dr. S.P. Singh, Ex. Joint Secretary, Ministry of Agriculture, P.N. Ramamurthy of Banking Division, Ministry of Finance; Messrs D.D. Guru, M.P. Pandey and A.N. Sharma of A.N. Sinha Institute of Social Studies, Sri Razi Ahmed of Gandhi Sangrahalaya, Dr. Ugra Mohan Jha of Bhagalpur University, Dr. S.S. Tulsyan of Patna University, Dr. Amrita Rangaswami of Centre for Relief Administration and my wife Dr. Usha Singh, Reader in Economics deserve special mention. Mr. Vincent Davies, I.C.S. (Retd.), Dr Sujay Guha of I.I.T., Delhi, Sarvashri D.P. Yadav, Kapildeo Singh and Rajendra Prasad Singh, Ex-Ministers offered me useful comments on the subject. I received much support from the Regional Office of the International Development Research Center (Canada), New Delhi.

Limitation of space does not permit met to thank all the persons individually for their valuable assistance in completing this book. Members of my staff who helped me in compiling the tables, typing and other miscellaneous work deserve special thanks for their ungrudging support.

The book draws on my doctoral dissertation presented to Patna

University in1993. It also draws on my earlier book, 'Planning for Developing a Backward Economy' 1988. I owe my inspiration to undertake the study of backwardness to my stint at London School of Economics in 1979-80, where the two renowned Development Economists—Professors P.T. Bauer and Hla Myint happened to be my tutors.

I am grateful to the Indian Council of Social Science Research for granting me financial assistance to publish the book under their aegis. The consultant, Prof. K.N. Kabra of I.I.P.A. provided me useful tips and helped me to recast the book and present the propositions coherently.

Abhimanyu Singh

1

Backward Regions: Bihar's Slide Down

Backward regions exist in all parts of the Country. Even the developed States of Maharashtra and Punjab have backward pockets. But development in the State exerts a beneficial pull over such backward pockets. Backward regions are those that have lagged behind in development compared to the rest of the country. The rate of growth in such regions is very sluggish, per capita income growth being less than 1% or even negative. They are less responsive to the modernizing influences because of apathy of the people and lack of awareness on their part.

The major urban agglomerations because of their developed infrastructure provide more income earning opportunities and, therefore, are better off. The industrialised areas are centres of production and are similarly better off. Agriculture being the main occupation of the country, the arid and hilly regions in the North and North-East of India lack the potential for development and inhabitants of the place are not naturally well off. But there are fertile agricultural areas also where productivity is low and the potential has been only partially utilised. This includes the area covered by Eastern Uttar Pradesh, Bihar and adjoining areas in West Bengal. The present study attempts to identify the constraints which are holding back progress of such backward regions.

It is not the pressure of population alone that is thwarting development. Kerala with equally high density of population has easily shown high propensity for growth, with remarkable improvement in human welfare. This has been attributed to high percentage of literacy.

Bihar has been at lowest rung of development. It was not always so. We analyse the situation in Bihar as it struggles against poverty, illiteracy and social unrest.

Historical Background

Bihar had a glorious past. In ancient India from 6th century B.C, for over 1000 years upto 6th century A.D, it was the seat of Maurya and later the Gupta Empire. Bihar dominated the entire Sub-continent. It enjoyed peaceful and benign rule under the Palas and Senas upto 12th century A.D. World renowned seats of learning at Nalanda and Vikramshila gained prominence during the period and attracted scholars from distant countries.

With Muslim invation, starting from the beginning of 13th century A.D., North Bihar and South Bihar Gangetic plains passed under the rule of Muslim conquerers. The hills and forests of Chhotanagpur plateau inhabited by tribals were probably never subjugated. The seats of learning were burnt and the numerous Vihars, after which the region was named, ruthlessly destroyed.

The Pathans established a strong base in Bihar and Sher-Shah Suri pushed Bihar into 'fame' for a short period during 16th century A.D.

Bihar was among the first region which were brought under British control. Bihar was a part of the Bengal 'Suba.' Mir Qasim made a brave attempt to thwart the British but was crushed in the battle of Buxar in 1761. Bihar developed only as a hinter-land for the commercial and industrial activities, which centred around Calcutta.

The earliest records which we have of the condition of the people of Bengal and Bihar relates to the period 1807-1816. Dr. Francis Buchanan was directed to enquire into the economic condition of selected districts in Bengal and Bihar by the East India Company, who were alarmed at the deteriorating condition of the people. The districts covered by the Survey included Patna (under Bihar district), Shahabad, Bhagalpur and Purniya. The annual wages ranged from Rs. 16/-to Rs. 22/- but then one could buy 70 seers of paddy for one Rupee. In Bhagalpur, the ploughman received this amount as advance and laboured for their master till this was worked off. The cultivators' rent was half the produce, after deducting the cost of harvesting, and this rent included the ground rent, the cost of irrigation, and free pasture. Spinning and weaving were the great activities, after cultivation, and majority of the women engaged in spinning during their spare-time. The women earned on an average upto Rs. 5.00 from this in Bhagalpur.

Thus the plight of farm labourers was more or less what it is to-day. Over one hundred and fifty years of British rule did not bring about any improvement. Towards the close of the nineteenth century, the Sone Canal was completed and it transformed the area covered by it. The cottage industries were, however, gradually eliminated in face of competition from thread and textile manufacturing in England, which obtained official patronage. The British developed the colonies primarily as market for their manufactured products or as suppliers of raw-materials which could be processed in England and sold as finished goods in the subcontinent at profit. The excellent net-work of railways developed by the British served their interests very well. The British developed huge indigo plantations in North Bihar, but they were liquidated after German invented artificial dye during the First World War.

Bihar and Orissa were carved out of Bengal in 1912, as the province of Bengal was too big and ignored the regional interests of Bihar and Orissa. In 1937, Bihar emerged in its present form, but lost some of its areas (Purulia and part of Kishanganj) when the States were reorgnised in 1956.

Bihar is rich in mineral resources. It has 63,400 million tonnes of coal deposits, nearly 1/3rd of the total deposits in the country, 3087 million tonnes of iron ore, more than 1/4th of the total deposits in the country and 154 million tonnes of copper, nearly 1/2 half of the total deposits in the country, besides rich deposits of bauxite and limestone. Coal mining operations were first taken up in this country in Jharia (Bihar) in the beginning of the 20th century. In the second decade the Tatas set up the first steel plant in the country at Jamshedpur. Later flourishing sugar industry emerged in North Bihar, which accounted for 25% of sugar production in the country upto the 1950s. Installation of H.E.C. at Ranchi, Steel plant at Bokaro, Refinery and Fertiliser factory at Barauni raised hopes of major industrial thrust in Bihar in the early phase of planning. But after 1980, the pace of industrialisation slackened.

Neglect of the Region

Since 1981, there has been increase in the share in total population for agricultural labourers and decline in non-farm employment. Census report of 1991, reveals that there was substantial decline in employment compared to 1961, in manufacturing (less by 296,000 or 21%), transport and communications (53,000 or 14%), allied agricultural activities (69,000 or 40%), construction (6,000) and mining and quarrying (11,000). Bihar was the only State in the country, where the percentage of persons employed in the primary sector has increased and confirms our fears about stagnation of the State economy. It is a matter of grave concern. Bihar is deficit in foodgrains. It has the highest illiteracy (62%) in the country. It is the least urbanized, just 13%.

The gross domestic product of the State at current prices in 1989-90 was Rs. 22,773 crores, of which the share of primary sector was 44.1% (compared to about 30% for all India), secondary sector 26.7% and tertiary sector 29.2%. Thus development of agriculture is crucial for development of the State.

Regional imbalance is natural in a country of continental dimensions. But the fact that Bihar's per capita income is only half the national average should be cause for concern at the national level. It calls into question the socio-economic policies of the country as well as the principles of federalism, on which our country is governed. Balanced Development has never been of much concern for planning in India. We were concerned about special areas, drought prone area, hill areas, etc. but problems of extreme povery, unemployment and backwardness were considered national phenomenon and no seperate strategy was considered necessary for tackling it at the regional level. N.E. States get preferential treatment but not the backward regions. Unfortunately, the data on unemployment suppressed the disguised unemployment and poverty in rural areas in North Bihar and other such pockets and the distressing situation in these areas did not attract adequate attention.

The State Plan outlays have not been able to arrest this slide towards extreme poverty. In the Fifties, Bihar's plan outlay was 3.30% of the total plan outlay. This declined to 2.83% in Seventh Plan. In the Eighth Plan it is projected at 2.99%. In the first three years of the Eighth plan, against the targeted amount of Rs. 6,900/- crores, the State was able to spend only Rs. 2,929/- crores, which was just over 40% of the proposed outlays. Per capita plan outlay in Bihar has been two third of the national average. This is also the level of per-capita central oulay.

The plains of north Bihar are the most densely populated in the country, with a density of 761 per square Kilometre in the country. The nexus between over-population, unemployment, tiny holdings, low-productivity, poverty, poor health, illiteracy, and poor infrastructural support, especially power is close and they are mutually re-inforcing factors. They constitute what Mydral appropriately described as a process of circular and cumulative causation in which low incomes lead to low levels of living (income plus poor health, education, etc.) which keeps productivity low; which in turn perpetuates low incomes and so on.

Declining Trend of Growth

Thus despite large and diverse potential, the progress made by the State in the last two and half decades lagged behind the rest of the country. The state's net domestic product, at the constant prices, exhibited growth rate of 3.11 per cent over the year 1970-81 as against 3.48 per cent for the country. Per capita income in the state in 1987-88 at current prices was Rs. 1846/- as against the national average at Rs. 3286/- and the gap between the two had increased from 32.7 per cent in 1972-73 to 43.8 per cent. At present it is less than one third of the per capita income in Punjab. The State's contribution to the national income has come down from 8.2 per cent at the beginning of the first five year plan (1950-51) to 6.67 per cent in 1975-76 and 4,98 per cent at the end of Sixth Plan. The State had 40.2 per cent of its population below poverty line, according to the NSS of 1987-88 as against 29.3 per cent for the country as a whole.

Investment under the Five Year Plans Priorities and Trend

Table 1.1—Summarises the sectorwise allocations of funds in the State since the Ist Plan. The major trends can be easily discerned. Social services got the top most priority in the Ist and IInd Plan. Power got this place in the IIIrd and IVth Plans. But, thereafter, irrigaton got the top most priority, and irrigation accounted for nearly 1/3rd of the total development outlay in the State between 1970-1990. In the VIIth Plan, Bihar spent more than any other State on major and medium irrigation, except Maharastra and it was more than Uttar Pradesh also. Surprisingly the results have not been commensurate with investment and actual area irrigated from major and medium irrigation projects has been steadily declining since 1989-90. The latest report indicates, that nearly 10 lakh hecters, though covered by irrigation projects, is not receiving irrigation.

Even with acute power scarcity in the State, the State Govt. has not considered it necessary to provide more resources to this critical sector. Situation has become worse because of deteriorating plant load factor and high transmission and distribution losses. The social services sector suffered during the IVth and Vth plan, but with greater awareness of the importance of human resources development there was higher allocation in the VIth and VIIth Plan. In the VIIIth Plan with 22.5% of the total allocation, social services has got higher priority than power (16.5%). and is only less than irrigation (25.2%)

Allocation on agriculture fell steeply after the IVth Plan, which was compensated by higher allocation to the rural development in the Vth and subsequent Plans. The transport sector, which means expenditure on roads, primarily, got as much as 11.4% of the total outlay in the VIIth Plan. Very few States spend as much on roads.

The thrust areas, i.e. those sector and activities which give higher return on investment must get preferential treatment in allocation of resources. Without this conditionality, higher allocation would not lead to higher production. The below capacity utilisation and unsatisfactory execution of irrigation and power projects has led to lower growth rate.

The share of central assistance in the total plan outlay since the Ist Plan is shown in the last two columns of the table. It has declined from over 60% in the earlier plans to around 40% in the VIth and VIIth plan. In the VIIIth Plan it is projected at only 36.23%. This has put stress on the states' internal resources. The inability of the State, further re-inforced by political reluctance to mobilise additional resources has led to serious resource crunch. There has been also lack of political will to restrict non-development expenditure. Since central assistance has continued at the projected level, its share was as much as 80% of the plan outlay in 1991-92 and 1992-93. The situation was not much different in 1993-94. During 1994-95 Bihar received nearly Rs.1,000 crores as central assistance, including assistance for externally aided projects and Centre's contribution to calamity Relief fund. Actual plan expenditure was only Rs. 900 crores, In recent times actual plan expenditure has been less than the total Central assistance received. Since the State was unable to honour its commitments in respect of various centrally sponsored schemes, their continuance is under threat.

The Growth Paradigm

The Strategy for tackling the problems of backwardness has therefore, to be multi-pronged, and we have to adopt programmes which provide employment to low income families, encourage literecy and family planning simultaneously. Thus land reforms, provision of basic rural services, and the provision of large scale job opportunities are policies that help us promote agricultural and rural development; policies designed to make education more relevant for development are a major force in promoting rural development. Policies designed to control population can be also an effective means for reducing unemployment and poverty.

In the present analysis we have focussed attention on some of the major economic activities that have critical role in economic development. Less developed economies can not afford to waste their limited financial and skilled manpower resources on unproductive- ventures. Investment projects are to be chosen not only on the basis of individual industrial capital output ratios, but also in the context of an overall employment programme that takes into account linkages, indirect costs, and long term objectives. More than lack of investible funds, it is human failure to adopt proper perspective, organising development activities efficiently and support rational institutions that is responsible for retarded development. It is due to inability of the people to exploit the available resources in the best possible manner and lack of dedication to achieve the development goals. Sustained commitment of a politically stable Government is the sine qua non for development. Where country's political leadership makes development a central concern, people can be also mobilised through a judicious use of economic incentives for achieving the goals.

It is difficult to introduce administrative and institutional reforms, but this is made easy if we have committed political leaders. It requires unusual ability and integrity to overcome the vested interests and take a long term view, and to place national social interests above functional, class, caste or ethnic interests. Rational decisions, which strengthen the economy, have catalytic role in development, and overcoming irrationality is far more difficult in practice than it appears. Decisions on economic issues are taken by politicians, who generally assign low priority to efficiency and take selfish and parochial view of issues.

There is no one strategy for development. It will differ with different situation. Since the problems we are required to tackle are multifarious and interdependent, the approach, too, as stated earlier, has to be multipronged. The strategy for growth would have to naturally concentrate on thrust activities and modal areas i.e. activities in which we have comparative advantage, so that we make best us of available resources and locations that are conducive to accelerated production. At the same time we have to economise on the use of resources of which there is scarcity. We must also keep under check those problems that are thawarting our development efforts e.g. unbridled population growth. Corruption similarly is corroding our system and providing the corrupt persons at help with huge sums of ill-gotten money for exploiting the weaker sections.

Chronic shortage of power seems to negate all development efforts. Power availability must improve if we are to raise agricultural productivity and strengthen and expand our industrial base. There has to be much better utilisation of irrigation capacity and existing assets, which have been created at great cost. It is a pity that excellent institutions of learning and for care of health of the people are languishing because of neglect. As poverty and unemployment is pervasive, and acts as a major debilitating factor, it has to be tackled on top priority basis. Lax execution of plan schemes by corrupt officials in league with unscrupulous politicians and greedly contractors has led to a situation in which benefits meant for the poor are not being fully realised by them. We should, therefore, be very careful and prevent corruption from subverting development efforts. The above in brief is the growth paradigm that has been propounded in the subsequent chapters.

REFERENCES

1. *Population Figures at a Glance 1991*, Directorate of Census Operations, Bihar.
2. *District Profile of Bihar*, Population Research Centre, Patna.
3. *Plan Documents*, Planning and Finance Department, Government of Bihar and Planning Commission, Govt. of India.
4. *State Income of Bihar*, 1980-81 to 1991-92, Directorate of Statistics, Government of Bihar.
5. R.C. Dutt, *Economic History of India*, Government of India.

Table: Occupational Distribution of Workers in Bihar

[The total number of workers is 256.2 lakh]

(Source : 1991 Census)	*No. of workers (Lakhs)*	*Percentage to total*
Cultivators	111.65	43.6
Agricultural Labourers	95.13	37.1
Allied Agricultural Activities	0.99	0.4
Mining & Quarrying	3.23	1.3
Manufacturing	10.25	4.0
Trade & Commerce	10.25	4.0
Other Services	19.70	7.7
Transport, Storage, etc.	3.29	1.3
Construction	1.62	0.6

Table 1.1: Planwise Expenditure 'Since Inception' by Main Sectors for Bihar

(Rs. in Crores)

Plan Period	Agri. Programme	Coop.R.D.& Panchayat	Irri-& Flood Contr.	Power	Industory & Mining.	Transp. & Communi.	Social Services.	Miscellanous	Total	Central Assistance
	Exp. with %	Exp. with %	Exp. with %	Exp. with %	Exp. with %	Exp. with %	Exp. with %	Exp. with %	Exp.with %	Exp. with %
1	2	3	4	5	6	7	8	9	10	11
Ist Plan 1951-56	14.42 (11.67)	1.63 (2.22)	12.94 (17.66)	9.46 (12.91)	1.04 (1.42)	10.78 (14.71)	21.19 (28.92)	1.82 (2.49)	73.28 (100)	55 (75.05)
IInd Plan 1956-61	28.59 (16.06)	25.62 (14.40)	26.98 (15.16)	31.14 (17.50)	8.47 (4.76)	15.20 (8.54)	41.28 (23.19)	0.70 (0.39)	177.98 (100)	84 (47.20)
IIIrd Plan 1961-66	38.51 (11.72)	29.28 (8.91)	81.77 (24.70)	94.05 (28.63)	16.53 (3.21)	17.44 (5.31)	56.85 (17.31)	0.27 (0.21)	334.70 (100)	216 (64.54)
Annual Plans 1966-69	44.57 (19.55)	10.75 (4.71)	60.23 (26.42)	68.84 (29.82)	6.22 (2.73)	10.34 (4.45)	28.51 (12.46)	0.18 (0.09)	229.94 (100)	156 (166.97)
IVth Plan 1964-74	72.08 (14.84)	17.63 (3.63)	145.74 (29.94)	135.77 (27.95)	17.39 (3.58)	35.61 (35.61)	61.71 (12.70)	0.13 (0.03)	485.76 (100)	173 (35.61)
V Plan 1974-78	130.02 (14.21)	9.08 (1.00)	270.57 (29.57)	248.83 (27.00)	36.26 (3.96)	86.89 (9.50)	119.19 (13.03)	14.12 (1.55)	914.96 (100)	411 (44.92)

(Contd.)

1	2	3	4	5	6	7	8	9	10	11
Annual Plans 1978-80	97.56 (14.41)	8.30 (1.24)	217.45 (32.44)	148.12 (22.10)	28.44 (4.24)	65.27 (9.74)	101.61 (15.16)	4.47 (0.67)	670.22 (100)	480 (71.62)
VIth Plan 1980-85	149.01 (5.07)	275.66 (9.38)	1043.80 (35.52)	601.57 (20.47)	108.17 (3.68)	295.79 (10.06)	447.55 (15.23)	17.16 (0.59)	2938.71 (100)	1260 (42.88)
VIIth Plan 1985-90	419.15 (6.95)	625.96 (10.37)	1851.05 (30.68)	1067.68 (17.70)	308.20 (5.11)	453.57 (7.52)	986.19 (16.35)	321.32 (5.32)	6033.12 (100)	2692 (44.62)
Annual Plan 1990-91	83.39 (6.63)	172.78 (13.73)	358.06 (28.47)	227.54 (18.09)	42.70 (3.39)	106.54 (8.47)	180.98 (14.39)	85.93 (6.83)	1257.92 (100)	625 (49.68)
1991-92	6254 (6.06)	182.18 (17.66)	259.18 (25.13)	150.00 (14.54)	26.12 (2.53)	87.44 (8.48)	218.46 (21.18)	45.64 (4.42)	1031.56 (100)	835* (80.95*
1992-93 (Recieved)	75.14 (6.83)	179.12 (16.28)	237.10 (21.56)	170.06 (15.46)	24.80 (2.25)	137.36 (12.49)	234.48 (21.32)	41.94 3.81)	1100.00 (100)	873 (79.36)*
Outlay for 1993-94	158.02 (6.87)	243.85 (10.60)	558.60 (24.29)	390.81 (16.99)	73.09 (3.21)	254.55 (11.07)	507.99 (22.09)	112.29 (4.88)	2300.00 (100)	873 (37.96)*
VIIIth Plan 1992-97	890.37 (6.85)	1170.80 (9.01)	3270.83 (25.16)	2145.58 (16.50)	458.14 (3.52)	1477.12 (11.36)	2918.54 (22.46)	668.62 (5.14)	13000.00 (100)	4710 (36.23)*
Approved Outlay										

N.B. * Tentative

** Figures in bracket indicates % of total outlay.

Source: State Plan Documents.

Table 1.2: Bihar State - 1992: A Profile

Sl No.		Total	Unit	Quantity	Remarks
1.	Population		Persons	86374465	
			Males	45202091	
			Females	41172374	
		Urban	Persons	11353012	
			Males	6156996	
			Females	5196016	
2.	Percentage of Urban Population to Total Population		—	13.14	
3.	Population (0-6 Years)	Total	Persons	177664186	
			Males	90655869	
			Females	8698317	
4.	Decennial Population Growth Rate		1971-81	24.06	
			1981-91	23.54	
5.	Area		Sq. km.	173877	
6.	Density of Population (Per km^2)		1981	402	
			1991	497	
7.	Sex Ratio i.e. No. of Females per 1000 Males		1981	946	
			1991	911	
8.	Effective Literacy Rate (Excluding 0-6 age group)		Persons	26402898	38.48%
			Males	18968636	52.49%
			Females	7434262	22.89%
9.	Percentage of Main Workers		Persons	25619038	29.66%
10.	Percentage of :		Persons	11164519	43.58%
	(i) Cultivators to main workers		Males	9867434	45.87%
	(ii) Agril. Labourers to main workers		Persons	9512892	37.13%
			Males	7078716	32.90%
			Females	2434176	59.29%
11.	Population of Scheduled Castes		Persons	12571700	14.55%
			Males	6569360	14.53%
			Females	60002340	14.58%
12.	Population of Scheduled Tribes		Persons	6616914	7.66%
			Males	3357563	7.43%
			Females	3259351	7.92%
13.	Population of Muslims (1981)				14.12%
14.	Population of Christian				1.06%
15.	No. of Occupied Residential Houses		—	12833123	

16. No. of Households	—	14012071	
17. No. of Villages	Inhabited	67503	
	Un inhabited	19191	
18. No. of Gram Panchayats	—	11835	
19. No. of C.D. Blocks	—	593	
20. No. of Sub-Divisions	—	112	
21. No. of Districts	—	50	
22. No. of Divisions	—	13	
23. No. of Towns	—	271	
24. No. of Civil Police Station	—	1097	
25. District with:			
(i) Highest D.G.R. (*)	Deoghar	31.64 (*)D.G.R. (Decadal Growth)	
(ii) Lowest D.G.R.	Gumla	13.44 Rate	
26. (i) Most Populous District (Density)	Patna	1130	
(ii) Least Populous District (do)	Gumla	127	
27. **District Having**			
Highest Sex Ratio	Siwan	1917	
Lowest Sex Ratio	Dhanbad	826	
28. Percentage of:	**As Per Census**		
		1981	**1991**
(i) Main Workers	Persons	29.68	29.66%
	Males	49.20	47.59%
	Females	9.06	9.97%
(ii) Marginal Workers	Persons	2.67	2.50%
	Males	0.98	0.32%
	Females	4.44	4.89%
29. Normal Rainfall	in mm	1211.7	
30. Percentage of Gross Irrigation to Gross Cropped Area		—	36.71
31. Percentage of Net sown area to total area		—	44.1
32. No. of Villages connected with all wheather Roads		—	25470
33. Total length of Surfaced and Unsurfaced Roads		Km	83643
34. Total length of Surface Roads		Km	40973

35. Total length of Railway track		Km	5362
36. No. of Post Offices		No.	11399
37. No. of SSI Units as on 31.3.88		—	55117
38. No. of Factories		—	4988
39. No. of Villages Electrified		—	46855
40. Energisation of Pump Sets		—	260540
41. Per Capita Income (at current Prices)		Rs.	2904
42. Per Hectare value of Agril. Output		Rs.	7893
43. Percentage of population Below poverty line		1987-88	40.7
44. **Motor Vehicles (1992)**			
(i) Truck		No.	77224
(ii) Three Wheeler		No.	23226
(iii) Bus		No.	15688
(iv) Car & Station Wagons		No.	73198
(v) Taxi		No.	23447
(vi) Jeep		No.	34871
(vii) Two Wheeler		No.	756241
(viii) Tractor		No.	56186
(ix) Trailors		No.	31394
(x) Others		No.	20172
Total number of motor vehicles on road		No.	1111747
45. Public Health & Medical Care (1992)	Number	No. of	bes. No. Drs
(i) Medical College/Hospital	9	7283	1514
(ii) District Hospital	47	5266	636
(iii) Sub-Divisional Hospital	32	1225	166
(iv) Primary Health Centres	2209	13245	5592
(v) Other Hospitals	154	6900	983
(vi) Referal Hospitals	99	2970	396
Total	2550	36889	9287
56. **Power**			
Installed Capacity	MW	1548	
Thermal	MW	1393	
Hydel	MW	149	
Total Generation (92-93)	Million Units	2967	
Per Capita Consumption of Power	Units	114	
Transmission & Distribution Losses (Average)		—	22%
Staff per MW	—	3.67	
Cinnected Load (1990)	MW	2579	
No. of Consumers (1990)		13,74,557	

Table 1.3: Land Utilisation (1990-91) in the State of Bihar

Particulars	**Area**
Geographical Area	17329649
Forest	2948995
Barren and unculturable land	1015692
Land put to non-agriculture uses	2109838
Total non-culturable land	6074525
Cultivable waste land	371706
Permanent pasture and other grazing lands	125870
Groves & Misc. Crops	291006
Other fallow land (2-5 yrs.)	998698
Current Fallow land	1765301
Net Area Sown	7702543
Total agricultural and cultivable land	11255124
Total Agricultural and non-agricultural land	17329649
Total Cropped Area	10405133
Area Sown more than once.	2782590

Source : Directorate of Statistics & Evaluation, Bihar, Patna.

Table 1.4: Number Area and Average Size of Operational [Holdings in Bihar] 1980-81 and 1985-86

Size Class (in Areas)	*No of Operational Holdings (per cent of total)*		*Area of Operational Holdings (per cent of total)*		*Average Size of Operational Holdings*	
	1980-81	1985-86	1980-81	1985-86	1980-81	1985-86
Below ! 1.24	6385300 (57.86)	6763392 (57.75)	385282.5 (14.09)	4113723.2 (15.28)	0.60	0.57
1.24 to 2.47	1935349 (17.55)	2212862 (18.90)	3438160.9 (12.58)	404368.0 (15.02)	1.77	1.82
Marginal (below 2.47)	83206.19 (75.44)	89762.54 (76.65)	7290743.4 (26.67)	8157407.12 (30.30)	0.87	0.90
Small 2.47 to 4.94	1217881 (11.04)	1327332 (11.33)	4069655.9 (14.89)	4617133.9 (17.15)	3.34	3.45

4.94 to 7.41	611986 (5.56)	621050 (5.3)	3588608.6 (13.13)	3660947.5 (13.6)	5.86	5.89
7.41 to 9.88	339212 (3.07)	329699 (2.82)	2818828.2 (10.31)	2744577.5 (10.2)	8.31	8.32
Semi medium 4.94 to 9.88	951198 (8.63)	950749 (8.12)	6407436.8 (23.44)	6405525.0 (23.8)	6.73	6.73
9.88 to 12.35	213873 (1.94)	191043 (1.63)	2312107.7 (8.46)	2064169.1 (7.67)	10.81	10.80
12.35 to 18.52	175399 (1.59)	143645 (1.23)	2632259.2 (9.63)	2166506.1 (8.05)	15.00	15.08
18.52 to 24.7	83498 (0.75)	69480 (0.59)	1747455.8 (6.39)	1433721.3 (5.33)	21.13	20.63
Medium 9.88 to 24.7	471770 (4.28)	404168 (3.45)	6691822.8 (24.48)	5664396.5 (21.05)	14.18	14.01
24.7 to 49.4	53072 (0.48)	42891 (0.37)	1750728.5 (6.40)	1403822.1 (6.21)	32.98	32.72
49.4 to 74.1	10414 (0.09)	7081 (0.06)	607548.37 (2.22)	408094.24 (1.52)	58.34	57.62
74.1 to 98.8	2709 (0.02)	1503 (0.01)	226844.8 (0.83)	120948.49 (0.45)	83.73	80.47
98.8 to 123.5	1011 (0.02)	524 (0.01)	109238.22 (0.83)	57057 (0.45)	108.05	103.88
123.55 and above	898 (0.008)	481 (0.00)	182970.19 (0.67)	82954.95 (0.31)	203.75	172.46
Large 2.47 and above	68104 (0.61)	52480 (0.45)	2877320.1 (10.52)	2072806.78 (7.7)	42.25	39.49
All classes	11029602 (100.00)	11710983 (100.00)	27336989 (100.00)	26917269 (100.00)	2.45	2.29

Source: Agricultural Census 1980-81 and 1985-86.

Table 1.4 (b): Estimated Acquired and Redistributed Surplus Land

Number & Area of Operational Holdings (Having Size Above 30 Acres) Number	Area	Estimated Average	Surplus land Surplus land	Surplus land Acquired (as Per cent of Estimated Surplus Land)	distributed (as Per cent of Estimated Surplus Land)
1	2	3	4	5	6
135105	58296742	43115	17766307	385013 (21.67)	262476 (14.77)

Table 1.5: Statement Showing Area Production & Yield rate of Important Crops in The State of Bihar

Sl. No.	Name of Crops	Year 1989-90 Area	Year 1989-90 Production	Year 1989-90 Yield Rate	Year 1990-91 Area	Year 1990-91 Production	Year 1990-91 Yield Rate	Year 1991-92 Area	Year 1991-92 Production	Year 1991-92 Yield Rate
1	2	3	4	5	6	7	8	9	10	11
1. (a)	Bhadai Rice	734526	645583	879	732421	685924	937	702927	681983	970
(b)	Aghani Rice	4470583	5596336	1252	4577140	5767671	1260	3997672	3634674	909
(c)	Garms Rice	80540	106928	1328	80942	109883	1358	91580	143811	1570
	Total Rice	5285649	6348847	1201	5390503	6563478	1218	4792169	4460468	931
2.	Wheat	1988052	3270192	1645	1965047	3360424	1812	1963297	3566021	1816
3.	Maize	702659	1205723	1716	665210	1037610	1560	667844	1195603	1790
4.	Course Cereals (Marus Jowar, Bajra,Barley)	176097	134339	763	166645	146207	877	156152	122337	783
5.	Pulses (Gram, Arhar & Masoor	427044	359579	842	421998	408141	967	396803	391429	986
6.	Oil Seeds (Mus-tered, Linseed, Gr-ound-nut, Caster)	183000	122963	672	192681	128516	667	179754	147941	823
7.	Jute & Mesta	140485	1092958 (Bale) / 196732 (tonnes)	1400	164607	119419 (Bale) / 214955 (tonnes)	306	171350	1362992 (Bale) / 245339 (tonnes)	1432
8.	Sugar Cane	124563	6694127	53741	148720	7805335	52483	144880	7076368	48843
9.	Chillies	6916	5909	854	4977	4867	978	5076	5472	1078
10.	To-bacco	15459	15848	1025	15285	12747	834	15218	8631	567

Unit
Area- In Hectares
Production-In-M. Tonne
Yield Rate-K.G. Per Hect.

Source : Directorate of Statistics & Evaluation, Bihar, Patna.

2

Underdevelopment of the Eastern Region

Bihar is the poorest State in India. Even in Eastern India, which has lagged behind the rest of the country, it compares unfavourably with its neighbouring States.

The statement below gives a comparative view of the level of development of different States in the Eastern region. It will be seen that the situation in Bihar is gravest of all and it has been least successful in tackling the problems.

Table 2.1: A Comparative View of the States in the Eastern Region

	W. Bengal	*Orissa*	*Bihar*	*U.P.*	*(83-84)*	*All India*
Population (in lakhs' 91)	681 (8)	317 (3.7)	864 (10.2)	1391 (16.4)		8463 (100)
Area (000 Sq. Km)	88.8 (2.7)	155.7 (4.8)	173.9 (5.3)	294.4 (8.9)		3287.3 (100)
Production of foodgrains (lakh tonnes in 94-95).	135.3 (7)	72.4 (3.8)	128.5 (6.7)	387 (20.3)		1911 (100)
Net State domestic product (average of '87-90 at current prices in Rs. Crores).	24,091	8,929	17,586	37,799		2,96,773
Per capita income in Rs. at current prices ('91-92).	5227	3907	2871	3979		5,583

Percentage of Population below poverty line (87-88).	27.6	44.7	40.8	35.1	41.6*	29.9
Percentage of unemployment rate (87-88) on currently, Weekly basis.	6.7	5.2	3.8	2.8		4.8
Density of population (1991)	766	202	497	471		267
Percentage of Urban population (1991)	27.4	13.4	13.2	19.9	12.6*	25.7
Percentage of Liberacy (1991)						
Males	67.2	62.4	52.6	55.3		63.9
Females	47.2	34.4	23.1	26.0		39.4
Percentage of main workers to total population (1991)	30.2	32.7	29.7	29.7	32.6*	34.1
Percentage of agricultural workers to total workers (1991)	53.0	73.1	80.6	72.1	79.1*	64.9
Percentage of agricultural labourers to total agricultural workers (1981)	45.9	37.5	44.5	26.1*		37.5
Number of agricultural workers per 10 hectares of best area sown (1981)	152	195	196	165*		105
Average size of holdings in hectares (1985-)	0.92	1.47	0.87	0.74*		1.68
Average size of marginal holdings, that is below 1 hectare	0.39	0.51	0.55	0.32*		0.39*
Irrigation						
(a) Percentage of ultimate potential utilised	39.1	28.5	28.4	30.8*		

(b) Percentage of grass cropped area irrigated (84-85)	26.1	23.1	36.7	42.6	48.5*	30.7
(c) Percentage of ground water resources utilised	24	10	25	32*		
(d) Cropping intensity (1980-81)	135	138	133	142*		123
(e) Percentage of utilisation of potential created Major & Medium (1984-85)	92.9	96.2	75.6	80.9		83
Percentage of Cereals under High Yielding varieties (in lakh hectares) 1994-95	41.4 (5.8)	30.2 (4.2)	57.8 (8.1)	144.9 (20.3)		712.7 (100)
Average yield in Kgs. per hectatre (1985-86)						
Wheat	1894	1912	1646	1992		2032
Rice	1555	1191	1128	1488		1568
Consumption of fertilizers Kg/hectare (1994-95)	86.2	22.5	64.5	99.3		75.7
Consumption of Electricity for Agricultural in Mill. KWH	257	113	1373	6042		38878
Foodgrains production-Mill.Tons. (1989-90)	11.0	8.0	11.8	34		171
Fish Production '000 tonnes (89-90)	601	154	157	94		3677
Milk Production (Lakh tonnes)	29.1	4.7	31.2	97		537
Value of output in Rs. (1979-80):						
(a) Per hectare of gross area	1655	1059	1170	1334*		1198

(b) Per agricultural workers	1517	1361	812	1249		1430
Industries (85-86)						
No. of factories	5619	1467	4988	7550		
Emp. in (000)	812	153	347	700		
Value of output (Rs. Cr.)	9542	2037	6520	8816		
Length of surfaced & unsurfaced roads per 100 Sq.KMs as on 1.3.91.	69.3	111.5	48.8	63.9		60.8

* Figures relate to Eastern U.P. Figures in brackets are percentage of All India.

The Marginal holdings (below) 1 hectare constitute 76 per cent of the holdings but cover only 30 per cent of the total operated area in Bihar.

In the intensively cultivated districts of Rohtas and Nalanda, the number of fragments per holding is between 15 to 20. The problem of fragmentation is becoming more and more serious. Between 1970-71 and 1980-81, the proportion of holdings less than 1 hectare increased from 64 per cent to 76 per cent.

Causes of Under Development of The Eastern Region:

It is difficult to isolate the main causes for poverty. They are so inter-linked and inter-dependent that most of them are both the cause and the effect of other factors. Thus poverty regards economic growth and low investment reinforces poverty.

The Eastern Region is predominatly rural with agriculture providing the main occupation to the population. Most of the culturable area has been brought under agriculture and there is little scope for extending the limits of cultivation. West Bengal because of Calcutta has larger urban weightage, and because of location of industries in and around the metropolis, the average per capita income of the State has been pushed up above the national average. From the above table it will appear the Eastern Region is characterised by high density of population, high incidence of poverty, low level of urbanisation, mass illiteracy, especially among women, heavy pressure of population on land with very small land holdings held in tiny plots, low per capita/ per acre yield of agricultural produce. Eastern India has the highest incidence of poverty. In absolute numbers it includes nearly one-third of the total population below poverty line in the country, of which Bihar contains about half. The high growth rate of urbanisation 66 per cent for U.P., 56 per cent for Bihar , 68 per cent for Orissa, 46 per cent for All India (1971-81) is a symptom of the growing poverty in the country side in the region. There has been declaration between1981-91. The growth in urban population in Bihar was only 30.4%, compared to 39% for UP, 36% for Orissa and 36.2% for All India.

Bihar's position is worst compared to other States in the Eastern region. It has the highest percentage of population below the poverty line, highest density of population after Kerala and West Bengal, lowest percentage of urban population after Orissa and Assam and lowest percentage of female literacy along with eastern U.P..

There is heavy pressure of population on land. The density of population in North Bihar plains is as high as 76 per Sw.KMs. It is 609 in South Bihar plains. Bulk of Bihar's population is concentrated in the Gangetic plains of Bihar, where there is not enough cultivable land to sustain the huge population. The number of agricultural labourers in Bihar is 9.51 million and landlessness has gradually increased over time. It has gone up from 30% of the total workers engaged in agriculture in 1961, to nearly 47 per cent of the total workers engaged in agriculture in 1991. This landlessness has created serious problems in rural areas, including agrarian unrest in rural areas. The economy of the State has to be diversified and the pressure of population on land has to be relieved by gradually shifting the rural population to other occupations.

The high percentage of population of children, aged 0-6 years, in the total population in Bihar (20.6%) and U.P. (20.3%) does not augur well for the future. It is 17.9% for the country. This means that at the turn of the century there will be higher per centage of people in the reproductive age group and without checks, population may grow more rapidly. Population of children in 'Orissa' (16.9%) and West Bengal (17.00%) is lower and provides encouragement.

Eastern U.P. resembles the Gangetic plain of Bihar and reveals the same characteristics. Eastern U.P. like Bihar depends overwhelmingly on agriculture but it has performed better. The intensity of cropping (1982-83) is 146.19, with average per hectare consumption of fertilizers being 66.30 Kgs. Irrigation coverage (per centage of net irrigated area to net area sown) in case of Eastern U.P. is 55 per cent, whereas in case of Bihar it is only 35 per cent.

National income of India increased from Rs. 1,731 crores in 1950-51 to Rs. 55,100 Crores at 1970-71, prices in 1983-84, that is, by nearly 329 per cent during the same period at 1970-91 prices, Bihar's net domestic product had increased from Rs. 1,166 crores in 1950-51 to Rs. 3,288 crores in 1983-84, i.e. by 282 per cent. Thus the growth in States's income was nearly 16% less. This worsened after 83-84. Between 83-84, and 88-89, net national product increased by 28%, Bihar's by 21% only. The per capita income figures over the years give better idea of inter-state growth rates. This information for the Eastern States is reproduced in Table 2.2.

Table 2.2: Trend of Growth of Income in Eastern States

States	*Per capita income in 1970-71 prices in Rs.*			
	1970-71	*1986-87*	*increase since 1970-71 in (Rs.)*	*in %*
Assam	535	605	70	13.1
Bihar	402	482	80	19.9
Orissa	478	533	57	13.0
Uttar Pradesh	486	607	121	24.8
West Bengal	722	860	138	19.1
All India	633	795	162	25.6

The above figures indicate that the growth of per capita income in the State has been nearly 25% lower than the national average. Bihar is the least developed state and the gap between per capita income in Bihar and rest of the country would go on widening, unless the growth rate in the State is substantially higher than All India growth rate. Efforts should be made to correct the imbalance. The poverty in East India is very glaring, and we cannot shut our eyes to it in the Ninth and succeeding plans.

Stagnation in Agricultural Production

Agricultural production increased at the rate of 2.5 per cent per annum for the whole country since 1951, but only 0.7 per cent in Bihar. Growth rate of foodgrains productions in the Eastern States upto 1985, lagged far behind the Northern and Southern States. Though foodgrains production at the All India level since 1950, grow at the rate of 2.32 per cent and was marginally above the growth rate of population of 2.24 per cent, growth rate of foodgrains production in Bihar was only 0.84 per cent (population growth 2.13 per cent), Orissa 0.42 per cent (1.82 per cent), West Bengal 1.29 per cent (2.09 per cent) and Uttar Pradesh 2.16 per cent (2.30 per cent). The higher growth rate of foodgrain production in case of Uttar Pradesh is explained by the major break-through achieved in Western Uttar Pradesh. Foodgrain production was far behind the growth rate of population which is indicated for comparison by the figure within brackets. Bihar has over 10% of the country's population but contributes only 6.7% to the total foodgrains production.

Distressingly, even in respect of milk production. Bihar laged behind rest of the country. Inspite of favourable conditions with nearly 10% population of the cattle in the country and higher prices of milk/milk products in the State, its share in milk production of the country declined from 8.3% in 1971-72, to 6% in 1987-88. In comparison, West Bengal has done remarkably well milk production increased nearly five times during the period; whereas in Orissa it remained almost the same.

It is agriculture, surprisingly which has served as a drag on development in Bihar. With 87.5 per cent of the population residing in villages and over 80 per cent dependent for their livelihood on agriculture, it is obvious that agricultural development holds the key to the economic growth of the State. Bihar produces less food than West Bengal, though it has much more arable land and far more area under irrigation. The hardships of agricultural labour and the reluctance of land owners in Bihar to invest in agriculture is attributed by some to the dominent land owning castes, who are either absentee landlords or who have been indifferent to improvement in agriculture as they can derive their profits by exploitation of agricultural labour, without trying to raise production. The solution which is recommended is to take away the surplus land from the big land owners and distribute it among the landless. This transfer of ownership, it is presumed, would automatically create the impetus for agricultural development, as vesting ownership in the landless would create the necessary motivation. Land reforms so far have been unsatisfactory and consolidation of holdings has been slow. The landowners have a powerful lobby and it is alleged that they have prevented effective transfer of ownership of land to landless. It is a fact that in Bihar, even according to official version, only about 1,00,000 hectares of land declared surplus under the Ceiling Act has been distributed. This accounts for less than 1 per cent of the total area under private ownership (115 lac hectares). In large number of cases the recipients of land have been ousted from possession.

West Bengal in sharp contrast to Bihar launched land reforms programme on a very high scale. 3,79,000 hectares of vested land was distributed among - 20. 43 lakh beneficiaries upto June,1992. Far more impressive has been the operation "Barga", under which 14.40 lakh bargardars (share croppers) were recorded as permanent tenants, covering 4.47 lakh hectares. The vested land and barga land together accounted for nearly 1/6 of the total land owned in the State and the total number of beneficiaries was 1/3rd of the total number of cultivators and agricultural labourers in the State. Agricultural production in West Bengal increased by 33% between 1986-1991. This increase in production is attributed to the motivation created by land reforms, among the peasant proprietors.

The agrarian unrest in Bihar is largely due to the pressure of population on land, landlessness being a conseqence of this phenomenon and the inability of the rural areas to absorb them gainfully. Agriculture in some areas is not remunerative enough to enable the land owners to pay even the minimum wages prescribed by Government. Agricultural labourers too, are not prepared to make a compromise and though they cannot get employment at the desired wage rates in their own village, they have always got the option to move to the cities and other places for higher wages and also for more durable employment. This seasonal migration of labour aggravates the scarcity of labour during the peak agricultural operations and increases the tension between landowners and agricultural labourers. In the Naxalite belts because of forcible harvesting and looting of crops, some of the big land-owners have preferred to leave their lands fallow.

But migration to other places always involves suffering which are not foreseen. At home the labourers could unite and fight for concessions and also bring pressure on the Government, away from home, especially in Punjab, they are subjected to tortures and humiliations reducing them to a worst form of bondage. It is said that nearly 1,000 Bihari labourers have been maimed by threshing machines alone. Lately they have been victims of gruesome and indiscriminate killings by the terrorists. Surprisingly it has not evoked any protest from any quarter. The labour from Bihar, Eastern U.P. and even West Bengal are welcomed by the Punjabi farmers, who get cheap labour and are thereby able to raise their profits from cultivation. They do not have to spend on their housing or on their welfare measures, as the labourers return to their permanent homes after the harvesting is over. This seasonal migration of labour to more prosperous agricultural regions in North India brings the cultivators in backward areas in Eastern India in competition with the well organised farmers in the North.

There is heavy concentration of Scheduled caste population in the Eastern States. In U.P. and West Bengal they constitute over 21% of the population. In Bihar and Orissa they constitute nearly 15% of the population. The two States have a large population of tribals. In Bihar they constitute 8.4% of the population and in Orissa as much as 22.4%. For historical reasons they are the most deprived class of the society and their presence in large numbers also creates social tensions.

This peculiar situation of confrontation with agricultural labour coupled with the insecurity to life in rural areas, has led the rural gentry to shift to the towns. They go to their lands in the villages only when necessary. Rural life has also decayed. There are no health and educational facilities. Ninety per cent of the health facilities in Bihar are concentrated in the urban areas which accounts for only 13.1 per cent of the population. There are no good primary schools, no electricity and no piped water supply. This has further accelerated the process of shifting to towns. Investment in "transport business" and "buildings" in cities by the rural rich is considered to be more lucrative, at least less risky. The landlords are reluctant to invest in agriculture because of the risks and uncertainty.

Inspite of all that has been said, agricultural developement would not have lagged behind, provided the inputs were readily available in time and in adequate quantity. Fertilizers and better variety of seeds have been always scarce and the farmers generally have to pay a premium to obtain them. Uncertainty of power has compelled the farmers to keep diesel pumps in reserve, and diesel, too, is in short supply.

The Gangetic plains of Bihar are the most fertile in the country and once happened to be the granary of the country. The low use of inputs and low utilisation of irrigation potential indicate the incapacity of the agriculturists to invest in the inputs and the failure of administration to make full use of the potential created through heavy investment in irrigation schemes, which has been made possible only by neglect of the social services sectors. Even though Bihar has large irrigated area and has surplus labour skilled in agricultural operations, it is deficit in foodgrains and the intensity of irrigation potential is 25 per cent less than the average for the country. Lower utilisation of potential implies either faulty planning by not providing adequately for distribution channels, or exaggerated estimates of irrigation potential, the latter is a pet device for taking up gradiose schemes which are not as beneficial as they are made to appear on paper. In case of irrigation scheme the lesson for the future is close scrutiny of irrigation projects, concentrating on higher irrigation intensity and optimum utilisation of the potential. In order to induce the farmers to make use of inputs, timely availability of inputs and larger support has to be ensured. Also more stable supply of power is required to enable the marginal and small farmers to use electric pumps and thereby making maximum use of ground water irrigation facilities. Only 25 per cent of the ground water potential is being utilised. It is a pity that the problems holding back agricultural production have not got the attention it deserved so far. The cheap availability of foodgrains from North India resulted in complacency and the need to utilise the full potential of the Eastern Region was not considered urgent.

Low Investment

The protagonists for the development of Eastern India argue that this region has been a victim of neglect. The investments have been much less than in rest of the country. Though this region is rich in mineral resources, underground minerals are the property of the Central Government. Though Bihar provides coal to the rest of the country, local industries have difficulty in obtaining coal. Bricks suppleid by kilns in the State are costlier than in Delhi, though coal is the most important input in the making of bricks. The royalty from minerals is not commensurate with the increase in the value of the minerals. Royalty is based on tonnage and not on "value", and since the revision in the royalty rates, does not keep pace with the increase in prices, the Eastern States are deprived of valuable resources for their development programme. This argument has some truth, for Gujrat and Maharashtra have been able to get much better terms for offshore oil and gas for their own industrial use at cheaper rate than the rest of the country.

The argument of low investment is also borne out by the per capita plan outlay/expenditure figures. This is summarised below for the three major States:

Table 2.3: Per Capita Plan Outlay/Expenditure at Current Prices in Rs. Under Different Plans

	I	II	III	IV	V	VI	VII	VIII*
Bihar	25.52	40.50	68.30	85.00	313.56	461.37	651.30	15.06
Orissa	12.20	52.44	122.61	113.62	184.62	568.83	930.80	31.73
West Bengal	55.37	48.54	81.61	82.14	164.78	641.45	677.80	14.35
Total (Av. of all States)	37.57	52.83	94.50	141.80	227.65	698.94	1029.81	22.05

* Based on 1991 population.

The per capita tax receipts is much lower in the Eastern States compared to the more developed States. The per capita tax revenue and expenditure on revenue account in 1987-88, and 1992-93, is given in the following table. Poor resource mobilisation naturally acts as a major constraint. Bihar's performance has been very sluggish.

Table 2.4

State	Receipt Rev. Acct. (in Rs.)		Expenditure on Rev. Acct.	
	1987-88	1992-93	1987-88	1992-93
West Bengal	478	870	474	952
Assam	548	1483	545	1167
Bihar	355	708	316	748
Orissa	506	993	475	1025
Punjab	735	1300	711	1833
Maharashtra	767	1336	747	1398
Tamil Nadu	533	1187	534	1298
Uttar Pradesh	364	743	387	819

The low per capita income and the poor tax base in Bihar, because of its small organised sector and agrarian character, does not offer much scope for intensifying resource mobilisation. The shortfall in investment can be made good only through higher central assistance. In fact, if the development of Eastern Region is to improve, then it has to be through more central assistance or through higher investment in this region in the Central Sector.

Table 2.5

(In Rupees)

	Per Capital Central Plan Outlay		Per Capita Central Assistance	
	1951-79	1980-85	1951-79	1980-85
Bihar	498	461	300	180
Orissa	737	569	464	250
West Bengal	621	641	297	125
All State Average	808	694	375	207

Table 2.5 indicates that among the three Eastern States, Orissa

is better placed with higher central outlay and assistance. In fact, it was the highest recipient of central assistance after Himachal, Assam and Punjab. Orissa also performed better in respect of mobilisation of resources and higher investment outlay. The allegation of step-motherly treatment to Eastern Region is, therefore, not without substance.

The credit deposit ratio for the Commercial Banks in the Eastern Region, except for Orissa (72%) is much below the national average of 61 per cent (March, 1992). For Bihar the credit-deposit ratio was only 39.5 per cent for U.P. 44 per cent and West Bengal 52.7 per cent. If the mobilisation of deposits and advances of credit in Calcutta are excluded, then the credit deposit ratio for the rest of West Bengal is lower than 30%. The lending policies of commercial banks in the region have led to net outflow of investible resources from the region. Obviously scarce savings of the region are being used to meet credit requirements elsewhere.

The low per capita plan outlay can be made good by larger flow of private investment. But investments by Commercial Banks have been much below the national average. The poor infrastructural facilities have been attributed as the main reason for low level of lending and credit absorption. However, there is no corelation between the two. The index of infrastructural facilities as computed by the Centre for monitoring Indian economy for West Bengal is 115, against the All India average 100, 111 for Maharashtra, 98 for Andhra Pradesh and 93 for Karnataka. Yet the C.D. Ratio for West Bengal is lower than the All-India average and those for the aforementioned States. In West Bengal,C.D. Ratio for rural areas is 46% compared to 59% for All-India, inspite of agricultural production showing higher growth rate in West Bengal. Bihar's index at 97 is higher than that for Orissa 86, yet C.D. Ratio in Bihar is lower than Orissa.

For Financial Institutions also the Eastern Zone is a shadow area. The State-wise assistance sanctioned and distributed by all Financial Institutions taken together (IDBI, IFCI, ICICI, SIDBI, LIC, ITI, CIC, SFCs, SIDCs etc) upto 1991, is summarised in the following table. We have included the more developed States for comparison. Bihar's share at 2.3% is lower than Orissa's 2.65%. Maharashtra and Gujrat between them got one-third of the total investments.

Table 2.6

Name of States	*Assistance Disbursed by All Financial Institutions cumulative upto 91 (Rs.Crores)*	*Percentage of the total for the country.*
1.	2.	3.
Bihar	1548.2	2.31
U.P.	6292.2	9.38
West Bengal	3616.8	5.39
Orissa	1912.9	2.85
Assam	458.9	0.68
Gujrat	8208.1	12.24
Maharashtra	13359.2	19.92
Tamil Nadu	6423.5	9.56
Andhra Pradesh	5481.9	8.17
Madhya Pradesh	3378.8	5.03
Karnataka	4336.1	6.46
Kerala	1581.9	2.36
Punjab	2338.3	3.49
Rajasthan	2670.4	3.98
All-India	67059.00	100.00

Sources: Report on Deveopment Banking in India 1990-91.

The great expansion of coal mines has not been a blessing to Bihar. Vast stretches of forest have been destroyed and land dug up. The ecological balance of the area has been upset. People have been uprooted. Jobs in the coal mines are becoming scarce because of mechanisation and have been grabbed by the big land holders as jobs have been linked with acquisition of land. Besides, the coal industry is faced with the problem of excess hands. Coal India has refrained from accepting its responsibility of rehabilitaion of displaced families or of preserving the environment and ecology.

Weak Infrastructure

It has been emphasised that availability of power and satisfactory transport and communication facilities are the prime movers of development. The position in respect of these essential infrastructure in Bihar is very unsatisfactory. The surfaced road length per 100 sq. KMs. of area (1991-92) was only 19.5 KMs. compared to the All-India figure of 21.8 KMs. The high density of population would imply that the State would require more and better roads to cope with higher traffic than the rest of the country. The total road length per lakh population is only 119 KMs. compared to the All- India figure of 211 KMs. The position in respect of power is equally alarming. The per capita consumption of power was only 110 units in 1988-89, compared to the All-India figure of 216 units. The per capita availability of power in the State till 1960-61 was better than All-India average. The position is much worse if we exclude the industries in Chotanagpur, which gets the major supply, 515 units per head. North Bihar is virtually bereft of power, per capita availability being just 26 units. The low consumption of power is not due to lack of demand but due to non-availability of power and low installed capacity in the State. It is surprising that the low consumption of power is used as an argument against increasing the installed capacity in the State. The result has been that private industries are reluctant to come to the State and the industries that have been set up are starved for power. Agriculturists, too, have failed to take advantage of the irrigation potential due to uncertain and short supply of power. Though N.T.P.C. set up Super Thermal Power Stations in U.P. and other states based on coal supplied from Bihar. Colgong in Bihar was selected only recently.

Disastrous floods have been a regular feature in Bihar, Assam, West Bengal and Eastern U.P. The large number of rivers emanating from the Himalayas, divide the plains into segments, making communication difficult between different parts. The discharge of the rivers increases manifold as snow begins to melt in summer and the rain water during monsoon over a large catchment area, major portion of which covers the heavy precipitation areas in Nepal and Tibet, seek an outlet across the North Bihar plains through Ganga and Brahmputra into the Bay of Bengal. The deltaic topography of the Gangetic plain naturally makes it flood prone. The taming of Kosi has been a major achievement in recent times. The river swung over an arc of 100 kilometres, devastating vast areas in North-East Bihar. The floods cause extensive damage to crops, property and human and animal lives. The flood prone area in Bihar covers nearly 1/3rd of the total geographical area and 3/4th of N. Bihar. Bihar accounts for nearly half of the total flood affected population in the country. Flood relief provides at present hardly ameliorates the hardship of the population and fails to touch the basic problem of controlling the floods. The damage caused by floods to the Eastern States is enormous and emphasises the need for it being tackled at the National level.

Thus low output per agricultural worker due to shortage of land and under-employment, inability to invest in inputs either due to non-availability or lack of credit support and also non-availability of power to utilise the irrigation potential have led to a situation of stagnation in agriculture. The few pockets of prosperity that have emerged are either due to favourable local factors or enterprise of individual farmers.

Lack of Commitment

Indicipline, among workers is common. Commitment to work is missing. The State public sector undertakings are over-staffed. The State Electricity Board has shifts of two days only in its power stations, which means less working hours and more rest through change of shifts. The workmen emerge over-time for doing maintenance work, though it is possible to perfom this job during the working hours, or they work as contractor's men for doing maintenance work. No doubt such workmen have vested interest in keeping the generating units sick most of the time, for it is more remunerative to them. Similarly, the State Transport Corporation has to depend on daily paid drivers to run their buses, as most of the regular drivers are either on leave or unavailable for duty for some reason or other. The daily paid drivers are naturally more interested in making extra income out of their jobs at the cost of the Corporation. These examples emphasise our point that we must evolve a system that is conducive to work and efficiency. Instead matters have been allowed to drift to such an extent that the system has degenerated into fostering inefficiency.

Efficienct police administration and satisfactory law and order situation is a basic factor in promoting development activities. The ability of the State administration to protect assets and enable the entrepreneurs, artisans and traders to pursue their activities without fear is a positive inducement. But when the law and order machinery breaks down and people lose faith in the police to protect them from the depredation of unscrupluous elements, there will be flight of capital. Confidence may be undermined to such an extent that it may be difficut to persuade entrepreneurs to pursue their activities in such areas. The record of criminal administration and law and order situation in Bihar has not been encouraging. The record of industrial relations, too, has been unsatisfactory.

Political instability in Bihar coupled with poor leadership has also been a retarding factor. The average tenure of Chief Ministers in Bihar between 1961-1990 was less than two years. No Chief Minister has felt strong enough to resist pressure groups and lobbies. The result is that succeeding Chief Ministers and Ministers took up schemes of their choice mainly benefiting their constituencies in haste without due consideration of their productivity. Large number of such schemes have proved to be bad investments of doubtful utility. The resources were thinly spread and naturally completion of schemes was delayed. Of late the contractor politician nexus has also grown, with the contractor being least concerned about completion of schemes and quality of work. Such a situation indicates why available resources are inefficiently utilised, and the income generated is much below the anticipated level. Narrow parochial consideration have dominated over fundamental issues of larger interest to the State. The frequent change of governments and ministers and officers entrusted with development work has meant that there is no continuity. There has been erosion of accountability. Though schemes were taken up to accomodate succeeding governments and ministers, there was no urgency to complete them. In Fact,many have been neglected as their patrons ceased to be in Power.

Concluding Remarks

Bihar, which was carved out of Greater Bengal in 1912, is not a homogenous unit. Apart from caste factions, there are subregions within the State, which are almost separate entities. Till 1956, when there was no bridge across river Ganga in Bihar, it was easier to travel to Calcutta from Patna than to undertake a journey from Patna to Muzaffarpur, only 40 miles away. The road bridge across Ganga at Patna which could be completed only in 1982, has proved to be powerful link between North and South Bihar and has also served as a catalyst for development by making the North Bihar areas easily accessible. This bridge it may be recalled was constructed at the initiative of the State Government, as the Centre was lukewarm to the proposal.

Almost entire investment in the Central Sector in Bihar has been in Chotanagpur. There has been very little Central investment in the rest of Bihar. The adivasis in Chotanagpur and Santhal Parganas have been violently agitating for a long time for a seperate Jharkhand State,. Surplus North Bihar labour is finding it extremely difficult to find jobs in Chotanagpur. With a strong Jharkhand movement, non-Adivasis naturally feel insecure. They prefer to go to Punjab, Haryana and even Maharashtra in search of employment.

The decay of sugar factories in North Bihar has created a void which has not been filled up as yet. At the time of independence 33 out of 138 sugar factories in the country were located in Bihar and they contributed 25 per cent of the total sugar production in the country. At the present Bihar has 28 Bihar factories, 15 of which are sick, and State's contribution to total output is barely 5 per cent.

The strong divisive forces have prevented the growth of regional feeling in favour of Bihar. Regionalism in other areas such as Assam, Andhra Pradesh. Tamil Nadu and to a limited extent in Orissa has served as a rallying point to promote the regions' interests. It worked as a lobby to bargain with the centre. Development in the present set up follows political influences. Regions which have strong political voice have been successful in obtaining development schemes. The development of Punjab, Haryana and Western Uttar Pradesh is a to large extent due to their close proximity to the Union Capital and the influence they wield with the central ministers. Bihar is politically important but Biharis have not been able to combine together to press for Bihar's interests. Naturally, Bihar's interests have gone by default. Because of conflicting pulls and pressures Biharis have failed to discover their identity.

It is obvious that Bihar requires more than proportionate share in Central outlay for eradication of poverty. The incidence of poverty being uneven, assistance should be linked with the incidence of poverty rather than with population or number of blocks. The same holds good in case of employment generation programmes. Assistance should be linked with the extent of unemployment. Further, the Centre has to provide the additional resource for investment in the infrastructure, especially power, transport and communication if it is to be brought up to All-India level, otherwise the State will continue to lag behind, the rest of the country.

REFERENCES

1. Seventh Five Year Plan, Planning Commission.
2. Aproach to the Eight Five Year Plan, Planning Commission, 1950.
3. Eighty Five Year Plan, Planning Commission, 1992.
4. Seventh & Eight Five Year Plans, Planning Department, Government of Bihar.
5. Annual Plans for Bihar, Planning Department.
6. Economic Survey 1985-86 to 1994-95 Govt. of India.
7. Draft Plan, U.P.
8. Basic Plan Statistics, Government of Orissa, 1985.
9. S.R. Sen Committees' Report on District Planning, Planning Commission, May 1985.
10. Diagnosing Bihars' Economic Backwardness (Statistical Table) Dr. K.N.Prasad.
11. Operational Statistics - I.F.C.I (91-92).
12. Bihar's Economy and Development of Rural Roads—CH-3 in Souvenir of Indian Road Congress, Dec. 1992.

3

Land Reforms for Raising Agricultural Productivity

With nearly 28% of the net national product being contributed by agriculture and 64% of the work force deriving their livelihood from agriculture, agricultural development holds the key to rural development. India's agriculture was virtually stagnant during the British rule. Neither change in population, in income or the organisational structure of the economy was such as to induce any significant change in agriculture. Transport and communication was very poorly developed, with the result that cultivation was primarily for self consumption or for meeting the needs of the village. Subsistence agriculture thus continued to be the principal characteristic of Indian agriculture till 1940s. Before this the impact of urbanisation was too weak to make production for market an important motive. Some non-cereals were grown for exports, e.g. tea, cotton, jute, sugar, etc., but these plantations were owned mostly by foreigners and dominated by ruling country's interests. The real challenge to Indian agriculture emerged in the post independence period with the population boom which was witnessed after the 1940s. The population of the Indian subcontinent was 280 million in 1901, and it had increased to 340 million in 1941, i.e. 60 million or 21.5% in 40 years. But the population of the subcontinent jumped to 745 million in 1975 i.e., by nearly 120% during the next 35 years. Till 1940 the requirement for more food was met by bringing in more arable land under cultivation. The Indian sub-continent is favourably placed as far as availability of arable land is concerned. India constitutes only 2.5% of the total geographical area of the world but has 143 million hectares of arable land which is 12.2% of the total arable area available in the world.

Ester Boserup in her book, "The conditions of Agricultural Growth" has propounded the thesis that it is the pressure of population and consequent increase in demand for food that is responsible for intensification of agriculture. According to her thesis the rise in price of foodgrains as a result of increase in population leads to fall in real wages of farm labour. The farm labourers in turn are induced to work harder to make up for the loss in their earnings. As the situation accentuates, adoption of improved technology follows. Boserup depicts a situation very similar to one we are facing in the Eastern Region of country. "A period of sustained population growth will first have the effect of lowering output per man hour in agriculture, but in the long run the effect might be to raise labour productivity in other activities and eventually to raise output per man hour in agriculture. People in rural areas, instead of voluntarily accepting the harder job of a more intensive agriculture, will seek to obtain more remunerative and less arduous work in non-agricultural occupations. In such period, large scale migrations to urban areas are likely to take place, with the result that the urban population must carry the double burden of finding employment opportunities and high food prices. Difficulties of this type have occured in most developing contries in the past, and they have been dealt with in different ways." As migration from rural areas to towns proceeds, the ensuing relative rise of food prices provides the necessary incentive for intensification for agriculture and is followed by rise in rural wages, which keeps migration within bounds. This analysis is very relevant under present conditions. Government policy should be to allow the natural effects of population change to assert itself. By keeping agricultural prices in check or by providing relief to farm labourers through other measures, we would only blunt the effect of this strong pull for inducing intensive agriculture. Availability of cheap food is necessary for industrial peace and political stability. Cheap food can be had through imports, but such a policy would not be conducive to agricultural growth. Similarly by forcing the food prices to be low, we are depriving the agriculturists of their main incentive to raise production. We also impose a heavy burden on the non-agricultural sector through heavy subsidies on foods and fertilizers. In 1989-90, food subsidies amounted to Rs. 2,480 crores, fertilizer subsidies being Rs. 4,540 crores. Since 1991, government has been trying to reduce the subsidy burden.

It was fortunate and a matter of coincidence that the Zamindari system, the big estate owners, holding intermediary rights between tenants and the state, were abolished immediately after independence. The institutions of Zamindars or the practice of permanent settlement of land which was established by Lord Cornwallis in the later half of 18th century had decayed into an oppressive system with the evils of rent racketeering and the extraction of begar (free-service) from agricultural labourers. The Zamindars enjoyed the patronage of the British rulers and the Zamindars in turn extended full support to the British regime. The Zamindars got identified as exploiters of the peasantry and with attainment of independence they were liquidated. The system failed to bring about improvement of land and development of agriculture as was originally intended. The liquidation of Zamindars was complete. The newly formed Congress Governments in the states showed much firmness and commitment, a feature which has been completely lacking in implementation of land reforms since then. Since independence we have also witnessed population explosion, industrialisation and rapid growth of cities. It is indeed fortunate that the peasants are now tenants directly under the state which has become the guardian of the tenants. The Zamindari system would have acted as an obstacle. The abolition of Zamindari and establishment of peasant proprietorship, laid the foundation for the technological leap forward into green revolution.

With the abolition of Zamindari, feudalism came to an end in Indian agriculture. However, mental habits and attitudes are slow to change and we may still witness incidents of oppression of agricultural labourers at the hands of big landlords. The conflict is no longer between big land owners and agricultural labourers. The stratification of the agrarian set-up, the mobility and cohesion of labour is the result of population explosion, industrialisation and urbanisation as described above. The bigger landlords have no option except to compromise with the situation in which the vast multitude of marginal farmers and agricultural labourers have the backing of popularly elected democratic government.

The principal features of Indian agriculture are the large number of agricultural labourers who are only partly employed, they constitute approximately 25% of the total work force and nearly 40% of those engaged in agriculture; the preponderance of small marginal holdings, they constitute nearly 75% of the total number of holdings, multiple fragments of holdings and tiny size of plots; low yield peracre and the extreme poverty and inability of the majority of the farmers to invest for higher production. Because of mounting pressure of population on land, per capita availability of land will decline to less than 0.30 hectares by the end of the century, even if half of the population shift to non-agricultural occupations. This will put pressure on the population to bring more and more of forest and pasture under cultivation. Besides, urbanization and industrialization will require 6 million hectares of additional land. Much of this will be provided only by surrendering agricultural lands. It is clear that additional requirements for food and agricultural raw materials will have to come through more and more intensive cultivation. How to tackle this grave problem is a major challenge before Indian agriculture. Agriculture is a private occupation and the state can only act as a catalyst for higher production. Far more attention has to be paid to Agricultural Research for introduction of quick maturing high yielding seeds for all major crops.

Satisfaction of basic needs of the family is a compelling necessity for the marginal and small farmers. Thus for the vast number of farmers, who are producing for self-consumption, the market prices are not very relevant. But it acquires significance when decision has to be taken for investing in inputs and developing the land for higher yields. Agricultural labour, too, is interested in protecting its real wage by putting in extra hours of work if necessary. Rational conduct implies that the peasats would try to improve their standard of living by adding to their incomes. This is possible only through higher yield per acre or through better price for agricultural produce. The former would result in more income only if the price for agricultural produce does not fall. There is no guarantee against this. It will depend upon the general buoyancy of the economy, i.e. if the economy is growing at a fairly stable rate with larger flow of incomes to the population to allow for increase in food prices also. In a poor economy, where food consumption is suppressed, income elasticity for food is positive. Rising prices for agricultural produce thus has the merit of providing a positive incentive to produce more and invest in development of agriculture. Nutrition level in the country is very poor. The average calorific intake is about 2,000 calories against a requirement of 2,400 calories. With increase in incomes, people would first impove their nutrition level. Food production in 1995 was 190 tonnes. The so called self-sufficiency in foodgrains does not mean that there is no unsatisfied demand for food. Because of poverty, poor are not able to buy enough food to feed their family members. If people could buy their full requirement, an additional 50 million tonnes of foodgrains can be easily absorbed. Our population is growing at the rate of 2% per annum. By the end of the century, our population would increase to 100 crores. Roughly 2.5 million tonnes of food is required to feed one crore people, i.e. @ 684 gms (3/4 seer) per head per day. This includes provision for seed and allows for reasonable loss in storage and transit. This means that nearly 250 million of foodgrains will be required in 2000 A.D. to feed the population at minimum nutritional standards. In 30 years, i.e. 1952 to 1982 food production doubled itself, i.e. increased by 75 million tonnes. Foodgrains production must increase by another 50 million tonnes in only 5 years if the above target is to be achieved. Foodgrains production increased at the rate of 3.0% per annum only during the Sixth and Seventh Plan. With increase in income and nutritional standard of the population, there will be shift to better food. The demand for oil seeds, pulses, sugar, vegetables and fruits will increase; so will the demand for commercial crops. This will make the task of increasing production more difficult as the food crops will compete with other crops, for there is very little scope for extending cultivation.

Thus there is insatiable demand for food and other agricultural produce, and there is no demand constraint for agricultural production and there is no fear of glut in the market either, Government has only to ensure that the farmers are adequately remunerated to take up intensive cultivation to meet their own needs and the growing needs of the country.

Tenancy Reform and Its Implications

It is argued that the institutional set-up in rural India and pattern of land ownership and cultivation are obstructing increase in agricultural production. The higher castes, who own bulk of the land, do not cultivate land themselves. The result is that land is not fully utilized. When family owns the land and also cultivates it, land is cultivated most intensively and the physical limit of output is reached. On the other hand, when cultivation is done with hired labour, production can be extended only upto the economic margin, i.e., upto the point when wage becomes equal to the value of the marginal output. This is presenting too simplistic a view of cultivation activities. Even family labour has cost. This is more than merely the cost over tools that have to be used for work. Labour beyond a limit is uncomfortable and may be positively hurtful, especially when less and less output is forthcoming with additional labour. Land and labour are not the only factors of agricultural production. Inputs like irrigation, improved variety of high yielding seeds, fertilizers, insecticides as well as labour saving devices are becoming increasingly important for extracting the maximum yield from land. This investment is not divisible labour wise. The capital investments in modern agriculture are more important than labour. It is for this reason that adequate provision of cheap credit has to be made available to the farmer in order to enable him to take recourse to the investment package cited above. With labour alone, productivity would be low and the physical limit of output per unit of land would be attained at a lower level. It is possible to attain higher level of production only by utilising additional labour with the complementary inputs mentioned above.

The contention that it is possible to reach the physical limits of production on family operated farms is therefore purely hypothetical and does not hold good in actual practice. A more plausible expalnation why family operated farms will be cultivated more intensively is that in case of family operated farms, marginal average output of family labour rather than marginal output of individual members will be equated with the value imputed by the family to its labour. This imputed value will be determined by the wage employment available to the family members in the neighbourhood.

Intensive (Scientific) cultivation as we have already mentioned requires substantial capital investment for which sufficient credit support is required. With step up in investments, agricultural production acquires an element of risk and uncertainty. A subsistence farmer will adopt a safe course and avoid risks. With availability of cheap credit he may venture to take risks. Credit market is very imperfect in India and more so in the Eastern Region. At present part of the requirement for credit is met by the bigger land owners. In Bihar this contribution is substantial. With peasant proprietorship this source would dry up.

Hard labour on a regular and continuous basis is a drudgery. Man temperamentally shirks hard labour. It is true that the necessity to grow sufficient food to avoid starvation is compelling necessity. It is argued that this compulsion would drive the farmer to cultivate his land more intensively till the physical limit of output is reached. But availability of wage employment in the neighbourhood would prevent this from happening. Public works are being taken up on an extensive scale. J.R.Y. aims at providing employment to those seeking jobs, at statutorily fixed minimum wages, which are generally higher than the economic rate of unskilled labour and are fixed in keeping with the social and moral objective of providing an acceptable standard of living to the weak and economically deprived classes. There is no doubt dignity attached to working on one's own land, and loss of face may restrain a land-owner to work as a wage earner on public schemes. But for those who are on the margin of subsistence this psychological barrier would not operate as a restraining force. Thus it may be argued that by hiking up wages through minimum wage legislation etc., the economic limits of cultivation would be curtailed. This can be averted if labour productivity increases. For labour productivity to increase, the farmer will have to take recourse to investment in better tools and equipments, like electric or diesel pumps, tractors, handtillers, etc., that provide him additional power. The burden of paying higher wages to labour can also be avoided by making the labour share in the cultivation process. This is a convenient arrangement for extracting more work from labour and also paying him in proportion to the produce he raises. Labour is also lured by the prospect of earning more through share in higher production.

Leasing out of holdings by bigger land owners is therefore dictated by purely economic considerations and is a common practice. Thus it is found not only in the poor countries which are heavily populated, but in comparatively developed countries also. The practice is widely prevalent and has persisted even in modern times in "Europe and other developed countries. In France, in 1946, as many as 33.5% of the total number of holdings were operated on rental basis and 10.3% of the holdings were operated on share cropping basis. In Spain (1952) the corresponding figures were 22.3% and 14.1% respectively and for Italy (1947) 18.6% and 33.3% respectively."

When agriculture is the predominant occupation and pressure of population on land is increasing and the inheritance laws allow devolution of land equally to all heirs, it is but natural that holdings will become smaller and more fragmented. Unless the inheritance laws are amended to give exclusive possession to those heirs only who opt for cultivation, we will be faced with a situation, in which those who migrated to cities and other places in search of better employment, will leave behind their paternal land to be cultivated by others, preferably their relatives or trustworthy people on rental basis. Besides there are widows, disabled persons, military personnel and old people who have no option but to lease out their land. Thus it is not only the big landlord who leases out land. The small and marginal farmers are also compelled to lease out their own land, and seek better employment in other occupations as their land holdings are too meagre to support the growing needs and aspirations of their families. Similarly there would be more and more of such people, who do not own land or who have very little land, and who would like to lease in more land to raise enough produce to feed their families. The transaction of leasing out land (Bataidari or share cropping) is therefore not be looked down as that of a pure rentier, but as also compelled by economic reasons and due to recalcitrance of labour. The terms and conditions of lease very considerably. When it is difficult for the landowner to supervise cultivation, he is generally satisfied by a fixed rental, either in cash or kind. Fixed rental in kind is preferred as it gives protection against rise in prices. The landowner who is in a position to supervise the agricultural operations and is willing to take risks by investing in agriculture, finds it most advantageous to go in for share cropping, i.e., sharing the costs and the produce, for thereby he gets more produce per unit of land.

The absentee landowners generally opt for fixed rent arrangement. It may appear that fixed rent would act as a spur to intensive cultivation to the lessee as he would try to compensate for the rent he has to pay through hard work. In practise this may not be so. As discussed above, this is possible only if the lessee is in position to invest sufficient capital and most of the tenants because of their extreme poverty cannot afford it, and they are also afraid of taking the risk of incurring higher expenditure and not being rewarded by commensurate increase in production and income. But there is no reason to presume why the share croppers should not be interested in investing over hired land, atleast short term investment related to raising of crops, the benefits of which would accrue entirely to the lessee. The real difficulty is the reluctance of financial institutions and even primary agricultural credit societies to finance such under tenants. The credit institutions should be persuaded to extend short-term credit to share-croppers against pledging of crops. The crop insurance scheme should serve to reassure the financial institutions. Under the present policy there is no arangement for giving short term loans to agricultural labourers or share-croppers. The few cases of such financing are the result of local pressures.

Under share cropping arrangements, under which the land-owner supervises the agricultural operations and shares the expenditure over inputs, there are obvious advantages both to the land-owner and the tenant. There is superior management. The land-owner utilises his spare time in gathering information about latest techniques and in arranging for the input which in Indian conditions is quite strenuous and time taking. Since the cost over inputs is shared, the risks are proportionately reduced and this provides stronger incentive for adoption of modern methods of cultivation. With a progressive land owner, residing in close proximity, share cropping would thus result in higher productivity. From the point of view of agricultural production share cropping is, therefore, not an inefficient arrangement. In fact it may be more efficient compared to peasant proprietorship who have no capital of their own and who do not have any institutional credit support either. From the point of view of equity, however, we may denounce share cropping as the tenant has to part with a portion of his produce as 'rental.'

Marshall's analysis of the tenant trying to equate his marginal output with the wage of labour has influenced thinking even during recent times on the subject. In case of sharecropping, it is argued the marginal product is proportionately reduced. Studies by S.N. Cheung and others have tried to refute this proposition. Whether the tenant will labour beyond the point when he cannot get equivalent of prevailing rate of wage depends upon the disutility of labour and the value imputed by the tenant to his labour. Tenancy takes diverse forms. The terms of leasing are determined by the bargaining strength of labourers vis-a-vis the tenats. It is also influenced by the capabilities of the two parties to take risks and invest in inputs for higher production. Tenants as share-croppers should have more incentive to work harder in order to improve their earnings, compared to ordinary wage earners. It is comon observation that piece rate workers work harder than daily wage earners. The share cropping arrangement offers even better motivation than piece rates. Piece rates induce harder labour but share cropping also encourages careful work, which is important for higher production and thereby the task of supervision by the land owner is made easier. Under share cropping risk is also shared, which encourages more intensive cultivation. The combined effect of all these enfluences is that the marginal productivity of labour is raised, leading to greater output for the same units of labour.

When the land owner hires labour on daily wages basis, the entire risk of cultivation is on the landowner. In case of fixed rent the entire risk is that of the tenant. The absentee landlord, who does not want to incur any supervision cost, is satisfied with low rental. This may result in larger gain to the tenant but as we have argued above does not necessarily lead to higher production. For higher production we require more than just 'labour.' There must be willingness to take risks and capacity to invest in critical inputs. In India we have a large number of landless agricultural labourers and marginal farmers competing with each other to hire a small bit of land from the landowners. At the same time because of social pressures, minimum wage legislation and public works, wages are tending to rise. In such a situation the landowners would prefer a share cropping arrangement under which he can avoid paying higher wages. In view of the legislations probibiting tenancy and leasing of land, the landowner tries to parcel his land in small bits to several tenants on an annual basis in order to safeguard himself against the possible application of legel measures and also to obtain the best terms. The tenancy legislations, therefore, have the opposite effect of reducing the bargaining strength of the under-tenants by preventing him from pressing for security of tenure for the law does not recognise tenancy.

To achieve total peasent proprietorship we will have to abolish the practice of leasing, enable tenants to acquire ownership and distribute land obtained by application of ceiling on larger holdings to landless agricultural labourers. Even if we succeed in our mission we will be still left with a very large number of landless labourers. According to the existing tenancy legislations, undertenants cannot acquire ownership over land belonging to small and middle land owners. They can do so over big land holding, which are already subject to ceiling law. This means that the number of marginal holdings, which are already half of the total number, will further increase. Without massive credit support, the need for which has been pointed above, the objective of intensive and scientific cultivation would not be realised. Large amount of compensation may have to be paid for conferring ownership, and there will also be large scale resumption of land from share croppers and other tenants by marginal and small land holders who can retain their holdings but cannot lease their land. On being pressed very much, they may prefer to keep their land fallow. The changeover may not be smooth and agriculture may receive a set back and there will be fall in production during the interim period. The reluctance of landowners, who are not self cultivators, to invest in agriculture is primarily because of the confusion over the status of tenants and the apprehension of being deprived of their land.

Leasing of land, except under extreme cases of disability, has been abolished by all the states. Informally this practice continues though in a disguised and concealed form on a wide scale. Thus the Agricultural census of Bihar, 1981, reports that only 0.4% of the land holders depend on leased in holdings which is less than 0.25% of the total owned area. This is obviously contrary to facts. It is to be found in all parts of the country though the incidence in some parts is more. The existence of the problem, however, is minimised by some states. These unrecognised tenants can get protection only if they go to the courts. The poor peasant who has chosen to take land on lease would not do so. Some political parties have chosen to rally these tenants to conduct a campaign against the big land-owners, especially in North Bihar. This has brought no benefit to the tenants but has served to increase the distrust between land owners and labourers, leading to disruption of agricultural activities. By not accepting the real situation we are only making the problem more acute. The entrusting of land by small owners, leaving the village for more gainful employment in the cities to the care of relatives is largely due to the fear of law. Such relatives entrusted with the care of land, take minimal interest in cultivation and have no urge for increasing production. Had there been no prohibitions, such land would have been leased out to those who needed it most and who would have made best use of it. The share cropper, under the existing law, cannot ask for long term leases or ask for loans for raising crops on the land over which he has cultivating possession. In the interest of intensive cultivation and for agricultural development it is necessary that the practise of share cropping and other forms of tenancy are recognised and the tenant is provided protection by regulating the conditions of leasing to his advantage, giving him sufficient security of tenure, extending up to 5 years atleast, and is also provided adequate credit support to take up cultivation more intensively. Land-owners would not object to these measures as long as there ownership is not threatened.

The short-term and long-term implications of family operated farms in terms of production, therefore, need to be looked into more closely. In the short-term, investment is primarily over imputs meant to raise crops and the share cropper would have motivation similar to any land owner. The long-term investments over providing source of irrigation, improvement of drainage, land levelling, field boundaries, irrigation channels, water conservation, social forestry, etc. will not be taken up by an under tenant unless he has permanent stake in the land or the leases are for fairly long periods during which the investment can be recovered. In view of the prevailing uncertainty due to anti-tenancy legislations and agrarian unrest and lately land grabbing the bigger landowners are also indifferent to such long-term improvement schemes.

The fall in incidence of share cropping or tenancy in green revolution areas is not due to inefficiency of share cropping. With intensive and scientific cultivation, the potential output per unit of land and consequently the anticipated earnings per unit of land goes up. This induces large and medium farmers to resume their land for self-cultivation. On the other hand, due to greater risks involved and rise in wage level, the inducement to lease in land by the marginal cultivators becomes weak. The opening of job opportunities outside agriculture further reduces the attachment of marginal farmers to stick to their holdings and they may opt to sell their land to bigger farmers. The large and medium cultivators, on the other hand try to increase their size of holding to take advantage of higher production techniques of cultivation. The combined effect would befall in the incidence of tenancy. This phenomenon is clearly visible in Punjab. But for major part of the country, including the Eastern Region, these forces are not operative.

What is our immediate task? As we have stated earlier, food production has to be raised to 250 million tonnes by the turn of the century to meet the full requirements of the population. The Ceiling Acts were adopted by the states in the 1960s. Our experience with application of ceiling on large land holdings and distribution of surplus land among landless has not been very happy. The surplus land which was obtained after much effort was enough to meet the needs of the landless and satisfy the hunger for land. The 1981, census recorded 55.5 million agricultural labourers in a total population of 222.5 million workers. Because of application of ceiling, 75 lakh acres of land was declared surplus. Even if we distributed 1 acre of land to each agricultural labourer not more than 7.5 million agricultural labourers, i.e., only 13.5% would get land. The problem is very grave in the heavily populated Eastern Region, especially the Gangetic plains. In Bihar the total population of agricultural labourers was 9.5 million (1991). Surplus land distributed so far has been less than 3 lakh acres , which means that not more than 4% of the total population of agricultural labourers were provided land. The above figures have been quoted only to convey the gigantic size of the problem and the ineffectiveness of ceiling laws in releasing enough surplus land for the landless. The hard reality is that out of 29.8 lakh hectares declared surplus for the whole country, government has taken possession of 23.5 lakh hectares and only 19.34 lakh hectares have been distributed. This leaves only 3.81 lakh hectares for distribution. The balance 6.65 lakh hectares are under litigation. In Bihar out of 4.74 lakh acres declared surplus, possession has been taken of 3.96 lakh acres and 1.03 lakh acres is still under litigation. In many cases the beneficiaries have been dispossessed by the erstwhile landowners. In large number of cases the beneficiaries have been chosen from non-agricultural occupations, and such beneficiaries lease the land at the earliest opportunity to others. It is doubtful if the application of ceiling laws has contributed to rise in production and majority of the beneficiaries continue to be below poverty line. It is quite understandable why the initial enthusiasm over application of ceiling on land holdings is over.

Our commitment to the socialistic pattern of society and considerations for equity would lead us to support the objective of transfer of ownership of land to those who till it. Self ownership confers status and dignity and eliminates the possibility of exploition which exists in the owner tenant relationship. But the limited availability of land and the needs of a mammoth population, which is growing rapidly, requires that we give more emphasis to higher production. Even the strong protagonists of peasant proprietorship concede that family operated farms yield lower output per unit of labour compared to large farms which engage hired labour. It is obvious that full potential of labour is not realised while operating on tiny family operated holdings. Is it not anachronistic that we should talk of tiny farms operated by family members on subsistence basis in an age of rapidly developing technology and higher standard of living to labour. It will be difficult to satisfy the marginal farmers or agricultural labourers with incomes which are only a fraction of the wage earned by the industrial workers. This is an untenable position. We cannot condemn our marginal farmers and rural population to penury for all items. Hunger for land is so keen that any talk of conferring ownership, however inadequate, is popular. But land is the most scarce and precious resource in India. We should try to have a system of land management that gives the best results in terms of production. Though suggestions have been made about community and village ownership of land and co-operative farming, we are reluctant to adopt it in view of the caste ridden and faction ridden society of ours. The Chinese have built up the foundations of a strong agricultural economy on the basis of co-operative ventures. The Chinese are of course, favourably placed because of their homogeneous society. When we are planning for agricultural development we have to look 20 or even 50 years ahead, when there would be atleast twice as many mouths to be fed. It is not suggested that there should be no ceilng on land holdings. Very large holdings are uneconomically managed and give undue control to the land owner over those who cultivate land for him. We cannot also afford the luxury of very large holdings, when so many are landless. But ceilings should not be made a fetish, and not much purpose would be served by revising it downwards at regular intervals.

We have to aim primarily at raising agricultural production and strive for security of tenure, so that our primary objective of providing enough food to all is not compromised. The statutory enactments, imposing ceiling on land-holding and abolition of tenancy have naturally created pressure for enforcement of these provisions. On the other hand the diffidence to enforce them has led to frustration among the landless and has also led to confrontation between the landowners and landless labourers and grabbing of land of the less resourceful absentee land owners. The latter development is the natural consequence of labour having been delinked from the big landowners and their erstwhile masters, and realisation by labour of the political power they wield because of their numerical strength. There may have been loss of 'insurance cover' provided by the earstwhile masters, but labour is now free to bargain for better terms and can migrate to other places in search of better livelihood. This attitude of lack of faith between land owners and labourers has upset the rural life and is having detrimental effect on agricultural production. Some may compare the present situation to the Marxian description of the preindustrial society, where serfdom yielded place to peasant proprietorship, attributing the present stagnation in agriculture to the greed of the landowners, who want to extract the maximum surplus, and their disinterestedness in agriculture. Though land is the bone of contention, it is the growing assertion of labour and the unwillingness of the farmers to take risks for raising productivity that is creating the stalemate.

Mr. Man Mohan Singh, Ex. Finance Minister, while Governor of the R.B.I. rightly observed. "The enactment of progressive land reform legislations, which are not effectively implemented, no doubt hurts the cause of equity, but it also gives rise to uncertainty, which hampers the growth of productivity as well. There have been complaints that in some parts of the country, the fear of land ceilings has prevented farmers to take advantage of the newly created irrigation facilities. It is time that, in the interest of both higher production and greater equity, uncertainty about the implementation of nationally aproved land reform legislation is brought to an end."[4] The Sen Committee on Agricultural Productivity in Eastern India also questions the appropriateness of present tenancy legislation when it recommends that "Small farmers having 2 hectares or less of land should be exempted from present tenancy legislations and permitted to lease out and lease in land freely. This will eventually lead to a more rational and economic operational holding irrespective of the nature of the ownership of the holding, so far as small farmers are concerned. Further, if a small and marginal farmer knows that he can get back his leased out land whenever he wants to resume cultivation, he may be more willing to lease his land to another interested small farmer and move to a non-farm occupation of his liking."[5]

"Land to the tillers" is a populist slogan which gives the political parties wide support. The measure implies creation of marginal farms operated with family labour in preference to middle and large farms. Such petty farms are certainly not conductive to modern agriculture relying on capital intensive inputs.[6]

It may be remembered that the period 1971-77 coincided with the drive launched by Indira Gandhi to enforce land ceilings and distribute surplus land among landless. This trend of disintegration of large holdings has continued though at slackened pace in recent times. According to 1985-86 Agricultural Census, the number of marginal and small holdings (i.e. below 2 hectares) increased from 66.19 millions to 74.63 millions, between 1980-81 to 1985-86, that is by 12.7%, whereas the area operated by such holdings increased from 42.91 million hectares to 47.13 million hectares, that is by 9.8%. At the other end, the number of holdings above 4 hectares declined from 10.24 million to 9.85 millions and the area operated by them fell 86.24 million hectares to 80.20 million hectares, that is by 7%. The total number of operational holdings recorded in 1986, were 97.73 millions and the area operated by them was 163.91 million hectares. The break-up of large farms and equitable distribution of land was not accompanied by significant gains in production. Marginal farms, which constitute nearly 90% of the total number of holdings and cover upto 40% of the cultivated area, in the densely populated districts of the Eastern Region cannot serve as a base for progressive agriculture. It is doubtful whether we can achieve agricultural transformation and take the great leap in agricultural production; the ambitious targets for higher production cannot be realised on the strength of such tiny farms. Under the existing tenancy requirements, the middle and large farmers are finding it more difficult to carry on cultivation with hired labour. The only alternative available to the middle and large farmers is to resort to mechanisation of cultivation. Because of the prevailing uncertainty, even the bigger farmers may be reluctant to undertake such heavy investments, benefits of which can be realised only in the long run. The situation may compel some of the bigger land owners to sell part of their land and transfer their resources to less risky trade and business in the cities. Such breaking up of large holdings is not welcome, for the bigger farmers generally take the lead in adopting better techniques of cultivation. It may be remembered that the so-called big land holdings in India are of pygmy size compared to the gaint farms in the West and much smaller than even the cammunes in China, which are collectively held and operated.

Interestingly the Agricultural Census of Punjab, 1981, reveals that between 1970-71 to 1980-81, the number of marginal holdings (below 1 hectare) had decreased by 69.4% and those of small holdings (1-2 hectares) had increased by 23.4%, whereas medium holdings (2-4 hectares) had increased by 2.3% and large holdings (4-10 hectares) had increased by as much as 8.6%. The average size of holdings had increased from 2.9 acres to 3.8 acres during the same period. This is in sharp contrast to the scenario in Eastern India. Agricultural Census of 1986, however, reveals that the general trend discernible in rest of the country is beginning to assert itself in Punjab also.

Thus a more rational approach is called for in which increase in agricultural production is accompanied by substantive gains to agricultural labour, so that, the deprived classes share in the agricultural development and participate with vigour in the process of change. It is rightly said that in our programme to launch the green revolution, as much attention will have to be given to fighting the famine of jobs as to working for adequate food supplies, nutritional levels and protection from diseases. All cannot be provided land, but jobs must be found for all, only through such a policy agrarian unrest can be checked.

Consolidation of Holdings

Consolidation of holdings is an important programme of land reforms. Through consolidation it is possible to bring together fragments and increase the size of plots. At present holdings are split into large number of tiny plots of different shapes making cultivation difficult and irksome. By bringing together far flung tiny plots and consolidating them into compact plots we certainly facilitate cultivation. Consolidation improves supervision, by enabling the farmer to save time, which is lost in moving from plot to plot for difficult operations. A small well also has a certain minimum capacity for irrigation. If the plot is very small, the potential is not fully utilized. A pair of bullocks similarly to be fully utilized require a plot of minimum size to be fully utilised. Certain overheads are indivisible, whereas others cannot be split below a certain minimum size. When land is scarce we cannot afford to lose it by way of unproductive field boundaries, passage or unnecessary extension of field channels. Apart from land being utilised unprofitably, tiny plots may be also wasteful of other resources. Besides, consolidation safeguards community land for future community use and development programmes of the village.

Consolidation of holdings done before independence (as in Punjab) or done immediately after independence (as in U.P.) was smooth and successful. This was because the problem of fragmentation was not so acute at that time. Holdings were fewer in number and fragmentation had not reached such absurd limits. The problem of absentee landlordism was also not there to the same extent. Persons who are absentee landlords and who are not present at site are disinterested in the consolidation process. The cumbersome consolidation law also makes the operation very time consuming and any dis-satisfied person can thwart the finalization of the operation. Apart from making the law simpler, there is also the need for an element of compulsion.

In Bihar, consolidation has proceeded at a very slow pace. The programme has been under execution for over 30 years but only 15% of the cultivable land has been consolidated. The land records are not upto-date with the result that much preparatory work is required. Even where consolidation is said to be complete, delivery of possession on the basis of revised maps has not been given. Thus the programme has not conferred much benefit to the farmers or boosted agricultural production. Village is the unit of consolidation and under the existing law upto four plots can be provided. Thus the reduction of plots after consolidation has not been substantial. The reduction has been around 50%. It is alleged that consolildation has helped the influential and richer farmers by giving them possession of better land and that it has proved to be source of harassment to the ignorant and illiterate landholders. Because of rampant corruption among the field staff, this allegation is not without substance.

The real objective of consolidation is to increase the size of plots by reducing the number of plots and thus enable better water and land management with a view to increase agricultural production. Why should village constitute the unit of consolidation? Why cannot panchyat be treated as a unit of consolidation? This may make the operation a little difficult but it can be managed. Similarly, why cannot holdings be consolidated into one or at most two plots? We cannot give concession to the argument that farmers are sentimentally attached to their land and would like to retain them as far as possible in original. We cannot permit multiplicity of plots also on the ground that certain plots are suited for cultivation of specific crops, as our objective is to replace subsistence cultivation by cultivation for the market. Again, why further partition of holdings cannot be restricted in future? Heirs who do not opt for cultivation can be compensated in money, to be lent on easy terms by the government to those heirs who want to acquire the share. This may appear to be rather drastic. But the problem of fragmentation has reached such alarming magnitude, that only such extreme remedies can help. When holdings fall below a certain minimum level in size, the landholders find it more convenient to sell it, and thus the rank of the landless goes on increasing in size. The problem of landlessness is a major social and economic problem in the villages. Though lack of consolidation of holdings has been stated as cause for slow progress of green revolution in Bihar, we have no reliable estimate of increased production as a result of consolidation. In the command areas of major irrigation projects, we have stretches of consolidated villages. It will be interesting study to ascertain their prodictivity vis-a-vis unconsolidated land holdings. The fact that even after 30 years, the need for such a study has not been felt indicates that the impact has not been significant. Naturally there is not much popular enthusiasm for the programme. It is also not surprising why several States have not opted for consolidation.

Updating of Land Records

It is really a sad commentary on land administration in Bihar, that land records continue to be unsatisfactory when it is basic to both agricultultural development and land reforms. The cadastral surveys were completed nearly a century ago and since then there have been a few rounds of revisional surveys as well. At the time of consolidation also the land records are updated. We have a well organised revenue staff, one of whose prime duty is to keep the land records up-to-date. It is claimed that land records in U.P. are more reliable as both the village map and ownership rights are updated every year during the agricultural season. The same is not the case in Bihar, where the village map is not touched and mutation of holdings is done for administrative convenience and does not carry legal sanction. Transfer of holdings by way of sales and partition, which are registered, are to be duly entered in the relevant land registers, embodying details of the ownership. The Registration offices are to give information of the sale deeds to Anchal offices. But the Anchal offices do not pursue this with the result the practice has fallen into disuse. The declining importance of land revenue and the repeated postponement of realization of loan dues has also introduced complacency in respect of land records. Special efforts will have to be made at the Anchal level to update the land records. It is the apprehension that Anchal officers cannot do this job honestly, that has prevented action. The survey operations are taken up after long intervals, some times after a gap of 50 years. The entire operation, in the circumstances naturally assumes the character of an original survey.

As has been discussed earlier modern agriculture has to rely on massive credit support for investing in the inputs as well as carrying out improvements in land. Land records will naturally constitute the basis for sanction of such loans by financial institutions. Dependable land records will be also required for monitoring of inputs. It is with this view that it is proposed to issue Khata-Pustikas or extracts of relevant land records giving details of land held by the land owner to all the land holders. In the Khata-Pustikas details of credit and other assistance provided to the farmers will be also entered. Such an arrangement presumes that the Khata-Pustikas would be authenticated by the Anchal offices at regular intervals and there would be a single agency for providing credit, inputs and other services to the peasantry, otherwise the practical difficulties in maintaining Khata-Pustikas would be insurmountable. The scheme has not been very successful so far. There is no denying that programmes for raising agricultural production have to be based on reliable land records. This is necessary for assessing the requirements of inputs for each family, i.e. operational holding, for fixing the targets and deciding the activities of each family to achieve the targets. The extension staff will also find their task immensely difficult in absence of such information. Though we have been very eloquent in emphasising the importance of updating land records, very little attention has been given to sorting out the difficulties that have prevented updating of land records.

Land tax, though insignificant as a source of revenue, served an important purpose, i.e. obliging the administration to keep the land records up-to-date. Land rent was one of the most important source of revenue to the state some 50 years ago. With expansion of trade and commerce and industrialization, the importance of land revenue has declined and the tax base has become broader. Dependence on land revenue implied that land records had to be kept up-to-date. It also involved the obligation on part of the state to keep the land assets and the services appertinent to land, such as irrigation, etc., in a state of repair. The receipt from land revenue for all the states taken together totalled a meagre Rs. 306 crores, slightly more than 1% of the total revenue in 1984-85. In view of the small amount, and the administrative expenses and difficulties involved in collecting it and also in their enthusiasm to grant relief to the poor land owners several states, including Bihar for small holdings, have abolished the land tax. Due to inflation, with passage of time, land tax has been reduced to a token amount and payment of land tax is now more an evidence of possession. With abolition of land tax, necessity of keeping land records up-to-date is also not keenly felt. But no alternative to rent receipts has been evolved. The abolition of land tax has, therefore, not been entirely welcome. Payment of tax was hardly a burden.

On the other hand the elaborate organisation set up for collection of land tax continue to exist.

REFERENCES

1. Ester Boserup, The Conditions of Agricultural Growth, George, Allen & Unwin. 1965 p. 118.
2. T.J. Byres, 'Historical Perspective on Share Cropping', *Journal of Peasant Studies,* Vol X 1 & 2 1982-83 p. 21.
3. Krishna Bhardwaj, Production Conditions of Indian Agr., Occasional Papers 33, Cambridge Univ., p. 84.
4. Manmohan Singh, *Agrarian Prospects of India,* R.B.I. Oct. 1984, p. 57.
5. Report of the Committee on Agr. Production in Eastern India, *R.B.I.* 1984, 8.2.5. (iii) p. 108.
6. *Agricultural Policy in India,* J.S. Sarma, IDRC,.
7. Abhimanyu Singh, Reform of Under Tenancy Legislation in Bihar, Yojana, Dec. 1976.
8. S. Cheung, "Property rights and Share cropping" *Journal of Political Economy,* Nov. Dec., 1968. "Theory of Share Tenancy", 1969.

4

Irrigation for Higher Agricultural Production

Water for irrigation is a critical input for agriculture. Excepting rain water, water for irrigation has to be stored and carried over long distance to fields. The pumping of water from underground or from rivers and canals requires power. The development of irrigational network along with power constitutes an essential infrastructure for agricultural development. Only with assured irrigation, benefits of modern bio-technology (use of fertilizers and high yielding seeds) can be availed to the maximum extent.

The irrigation potential realised in the country had reached 68 million hectares by the end of the Sixth Plan. Of this 30.5 million hectares was by major and medium irrigation schemes. The ultimate irrigation potential from major and medium irrigation schemes is estimated at 58.8 million hectares. The Seventh Plan document proudly claims that India ranks first among the countries of the world in respect of irrigation facilities. It has twice as much area under irrigation than U.S.A. Apparently the investment in expanding irrigation facilities has paid off though not to the extent we had hoped. The 1986-87, Economic survey of Government of India rightly emphasises that increasing trend of unutilised potential, especially in the case of major-medium irrigation projects is a cause for serious concern.

Table 8.1 shows that irrigation in Bihar has been favoured with much higher allocations compared to the All India level.

Since Third Plan the State has been allocating 25% to 33% of the total plan outlay on irrigation, compared to only 10% at the All India level. Massive investment over irrigation has, therefore been the king pin in the development strategy of the State. During Seventh Plan, Bihar's outlay on major and medium irrigation projects at Rs. 1332 crores was highest in the country after Maharashtra. It was more than that of Uttar Pradesh, Rs. 1245 crores. On flood control, Bihar spent Rs. 208 crores during the Seventh Plan which was as much as the combined expenditure by U.P. (Rs. 102 crore) and W.B. (Rs. 112 crores). In contrast Bihar spent only Rs. 28 crores on command area development. This was much less than that of Uttar Pradesh Rs. 91.6 crores, Maharastra 273 crores and Madhya Pradesh 116 crores. At the end of 1984-85 available irrigation potential of major and medium irrigation projects in Bihar was 28.8 lakh hectares, whereas utilisation was only 21.76 lakh hectares or 75.6% of the potential. Utilisation was lower than the All-India level of 83% as well as that of 81% for U.P. Punjab utilises nearly cent per cent of its available potential. The policy implication is that there should have been greater concentration on utilisation of the potential that has been created, instead of taking up new projects for creation of additional potential. The intention to utilise available potential fully is also not supported by the expenditure on development of command areas. Bihar's outlays was Rs. 28 crores, which was only 2% of its outlay on major and medium irrigation schemes, compared to 7.5% by U.P. and 14% for All India during Seventh Plan.

The case for lion share of plan allocation for irrigation has been based on the assumption that in Bihar only 44.3% of the ultimate potential (65 lakh hectares) has been covered by major and medium irrigation schemes, which is lower than the average for All India at 52.2% and therefore larger investment is required in irrigation to bring the state at par with All India levels. Creating irrigation potential cannot be an end in itself. The utility of irrigation schemes is to be judged by the benefits actually accruing to the cultivators through irrigation for raising agricultural production. The concept of ultimate potential is also illusory. The wisdom of creating additional irrigation potential has to be judged against the additional cost to be incurred on bringing additional areas under irrigation. Possibly all the best diversion sites and to a lesser extent dam sites have been utilised. Naturally cost of bringing additional area under irrigation will be very much higher. It is economical to go in for rationalisation and modernisation of the vast network of existing irrigation schemes. The cost of such modernisation schemes is about one/third of that of new projects. The costs may rise considerably if extensive field drainage and reclamation becomes necessary.

Among the Ganga basin states, Uttar Pradesh, Bihar and West Bengal, only U.P. has developed major irrigational schemes by building dams and barrages in the upper reaches and has lately installed powerful river pumps in the lower reaches. Bihar has lagged behind. The agreement with Bangaladesh on sharing of Farakka waters means that nearly 60% of the water reaching Farakka has to be diverted to Bangladesh. West Bengal has been lately complaining of inadequate flow during the lean season i.e., January to May. River Sone, a major tributary of river Ganga, which flows through Madhya Pradesh and Uttar Pradesh, is almost dry, down of Indrapuri Barrage during the lean season. Because of heavy drawal of water by Thermal Power Stations and for other uses at Rihand, there is dearth of water in Sone during the Rabi season, and the fertile area falling within the Sone Cannal system is facing a crisis. There has to be scientific water management in the Ganga basin so that full agricultural potential in the basin is utilised, and use of water for drinking, power generation, industrial purposes, aquatic life, navigation, etc. is fully taken care of. This may call for restricted use of water in the upper reaches in U.P. To permit river pumps installed in U.P. to draw water without restriction, even during the lean season, and allow pumps proposed in Bihar to draw water only during Kharif is not a fair arrangement and also not conducive to rational use of water for attaining maximum agricultural production.

The gap between potential and utilisation at the end of Sixth Plan in Bihar was 703 thousand hectares. It was expected to create additional potential of 315 thousand hectares during the Seventh Plan. Additional utilisation was targeted at 500 thousand hectares, which would have still left 518 thousand hectares, of unutilised potential. At current All-India average rate it cost about Rs. 30,000 per hectare for additional irrigational potential. In Bihar the cost was unofficially estimated to be Rs. 45,000 per hectare. This means that the unutilised potential at the end of the Sixth Plan was equivalent to an investment of Rs. 3,164 crores and Rs. 2,331 crores at the end of the Seventh Plan. There is no consistency in the figures for irrigation being reported for Bihar. The potential created was reduced from 28.8 lakh hectares at the end of at the end of Sixth Plan to 27.15 lakh hectares at the end of Seventh Plan as it was said to be an overestimate, though investment of funds had taken place as per earlier estimate. The potential which could be utilised was reported to be 24.25 lakh hectares, but actual irrigation was only 21.48 lakh hectares (Table 4.2). This was 5.67 lakh hectares less than the potential created for which huge public investments have been incurred. In 1991-92, the area irrigated further declined to 18.85 lakh hectares. Robert Chambers in his book, "Managing Irrigation" aptly observes, "Canal irrigation systems are huge, inert and deteriorating complexities, trapped in physical forms and by set routines and entrenched interest which lock them into low performance. "He asserts, "to improve the anti-poverty performance of canal irrigation systems is now one of the great practical and intellectual challenges facing the mankind."

Shri Rajiv Gandhi, while addressing the conference of State Irrigation Ministers in July, 1987 observed, "Since 1951, 246 big irrigation projects have been initiated of which only 65 have been completed. We need some definite thrust from the projects which we started after 1970. Perhaps we can safely say that almost no benefit has come to the people from these projects. For 16 years we have poured money out. The people have got nothing back, no irrigation, no water, no increase in production, no help in their daily life. By pouring money out to a few contractors and labourers to build canals, we are not really doing any favour. The favour comes when the benefits from the projects start flowing. "This may appear to be a sharp indictment but it correctly reflects the popular frustration with irrigation schemes. The Tenth Finance Commission reports that the losses incurred by irrigation projects have increased from Rs. 367 crores in 1987-88 to Rs. 881 crores in 1991-92, for the whole country. There are 15 major and 29 medium irrigation schemes in Bihar, Which have spilled over to the Eight Five-Year Plan. Nine of the major schemes were taken up in the 1970. The 15 major schemes were originally estimated to cost Rs. 1070 crores, the revised estimate is Rs. 4,894 crores and Rs. 1661 crores have been spent. The cost of Subaranrekha project has gone up by four times; till February, 1993, Rs. 576 crores had been spent which was 50% more than the original estimate. New projects add to the constraint of funds. Inflation makes matters worse. Paucity of funds becomes a convenient pretext for delaying the completion of schemes. The cost of creating additional potential went up from Rs. 1,200 per hectare in 1950, to Rs. 30,000 per hectare in 1985, i.e. by 25 times, though wholesale and consumer price indices rose by only 7.5 times during the period. Obviously the escalation costs have gone to enrich the middlemen and contractors.

To complete the pending major schemes alone at 1993 prices Rs. 3,233 crores would be required. The cost would further escalate. Expenditure in 1990-91 and 1991-92, was only Rs. 257 and Rs. 130 crores respectively. Therefore, we cannot predict with any certainty when these schemes will be completed, unless strict prioritisation is done. The allocation in 1993-94, was only Rs. 319 crores. Assuming that higher allocations would be able to take care of escalation in prices (which is unlikely), it will take 10 years to complete the schemes. The sacrifice entailed by this long period of waiting can be well imagined. To complete the schemes there has also to be complete embargo on new schemes, which is unlikely. The tendency to take up more schemes than what the State Government can fund, is encouraged by the practice of giving go-ahead to schemes without proper techno-economic appariasl on political considerations. Central Water Commission and Planning Commission also take several years in examining and granting approval to schemes, and thereby fail to check expenditure on schemes of doubtful utility.

The rich contractors enjoying political patronage influence the allocations for major and medium irrigation schemes in connivance with corrupt engineers. Prioritisation on the basis of benefits or economy has been ignored. Priority schemes, like konar, where reservoir is in existence, has dragged on for years. However, money has not been scarce for schemes of dubious worth. If only leadership in Bihar had strength to prevent this squandering of public money, Bihar's agricultural performance would have been much better.

Irrigation and power account for 55% of the total plan outlay in Bihar. Whereas irrigation projects are financed totally by Government, power projects depend largely on borrowings from Government and other financial institutions. The budgetary support which is extended to the S.E.B.s by the State Government is 50% grant and 50% loan. The State Government has to compensate the S.E.B. for the loss incurred over rural electrification. But only rarely cash payment is made, the interest owed by the S.E.B. is adjusted against the compensation due to them. The loss of S.E.B. are highlighted and it finds itself in a weak bargaining position with government. The performance of the irrigation schemes, on the other hand, is seldom brought into focus. As the claims for additional fund is made in the name of agricultural development it is never questioned. The results of investment in power projects are transparent. There is no such transparency in irrigation projects. The ultimate test of irrigation projects is the actual irrigation provided by them. The principles governing rational allocation of resources, i.e. obtaining maximum social benefit at least cost (which includes prevention of time over-runs as well) apply with equal force to the irrigation schemes and by ignoring it, we are only encouraging wasteful utilisation of resources. The Tenth Finance Commission is very generous when it recommends that receipts from irrigation projects should give a return of 1% only over and above the cost of maintenance.

Ground Water Irrigation

The ultimate irrigation potential in the country from minor irrigation schemes (schemes which have cultivable command/ area of less than 2,000 hectares) is 54.9 million hectares of which ground water potential is 42 million hectares. The States in the Gangetic Plan, U.P. (13.2 million hectares), Bihar (5.9 million hectares) and West Bengal (3.8 million hectares) cover more than half of the potential. Ground water irrigation is a very convenient source of irrigation for small farmers. The total ground water resource for Bihar have been estimated to be 33,521 million cubic metres. After allowing for drinking water and industrial use, the ground water recharge available for irrigation is 28,493 cubic metres, against which the net draft on 31.3.1991 was only 5,470 cubic metes of 19.2% of the total availbility. At present ground water explitation is only 10% of the potential in Orissa, 25% in Bihar and West Bangal and 32% in East U.P. The inability of the Eastern States to exploit their ground water potential calls for concerted effort, backed up by adequate central assistance in a big way to make up for the gap. Power is crucial for ground water utilisation. Better exploitation of ground water in U.P. is largely due to greater availibility of power for tube-wells. Nearly 3,510 million units or 34% of the total available power in U.P. in 1983-84, was provided to agriculture. This compares very favourably with Bihar, (only 650 millin units, 12.5%), Orissa, 3.2% and West Bangal 1.5%. The agriculturlly progessive states were able to allocate larger share of power to agriculture; Punjab 35% (2,190 million units), Tamil Nadu 27% (2,210 million units), Maharashatra 15% (2,540 million units), Gujrat 15.4% (1,430 million units) and Haryana 40% (1,300 million units).

Ground water irrigation has distinct advantages. Source of water can be sited adjacent to the areas to be irrigated and therefore the need for costly disribution channels is avoided. The gestation period for such schemes is less. Water is available when required and the problems of water-logging, salinity and loss of water by evaporation and seepage is greatly reduced. The tube-wells by providing copious source of clean drinking water also fulfil a basic need of the rural community. Large reservior and dams lead to environmental damage, and larger the area of water storage, the greater is the risk of water borne diseases. Since most of the tube-wells are constructed privately, government is relieved of the burden of finding sufficient resource for their installation and maintenance. Proper supervision and maintenance of State tube-wells has proved difficult. Less than one third of the State tube-wells in Bihar are in running condition. In all cases of resource use, economic efficiency will be higher where the consumer pays the real cost of supplying the various inputs or service. In case of private tube-well, the user meets the full cost, and it is expected that he will use water for irrigation only to the extent the marginal returns from irrigation are equal to the marginal cost of pumping water. A strong argument in favour of State tube-wells is that multiplicity of private tube-wells in close proximity leads to fall in water table, and reduced flow of water as well as higher cost of pumping. Such a situation can be prevented by regulating the location of tube-wells at the time of sanctioning application for power connection.

Pumps and tube-wells at subsidised cost to the weaker sections of the population serves an important social purpose but does not meet the criteria of efficiency. What is received gratis has no costs, and if it fails to give any return it does not mean any burden to the beneficiary. It is not surprising that pumps which are received free or at nominal cost are transferred at throw away price to other farmers. There is profit for asking in transferring the assets; whereas improving income through cultivation would require hard labour and sustained effort.

Bihar is very favourably placed as far as ground water irrigation is concerned. Water is available in some areas within 10 to 20 feet of ground level. It is said that the whole of Gangetic Plain is floating over an underground sea of water. Over fifty thousand square kilometres in the alluvial plains in Bihar has the advantage of ground water.To utilise this potential, we require adequate supply of water and credit support to the farmers. It is the non-availability of power that has proved to be the biggest obstacle in exploitation of ground water. Irrigation by diesel pumps is costlier. Obtaining diesel and carrying it over long distances in the interior is also difficult and irksome.

It may be pointed out that creation of infrastructure does not ensure results. Efficient operation and maintenance of the system is more important. Bihar at the end of Sixth Plan had 28.8 lakh hectares potentially under irrigation, which was higher than 24.6 lakh hectares potentially under irrigation in Punjab. Even under minor irrigation, Bihar had more land, 34.2 lakh hectares as against 31.7 lakh hectares in Punjab. Inspite of larger area under irrigation in Bihar, production of foodgrains in Punjab was 50% more; the other inputs for higher production, fertilizers and high yield seeds made the difference. It is to be attributed largely to better water management. The per capita consumption of electricity for irrigation in Bihar is only one-third of the national average. Larger availability of credit enhances the risk bearing capacity of the farmers and emboildens them to adopt modern means of intensive cultivation. It is thus the critical input of cultivation. The total of short term, middle term and long term loan by co-operatives in 1985-86, in Bihar was only Rs.55.4 crores compared to Rs.373.5 crores in Punjab, Rs.575.4 crores in Maharashtra and Rs.338.7 crores in Uttar Pradesh. The diffidence and unwillingness of the farmers in Bihar to opt for intensive cultivation is understandable. Per hectare consumption of fertilizer in Bihar was only 56.8 Kgs. in 1990-91, and was thus less than one-third in Punjab (171.2 Kgs. per hectare). Table 4.1 gives the level of utilization of the inputs in Bihar between

1989-90 to 1991-92. Only 45% of land area under rice and 76% of the area under wheat is covered by H.Y.V.s. Availability of credit is less than Rs.100 per hectare.

Bihar Government has adopted over generous approach in promoting minor irrigation schemes. S.C./S.T. applicants get cent per cent subsidy. Even the bigger farmers, with holdings upto 10 acres, were given 45% subsidy for encouraging adoption of ground water irrigation at one time even though return on such investment is very high. Such high subsidisation is not necessary. The banks are keen to grant credit for minor irrigation schemes. The enterprising farmers would be encouraged by the gains from the scheme to take loan for the purpose. In retrospective it appears that much of the enthusiasm has over-spilled and there has been abuse of subsidy. The total potential created (cumulative) for minor irrigation schemes in the State upto March,1992 was 48.74 lakh hectares. With 5% depreciation per annum, the effective potential available at the end of 1991-92 was estimated by the department at 25.5 lakh hectares . No explanation has been given for this depreciation, when maintenance is also provided for. There is the possibility that the potential which has been claimed is over estimate, for many who received the subsidy did not create the assets, and therefore this deduction is made to make the estimates realistic. Only 18.92 lakh hectares was irrigated from such sources in 1991-92, thus utilisation was only 74% of the effective potential. This is a very low figure for minor irrigation schemes and is explaind by utilisation of government achemes much below their rated potential. Irrigation from different minor irrigation schemes from 1889-92 along with their potential is shown in Table 4.3. Irrigation from Government sources is less than 10%. The State Government spent Rs. 400 crores between 1985-92, which resulted in an increase of 4.14 lakh hectares of effective potential. Since only 3/4 of the availble potential is utilised for irrigation, it implies investment of nearly Rs. 13,000/- per hectare of additional irrigation. The expenditure was incurred between 1985-92, therefore, at current prices the cost may be taken as Rs. 25,000/- per hectare. This does not include the farmer's contribution. The cost is certainly on the higher side, considering the fact that life of minor irrigation schemes is assumed to be only 20 years. In respect of irrigation schemes we have been pursuing the goal of achieving the ultimate potential irrespective of the cost and benefits.

The so called ultimate potential for irrigation schemes apears to be elusive. The State Government has given two estimates for ultimate potential of minor irrigation, 59 lakhs hectares (as reported to the Planning Commission and 90 lakh hectares (for internal reference). Till 1992, expenditure had been incurred for creating total potential (cumulative of 48.74 lakh hectares. In VIIIth Plan it is proposed to create additional potential of 18.32 lakh hectares. Thus the total potential created by the end of VIIIth Plan would be 67.06 lakh hectares, which would be much more than the ultimate potential of 59 lakh hectares. However, at 5% depreciation per annum, effective potential at the end of VIIIth Plan would be only 35 lakh hectares. The ultimate potential for major and medium irrigation schemes is 65 lakh hectares. Thus the total for major, medium and minor irrigation schemes is 124 lakh hectares, and if the latest version of minor irrigation department is to be accepted, 155 lakh hectares; whereas, net area sown is only 76 lakh hectares. With cropping intensity being less than two (2), even in irrigated areas at present, the ultimate potential is certainly exaggerated, with the avowed purpose of obtaining higher allocation of plan funds, and completely ignores the cost benefit consideration.

REFERENCES

1. *Agricultural Situation in India,* June, 1990.
2. *Agricultural Census,* 1985-86.
3. *Annual Report,* Ministry of Agriculture, Government of India.
4. *Indian Agriculture in Brief,* Ministry of Agriculture, Government of India, 1988.
5. NABARD, *Annual Report,* 1991-92.
6. *World Development Report,* 1982, World Bank.
7. Robert Chambers, *Managing Canal Irrigation,* Oxford & IBH,1988.
8. *Report of the Second Bihar State Irrigation Commission,* 1994.

Table 4.1. Utilisation of Inputs H.Y. Seeds/Crop Loan in Bihar

S. No.	*Particulars*	*1989-90*	*1990-91*	*1991-92*
1	2	3	4	5
1.	**Area and Yield Under H.Y.V.**			
	(a) Rice-Area in Hect.	2349441	2402792	2247515
	Yield Rate (K.G. per Hect.)	1383	1393	1126
	(b) Wheat-Area in Hect.	1471137	1463888	1502558
	Yield Rate (K.G. per Hect.)	1757	1937	1945
	(c) Maize-Area in Hect.	385536	379821	399837
	Yield Rate	2135	1988	2338
2.	**Distribution of Crop Loan** *(Rs. in Crores)*			
	(a) Commercial Bank:			
	(i) Kharif	25.28	22.46	
	(ii) Rabi	29.32	25.12	
	Total:	54.60	47.58	10.80
	(b) Co-operative Bank:			
	(i) Kharif	58.58	18.54	
	(ii) Rabi	27.41	24.35	
	Total:	85.99	42.89	86.12
		140.59	90.47	96.92

Source: 1) Agriculture Department.
2) Department of Institutional Finance.

Table 4.1b Source and Cropwise Area Irrigated in Bihar

Sl. No.	Name of Source	Year 1989-90	Year 1990-91		Name of Crops	Area in Hectares	
						Year 1989-90	Year 1990-91
1	2	3	4		5	6	7
1.	Canal	1472949	1411412	1.	Kharif Paddy	1799747	1840042
2.	Tanks	116307	139996	2.	Garma Paddy	70282	69561
3.	Tube Wells	1624321	1753927	3.	Kharif Maize	19688	29881
4.	Other Wells	139594	153581	4.	Garma Maize	261618	257043
5.	Lift Irrigation	9770	37598	5.	Wheat	1604151	1680575
6.	Others	759364	695941	6.	Gram	4316	5015
				7.	Sugar Cane	27419	20937
				8.	Kharif Potato	37953	37063
				9.	Rabi Potato	91033	93139
				10.	Vegetables	65773	68736
				11.	Fruits	10545	9544
				12.	Others	129729	80928
Total Area Irrigated		4122305	4192455		Total Area Irrigated	4122254	4192464

Source - Agriculture Department.

Table-4.2 Irrigation Coverage Throuth Major and Medium Irrigation Projects (Bihar)

(Unit: In Thousand Hectares)

Sl. No.	Year	Potential created	Utilisation of Potential	Area Irrigated as per Irrigation Department			Area Irrigated as per
				Kharif	Rabi	Total	Directorate of Statistics and Evaluation
1	2	3	4	5	6	7	8
1.	By the end of VIth Plan 1984-85	2879	2176	–	–	–	–
2.	1988-89	–	–	1472	500	1972	1500
3.	1989-90 By the end VIIth Plan	2715	2425 (2525)*	1552	596	2148	1473
4.	1990-91	15	–	1560	548	2108	1411
5.	1991-92	20	–	1323	562	1885	–

* 2525 is the figure reported to Planning Comission.

Source – Complied from data reported by Major Irrigation Department/Directorate of Statistics.

Table- 4.3 Irrigation Coverage Through Minor Irrigation Schemes (Bihar)

Sl. No.	Name of Schemes	Cummulative up to March 92		Area Irrigated in Hectares		
		Schemes Completed (No.)	Potential Created (Hect.)	1989-90 (Kharif Rabi)	1990-91 (Kharif Rabi)	1991-92 (Kharif Rabi)
1.	Departmental Medium Irrigation Schemes	686	72237	32352	10462	36082
2.	Department Lift Irrigation	2074	166164	14950	48799	13455
3.	BHALCO Lift Irrigation	279	26600	1948	1186	–
4.	E.R.P. Sets	77	6160	–	–	636
5.	Total Surface Water Schemes	3116	271161	49250	60447	50173
6.	State Tube Well Boring	4950	495000	34914	22880	15103
7.	**Private Irrigational Schemes**					
	(i) Private Boring	658482	1975446	1196422	1293637	1448660
	(ii) Bomboo Boring	106938	213876	202423	241558	294079
	(iii) Dug Well	105340	105340	67488	72868	84272
	Total (i) to (iii) (From Private Irrigation Schemes)	870760	2294662	1466333	1608063	1827011
8.	Grand Total (5+6+7)	878826	3060823	1550497	1691390	1892287

Source– Complied from data reported by Minor Irrigation Department.

5

Eradicating Unemployment and Poverty

"To a people famished and idle, the only acceptable form in which God can dare appear is work and promise of food as wages."

Mahatma Gandhi, *Young India*, Oct. 1921.

With more than 75 per cent Indians residing in villages, rural development is the corner stone for development of the Indian economy. Economic planning is essentially the process of utilising the available resources to tackle the urgent problems, or fulfil the needs of the people for whom the plan is meant within an assigned period. It implies mobilisation of resources, natural as well as human endowments to the maximum extent, and utilising it judiciously over schemes that are capable of giving the maximum benefit. It necessarily involves taking decision on priorities and choice between alternatives. We are short both of resources and time. Our life span is short and every individual strives to improve his living during his life time. He wants to assure his off-spring a life better than his own. Planning is therefore, a conscious effort for improvement which can be judged in terms of physical well-being.

Due to centuries of alien rule and drain of wealth, the Indian sub-continent has been impoverished. Exploitation of labour, low wages and inhuman working conditions have reduced the bulk of the population to subsistence level. The economy is thus in the grip of vicious circle of poverty. Low incomes do not enable enough savings to be generated for investment in capital assets. The population, therefore, continues to languish in poverty. The common man was always neglected, both during British rule and prior to British rule. The economy was virtually stagnant for nearly two centuries. Aggregate food production increased at the rate of 0.11 per cent per annum between 1891-1947 and lagged far behind the growth of population. Ignorance and disease pervaded the country. The average life of an Indian was just thirty years. When India attained independence it was hoped that the right to work and living wage would be embodied as a fundamental right, as in several socialist countries. But due to the immensity of the problem, the makers of the constitution were daunted and right to work and living wage could find a place only in the Directive Principles of State Policy.

Tackling Rural Unemployment

Article 39 states that 'the State shall direct its policy towards securing its citizens, an adequate means of livelihood. Article 41 emphatically asserts that the state shall within its economic capacity make effective provision for securing the right to work. Articles 43 and 47 leave no doubt as to the intention of the State, "the State shall endeavour to secure... to all its workers a living wage and condition to work ensuring a decent standard of life." Article 47 states, "The State shall regard the raising of the level of nutrition and the standard of living of its people and the improvement of public health as among its primary duties." The directive principles were to guide the policies of the government. When planning for development was undertaken, the objective of industrialisation became paramount, and poverty eradication and employment generation become incidental, with the result that the first five plans had really no impact on the incidence of poverty and unemployment. The well to do benefited more from development programmes. Only in the Sixth Plan it was decided to attack the problem of poverty directly and there was some decline in the incidence of poverty. Though importance of rural works programmes and raising the income of rural people was well recognised, there was no clear policy or urgency to achieve it. Only in 1975, when the 20-Point Programme was announced, rural problems were emphasised. The 2nd to 6th points included programmes for distribution of land declared surplus through application of ceiling on land holdings, housing for homeless, application of minimum wages to agricultural labour and protection against debt to peasants. The 1982, version laid more stress on productivity. Rural employment programmes became the most important programe for rural development. The other programmes, except for minimum wages and protection against debt were retained. The intractable nature of land reforms under Indian conditions is proved by the fact that it still finds a prominent place in the 20-point Programme (1986 version) even though we have been committed to it for over two decades now. Poverty eradication gets the top place in the latest programme.

The basic objectives of rural development are raising agricultural production, providing gainful emploument to all able-bodied persons and eradication of poverty. Unemployment is linked with poverty. If a person is employed he is able to earn enough to sustain himself. Thus the anti-poverty programmes and the employment guarantee programmes have been tagged to each other.

There is heavy pressure of population on land. Due to rapid increase in population the holdings are getting fragmented into even smaller holdings. Even these small holdings are held in tiny plots. The small holdings distributed over tiny plots makes scientific cultivation difficult and utilisation of ground water potential uneconomic. In such a situation the marginal farmer hardly derives enough income to sustain himself. Landlessness is on the increase and in Bihar nearly 25% of the rural households are without land. They seek employment by taking land from others on lease or work as labourers for others. Agriculture as an occupation is gradually offering less and less prospect to enterprising youth, besides the gap between urban and rural standards of living is widening, the result is migration to cities. The per capita income in rural areas is less than half of that in urban areas. Educational and health facilities are minimal. Piped water supply and electricity is available to less than 10% of the rural households. But, the pressure of population on land is not relieved by migration to cities, for those who go to city, continue to retain their right over their parental land.

The agrarian unrest in countryside is manifestation of the increasing landlessness in rural areas. It increased by nearly 50%

between 1961 to 1981. There has been mass awakening and demand for higher wages and better living conditions in the rural areas. But in several parts of the country, the rural economy cannot afford the higher wages. The landlords are reluctant to concede the demand, leading to confrontation between the haves and have nots. There are violent caste feuds. But the same two castes are not involved in all such incidents. One of the groups is the land owning class and other the deprived class, who belong to the weaker group. This situation of unrest in the countryside is not conducive to investment in agriculture, by landholders for higher production.

The path to agricultural development is well known. It is to be achieved through raising agricultural yield to its full potential. This is possible through larger coverage by irrigation, adoption of seeds of high yielding varieties and more use of fertilisers. In order to enable the farmer to take recourse to these means, he has to be provided with larger credit support. To induce the farmer to accept these intensive techniques for cultivation, he has to be educated through an extension machinery and also encouraged to introduce new crops, which are agroclimaticaly more suitable. He may also be provided price support and marketing facilities for his produce so that his labour and investments are justly remunerated. All this calls for a very efficient organisation which should ensure assured quality of inputs and timely supply to the farmers in adequate quantities.

Increase in agricultural production brings prosperity to land owners primarily. It is only indirectly that agricultural labour benefits from increase in agricultural production, i.e., through more employment opportunities and through higher wages. There-fourth of land holders in Bihar are marginal farmers having holdings less than 1 hectare, who own 30% of the land and average size of such marginal holdings is 0.9 acre. This implies that agricultural development alone cannot bring prosperity to rural population at large. Landless agricultural labourers constitute as much as 25% of the population in some regions. The 1991 census enumerated 95.13 lac agricultural labourers, constituting over 37% of the total population of main workers in the State. A recent estimate puts 47% of the unemployment from amongst the agricultural labourers. Due to the above constraints, the impact of higher investment in agriculture on poverty alleviation and employment generation is reduced. The treacle down effect or percolation of benefits of agricultural development and general development of the economy to the rural poor, therefore, cannot be relied upon for eradication of poverty in rural areas in the short term. Gains over long term are of little relevance to the present generation. It is realisation of this fact that led to the evolution of the policy for direct transfer of resources to the rural poor for eradicating them from poverty. The self employment programmes (I.R.D.P.: Integrated Rural Development Programme) backed up by the programme for training of youth for self-emploument (TRYSEM), along with the wage employment programmes, the Jawahar Rozgar Yojna (J.R.Y.), constitute the main weapons of the government strategy to tackle the problems of poverty and unemployment in rural areas. All the three are centrally sponsored programmes.

The total work force in the age group 15-59 is estimated to be nearly 60% of the total population. Assuming that the population of the country was 860 millions in 1992, the total number in the age group 15-59 may be estimated at 516 millions. Further assuming that only 2 out of 3 in this age group are in need of job or willing to work, the total number available for employment can be roughly estmated to be 344 million. With aspirations of better living standards and exposure to modern influences, a work participation rate of 2 out of every 3 among the adults may be considered to be realistic. Many women would be fully engaged within the household. There are substantial number of disabled persons and those who are very well off, do not like to offer themselves for employment.The Eighth Plan estimated total employment at the beginning 1992-93 to be 301.7 millions on weekly status basis. Thus the total number of unemployed at the beginning of Eighth Plan were approximately 42 millions. This estimate is not very wide off the mark, for the number of job seekers listed with the employment exhanges in June,1992 was 37 millions.

The unemployment problem is increasing in magnitude as far more people are coming into the employable age group than the natural growth of employment opportunities can take care of. Between 1977-78 and 1987-88, employment increased at the rate of 1.95% only. This was not even enough to take care of the growing numbers joining the work force. New employment opportunities are expensive and difficult to create. Employment in the organised sector has been virtually stagnant. If we cannot create the additional jobs, the only remedy is to check the number of those seeking jobs. Only a vigorous policy of population control can redeem the situation. We have still not awoken up to the grim realities of the situation. Even such a policy for population control would yield results only 15 to 20 years from now. With spread of education and rising aspirations due to ;modernisation, the problem of containing unemployment would be far more problematic in future.

It is this huge number of unemployed and underemployed who are responsible for the subsistence wages and extreme poverty of labour force in India. Agricultural labour and the marginal farmers constitute the most vulnerable group. The marginal farmers are the first to suffer during a bad agricultural year. Agricultural labour is only seasonally employed. It is idle for nearly 4 to 8 months in a year. This has naturally led to large scale migration of agricultural labour from the less developed regions to the cities and agriculturally more prosperous regions in search of better wages and durable employment. Availability of agricultural labour is a potential resource and when migration takes place, it creates dearth of labour in the villages from which migration occurs. The tea plantations in Assam gained from such migration from Bihar and Eastern U.P. in the past. Now it is agriculture in Punjab and Haryana that is deriving benefit from cheap labour from East. The migration to cities has led to growth of squatter settlements, pavement dwellers and consquent health hazards and social problems leading to rapid deterioration of environment in the cities. This labour force takes up trades like rickshaw pulling, rearing of cattle on the streets, shoe-polishing or make living as petty hawkers. Such urban poor live on a pittance and lead a very insecure life. They come from rural areas in search of better life, but only suceed in finding shelter in jhuggies and jhoparies of the slums in the city-outskirts, where life is more miserable. The urban poor have attracted attention recently and programmes for upgradation of urban basic services have been introduced.

Poverty can be looked upon as a grave malaise afflicting the economy. Desperately poor people can accept any opportunity for survival. Desperate economic circumustances breed social instability. Despair is the fodder of religious fundamentalism, of populist political parties, and of criminal activity.

The large working population is no doubt a vital resource, provided it can be harnessed for productive purposes. Ragnar Nurkse an eminent economist, had propounded the theory that idle labour can be mobilised for capital formation. His argument was that society was maintaining this idle labour force, though at subsistence levels, so if they could be utilised over productive schemes, which had labour content mainly, useful physical assets could be created. W.A. Lewis also stressed this point in his famous article on "Economc Development with Unlimited Supplies of Labour." Gunnar Myrdal in his book, "Asian Drama", too, found it paradoxical that there could be mass idleness, when so much remained to be done in the villages in India. The conditions which Nurkse imposed were that the work site should be close to the villages where the labour resided, and only a small wage was given to the labourers in order to do work to generate higher savings. The presumption is that though there is surplus food, people are not able to buy it because of lack of purchasing power. There are many loopholes in this argument but the underlying idea is sound in principle. China utilised its surplus labour for development of rural infrastructure. China guaranteed through its communes at least 200 Kg of grains per person per year. This eliminated starvation. Everybody is obliged to work for the commune. Even the elderly usually find some lightwork to claim a share of the community income. All communes maintain adequate grains reserve and in normal years sell grain to the government. In years of distress, however, they recieve relief. The administrative savings by way of dealing with communities rather than individual members and households is considerable.

The employment generation programmes of the government intend to mobilise the surplus labour for building up durable assets and providing the rural poor much needed wages to survive the difficult lean agricultural season. Under J.R.Y. scheme 80% of the funds is allocated by the Centre on the basis of incidence of poverty in the State. The scheme is being executed through the Panchayats. It is argued that resource transfer in case of these employment generation programmes is direct, the leakage being very little. The target group are the landless labourers who are idle during off season, and who in absence of regular employment would be in much distress. 6% of the resources under J.R.Y. are earmarked for houses for the homeless (Indira Awas), 20% for ex-ploiting ground water (Million Wells Scheme) and 3% is allowed for meeting administrative expenses and 10% for maintenance. But a recent survey conducted by the Planning Commission revealed that less than 20% of the target group were benefited and the individual beneficiary got employment for fewer than 20 days in a year on an average. Expenditure report on J.R.Y. in Bihar in 1992-93, indicates that nearly 50% of the funds are being retained at the district level on the plea of completing on-going schemes and that expenditure on establishment is more than 10%. The unit cost of employment is Rs. 41 though the minimum wage is only Rs. 24. This indicates that there is substantial expenditure on materials. With such diversions effectiveness of the programme in providing employment is much reduced. Under the programme wages are paid at the statutorily fixed minimum wages, part of the wages (2 Kg. per head per day) is given in wheat at concessional rates. Due to unsatisfactory delivery system, however, the wheat component of wages falls much short of the actual demand figure. These programmes are expected to provide employment to at least one member from each family upto 200 days in a year. To facilitate construction of durable assets and thereby strengthen the rural infra-structure, expenditure upto 40 per cent on material component is allowed. J.R.Y. provides guarateed employment, and it is widely dispersed. We can not think of a better arrangement at present for insuring the rural labour from prolonged unemployment and distress. We must ensure that the benefit of the entire expenditure goes to labour and the durable assets that are created are useful and really serve the needs of the rural population. The assets that are created are mostly ephemeral and very few survive beyond two years. In a country ridden with scarcities, cost effectiveness of schemes cannot be ignored. The leakages by way of substantial share being pocketed by executing agents have to be closely guarded. There are complaints of muster rolls being interpolated. The part wages which is paid in kind is seldom given in full and the labourers do not have the patience to collect the balance later. The schemes are loosely prepared, the costs are over-estimated and large number of schemes are being wound up before completion. The so-called durable assets should survive for atleast two or three years and serve genuine needs of the rural population.

Creating assets is not enough, if they do not lead to higher productivity. The assets may be conducive to rural development but would have little impact on poverty. Village link roads, school buildings, community halls are welcomed by the affluent villagers, as they enable them to enjoy better amenities without spending for them. There is no contribution from them, either, for maintaining these assets which explains the short life of such assets. The character of the assets have to be primarily production oriented. We should identify the unemployed, and list them according to their capabilities and device schemes suited to each group.

The more capital intensive projects like power and irrigation also have labour and wage components. In the case of buildings the wage component is about 22%. In the case of latter, the assets that are created to generate income in turn, and have strong multiplier effect. Thus we have different options in deciding our investment outlays. Bihar was allocated nearly Rs.300 crores under Jawahar Rozgar Yojna in 1989-90. This amount if invested in power sector would have created an additional capacity of 150 M.W. and at 40% P.L.F. would have provided 60 M.W. power on a continuing basis and generated an income of approximately Rs. 25 crores annually at the prevailing rate of sale for power. Further by providing additional power to the power starved sectors it would have boosted development activities. The emphasis in employment generation Programmes is on social forestry, social sanitation, village link roads, housing for weaker sections, school buildings, etc. No doubt, such schemes would lead to greater social justice and also contribute to improvement of rural life. But the effect of such schemes on increasing the income earning capacity of the people, is significant. Leakage of funds in implementation further weakens the prospects. In the circumstances, it may be questioned, whether we should depend upon the employment generation programmes for eradication of poverty in face of persisting deficiency in infrastructure.

The employment generation programmes cannot be looked upon as permanent programmes. These programmes serve to support people in poverty. They have to be looked upon as transitional programmes till such time lasting jobs are created for the rural unemployed. But the manner in which these programmes are being expanded, there is apprehension of the real objective receding into the background. It is not desirable to relegate the rural poor permanently into the category of unskilled labourers.

During the Eighth Plan the addition to labour force is estimated at 35 millions, but the plan hopes to create 40 million jobs and thereby keep the situation under control. This is based on the assumption that G.D.P. would grow at the rate of 5.6% which would result in employment growth between 2.6 to 2.8%. This in turn would depend upon a combination of favourable factors.

These targets have also to be viewed inthe context of plan's commitment to increase competitiveness and raise productivity. The Seventh Plan observes "employment guarantee as an objective does not mean the adoption of a static technology. Technological upgradiation, modernisation and scientific advances in production process constitute the essence of growth of productivity whether in organised industry, agriculture or small industries if they are to become viable and compete internationally. "The trend is towards managing with minimum labour force, better utilisation of idle capacity and available labour. Most of the public sector undertakings are carrying excess staff. The prospect of surplus labour of rural areas being absorbed in cities is therefore bleak. Agricultural labour under distress can take up earth work, but it cannot take up other skilled jobs. The surplus agricultural labour has to be trained in requisite skills if they are to improve their well being and take advantage of the job opportunities created by industrialisation. Marginally well to do families may not take up physical labour even though they are idle. To harness them for productive purposes, vocational institutions have to be established. Thus the rural economy has to be diversified and the village and small scale industries greatly expanded for which a much larger outlay is required. More than investment, the necessary suppoting institutions have to be created, along with availability of inputs and acceptability in the market for the goods that are produced by the village industries. Such a strategy has not been clearly spelled out. The TRYSEM programme is only a token effort and falls far short of the requirenents due to unsatisfactory implementation.

Encouraging Self Employment

The Jawahar Rojgar Yojna Scheme can take care of the idle work force who can do manual labour. The number of such people who can be trained and motivated to take-up skilled jobs as well as those who are educated, including technically qualified persons would require other special schemes. Vegetable and fruit cultivation, dairy, poultry, fishery, sericulture, small scale indutries, transport services have a big potential market and provide vast opportunities for expansion. Readymade garments, leather goods, handicrafts are popular export items form India. We can avail of the comparative advantage in these activities by expanding production of such items. We can take help from international financial institutions and negotiate with multi-national firms for technological upgradation and expansion of S.S.I. units engaged in such production. International assistance would be also forthcoming for fruits cultivation, food processing and fisheries. We can thus plan for export promotion by tagging of small scale and household units. But we will have to ensure quality by apropriate technical guidance and counselling.

In developed countries people whose annual income is less than 1/3rd of the national per capita income are said to be below the poverty line. But in less developed countries, povety is linked with minimum food consumption. Lately this concept has been questioned. An individual also requires cloth, shelter and some medicine to live. For our country, people whose food intake is less than the equivalent of 2,400 calories in rural areas and 2,100 calories in urban areas are said to be living in absolute poverty. Considering the consumption pattern, this is supposed to correspond to annual household income of Rs. 7,300 in urban areas and Rs. 6,400 in rural areas at 1984-85 prices. This has recently been raised to Rs. 11,000 for both rural and urban areas. A household is assumed to consist of 5 members on an average. The latest estimate puts the number below the poverty line at 29.9% (1987-88). It is planned to eliminate poverty by the end of century. The per capita income which was Rs. 2,616 in 1984-85, is expected to go up to Rs.4,163, at 1984-85 prices by then. The increase is really at a snails pace, a pittance, for we will still continue to be classified among the poorest low income countries in the world. By present day standards also, countries having per capita income of less than $ 400 per annum are placed in the poorest group. The advent of 21st century, therefore, does not appear to hold much promise.

The Integrated Rural Development Programme (IRDP) seeks to provide self-employment opportunities to families below the poverty line by encouraging them to take up selected production activities by subsidising them and by providing the balance amount as Bank loan on concessional terms. For the educated youth including the technically qualified persons, the Prime Minister's Raojgar Yojna (PMRY) was launched in 1993-94. This envisages loan upto Rs. 1.00 lakh and maximum subsidy component of Rs. 7,500.

It may be recalled that it was proposed to bring initially 600 famillies above the poverty line under I.R.D.P. in each block per annum. Since there are 5000 blocks in the country the annual target was 3 millions. With 50 to 60 million families below the poverty line, it was assumed, hopefully, that poverty would be banished within 15 years. This was being too optimistic and a very simplistic approach to the gigantic problem of poverty. Poverty in rural areas has been pervasive since centuries, and the poor people have come to accept destitution and have developed an attitude of non-chalance to poverty, having resigned themselves to hunger, suffering and disease. They have succumbed to exploitation. In such situation activising people to take recourse to development through their own efforts is indeed difficult. Besides the return from investment from anti-poverty programmes were also overestimated. During Sixth Plan the incremental capital output ratio (I.C.O.R.) was assumed to be 1.5. On an average an expenditure of Rs. 1,000 per family by way of subsidy and Rs. 2,000 as credit support was envisaged for each family. With Rs. 3,000 it was estimated that income of the beneficiary would go up by Rs. 2,000 per annum. This was projecting too rosy a picture. Estimate of return of 66% on investment was totally unrealistic. The Seventh Plan assumed the I.C.O.R. to be 2.7 and provide Rs. 1,333 as subsidy and Rs. 2,666 as credit support, raising assistance to each family on an average to Rs. 4,000. With I.C.O.R. of 2.7 or a return of 37% it estimated an additional income of Rs. 1,480 per annum. This was also an over-estimate. Even with this additional income of Rs. 1,480 per annum, families which were much below the poverty line could not have come above the poverty line.

In Bihar per capita investment was Rs. 2,300 only on an average during the Sixth Plan. The per capita investment figure is reported to have gone up to Rs. 5,916 in 1991-92 the loan component being Rs. 3,749 and subsidy being Rs. 2,167. This was nearly 20% less than the prescribed norm of per family investment of Rs. 7,500. To be really purposeful the per family investment should be much higher. There are glaring lapses. Since the beneficiaries are not correctly identified, the programme is not confined to the target group only, and families which are above the poverty line also manage to get assistance under the programme. The field functionaries have drawn attention to the genuine difficulty of identifying families below the poverty limit. Since poverty line decides the eliglibility for government assistence, families which are clearly not poor, also have a strong incentive to record themselves as poor. This difficulty can be got over by entrusting this task to village or Panchayat committee consisting of representatives drawn from all sections of the population who have personal knowledge of the families in need of assistance. There were leakages in the sense that the assets were not created or were transferred to non target groups by the beneficiaries and therefore the assets did not result in regular flow of income to the beneficiaries. It does not speak well of the programme that 50 to 60 per cent of the Sixth Plan beneficiaries may not have actually crossed the poverty line and were targetted to be given a second dose of assistance. The leakages in I.R.D.P. are also due to wrong selection of schemes, lack of support for supply of raw materials and marketing of produce and diversion ot the assets provided under the programmes by manipulation of the well to do classes for their own benefit and corruption and delay in the release of the amount of assistance. Assistance under the programme comes as subsidy from Government (25 to 33 per cent for individuals and 50 per cent for group schemes) and the balance as loan from banks. The very nature of schemes makes it obligatory for the Government to establish close and effective coordination with the banking institutions to facilitate timely release of credit. The banks have been rather conservative and technical in their aproach creating obstacles for the programmes. The bank staff have been also accused of corruption in disbursement of loans.

C.H. Hanumantha Rao in a study analysing the distribution of poverty and decline in poverty since 1977-78 has pointed out that incidence of poverty in Eastern India is highest whereas decline in poverty is lowest, with the result that this regions' share in the number of poor in the whole country has increased. Similarly the incidence of poverty among scheduled castes and tribes is more than for the rest of the population and decline in poverty among these groups is also less than for the rest of the population. The condition of scheduled castes is worse as the problem of landlessness is more acute amongst them. The percentage of agricultural labourers to main workers in Bihar is as high as 73% among scheduled castes but is only 22% among schedule tribes. The study advocates greater effort to increase food production in Eastern India, if poverty is to be reduced is to the same level as the rest of the country. That is food production must increase at 4.5% per annum in Eastern India compared to 3.7% for the country as a whole. It was with this objective that the Special Rice Production Programme was launched during the Seventh Plan as a centrally sponsored scheme in the Eastern Region for exploiting the higher agricultural potential of the region.

Towards Better Rural Life

When we talk of self-employment programmes (I.R.D.P.) or the employment guarantee programmes (J.R.Y.) we are looking at the purely income aspect of rural development. But there are other aspects which have a vital bearing on the quality of rural life, for example, health and medical services, supply of clean drinking water, sanitation, primary education facilities, housing, etc., which have to be given due recognition if we are to ensure that the rural masses share in the benefits of development, modernisation and latest scientific and technological advances. The Seventh and Eighth Plans have rightly emphasised human resources development and expansion of the social infrastructure for education, health, water supply and sanitation. The Eighth Plan seeks to achieve universal elementary education and eliminate illiteracy in the age group (15-35), universal immunisation and extend health services to all under privileged population. It also seeks to provide atleast one source of safe drinking water for every 250 persons. The Government had the ambitious programme of electrifying all village by 1990. But the large and populous states, including U.P. and Bihar have fallen far behind the target. Similarly it was planned to provide link roads to all villages having more than 1,000 population. This goal was planned to be achieved during the Eighth Plan. The basic needs programmes are covered under the M.N.P. for which seperate allocation of funds and targets have been fixed. The Seventh Plan rightly sought to integrate the M.N.P. with rural development and anti-poverty programmes so as to create the necessary linkages in the delivery services.

Projecting The Weak

Planing for rural development requires identification of the target group, i.e., the weakest who are in need of employment. Identification of the target groups on the basis of 'caste' or 'religion' is artificial and can create social conflicts. The weak irrespective of caste and creid deserve our prime attention. Agricultural labourers constitute a distinct target group. But all who are landless and weak cannot do physical work.

Children upto 14 years have been pervented by constitution and different legislations from being engaged in arduous physical work. We have to look for better future for children by providing them suitable elementary education. Child labour is a major social problem and confirms the acute poverty in India. Though we are very much concerned about bonded labour, we are not bothered about child labour. A UNICEF study estimated the total number of child workers in 1971 at 10.7 millions, the total child population being 230.3 millions. 87 per cent of the child workers are engaged in agriculture. The position has further deteriorated and the 1981, Census estimates the number at 14.5 millions. The number of child labour in Bihar is estimated to be 1.1 million. According to the findings of the Asian Labour Monitor, every third houehold in Indian has a working child. On this basis the number of child labour would be around 40 millions. Government estimates are understandbly under-estimates. Child labour is employed extensively in cottage based production units. In Bhadohi-Mirzapur carpet industry as many as 75,000 child workers were engaged in 1985. Child labour is extensively employed in glass factories, in building construction, match, wool cleaning, in the informal sector and in the households in Bihar. Child labour displaces adult labour, keeps down wages and restricts employment opportunities. The increasing incidence of child labour inspite of the legel embargoes also defeats our policy of providing universal elementary education and elimination of illiteracy. They work under hazardous conditions on petty wages and their health is ruined when they grow up, reducing their capabilities as adults.

The aged, disabled and infirm similarly cannot be expected to work. Women, especially nursing mothers require special care. Thus with focus on the landless labourers we must provide for protection of the above vulnerable categories of population also to promote greater well-being of the rural society. The Social Security Scheme in Bihar covers the aged, disabled and widows. The amount of pension has been recently raised from Rs.30 to Rs.100 per month but, there is substantial deduction at source by the corrupt distributing functionaries. In August, 1995 the National Social Assistance Programme (N.S.A.P.) was adopted. It is a multi dimensional programme, which encompasses old age pension @Rs.75 per month to destitutes and above 65 years of age; family benefit (Rs. 5,000) in case of death due to natural causes and Rs. 10,000 in case of accidental death; and maturity benefit of Rs. 300 per pregnancy upto the first two live birth. It is centrally approved programme with 100% central funding and aims at providing social protection to the weak uniformally throughout the country. The impact of this programme is yet to be known.

The Public Distribution System in our country can be an effective cover for protecting the poorest families from seasonal rise in price of foodgrains and scarcity of essential commodities. Through P.D.S. wheat, rice, sugar and kerosene oil are being supplied at subsidised rates to consumers. According to present arrangements, however, the system is to benefit all, rich and poor alike. The per capita availability of commodities becomes so little, that it fails to satisfy the needs of the people. In normal times when market prices are low, the well off do not bother to take their quota from P.D.S. Their share generally leaks into the black market. During scarcity the pressure on P.D.S. increases and whatever relief that is available to the poorer section from P.D.S. assumes much significance. It is the really poor who should be entitled to the benefits of subsidized commodities, and the benefits from P.D.S. should be restricted to the families below poverty line.

Preserving the Environment

Some programmes, hold much potential and they can be adopted with local variations for rural development. Scarcity of fuel wood is increasing in rural areas and there is indiscriminate felling of trees leading to reduction of much green coverage which in turn renders vast area waste through erosion of top soil, as the volume of run-off water increases because of the lower retentivity of water by land.

The desirable norm for forest cover is 33%. Recent estimate of forest cover during the period 1981-83, puts the figure at 64.20 million hectares or 19.5% of the total geographical area of this country. But of this only 35.77 million hectares or 11% is closed forests (defined as forests with crown cover of 30% and more) and the rest is open forests or mangroves. This should not make us complacement for the existing forests are being destroyed at the rate of 1.5 million hectares per annum. Bihar has only 16.8% of land under forests and most of it in Chotanagpur. The pressure of population and cattle grazing has led to large scale cutting of trees and loss of forest coverage in Bihar. The Forest Department has brought 15,250 hectares under plantations between 1985-93, but this has had no impact because of the depradations. The thickly populated Gangetic plains has no forests. The extensive orchards have been gradually brought under cultivation. Fortunately there is nearly 4.5 million hecatres of wasteland (nearly 25% of the total land area), on most of which plantation is possible.

The prospects look really grim and stresses the need for reforestation on large scale. Energy and fuel plantation on waste lands, a part from meeting the basic requirement for fuel and timber in rural areas, would also serve to restore the ecological balance. Quick growing trees have to be identified for each region. Otherwise, also, fodder, orchard or timber plantations on non-agricultural land would serve pressing social needs. The emphasis on social forestry programme by the Government is laudable. Government in its enthusiasm to encourage plantations has adopted the policy of leasing Government land to private individual organisations for growing trees. Money is also provided to the parties for nuturing and protecting the plants. The usufructs of the trees when they mature is granted to the parties concerned. It may be recalled that majority of such wasteland is either Government land or community land for common pasture, etc. Considering our commitment to eradicate rural poverty, it will be advisable to grant such leases to group of villagers, rather than well-to-do individuals. Such joint ventures will make rural people conscious of the importance of plantation for healthy environment and its benefits to agriculture. Protection of plants is as important as planting of trees. The plantation programme like family planning has to involve the masses. Also little attention is being given to the kind of plants that are being raised. There is much objection to Eucalyptus and Acacia plantations in several parts of the country. We should be careful in selecting the plants, even if it is costly, for ultimately it is the utility of the plantations that will matter.

Meeting the Requirements of Rural Energy

In rural areas 70 per cent of the energy requirement is met by wood and is utilised largely for cooking purposes. Wood being consumed as fuel was estimated largely for cooking purposes. Wood being consumed as fuel was estimated to be equivalent to about 130 million tonnes of coal (1982) which was nearly as much as the total production of coal in the country in that year. Fuel and wood prices have shot up adding to the misery of the rural population. Conservation of fuel wood and devising more efficient methods for use of fuel is very vital. Traditional varieties of chullah (cook-stove) have fuel effieincy of only 10 per cent (i.e. they are able to tap only 10 per cent of the potential energy of the fuel which is used by them). Improved varieties of chullah have been evolved which give fuel efficiency upto 25 per cent. It is thus possible to economise on the use of fuel up to 50 per cent, by the use such improved varieties of chullah. An additional advantage is that smokeless chullahs are harmless for health of women. The large incidence of cataract among rural women is due to use of chullahs which emit large quantities of smoke. The use of improved varieties of chullah has to be widely propagated through voluntary agencies and panchayats.

Bio-gas plants similarly would help in utilising cow-dung and agricultural waste for meeting the fuel requirements, and in converting cow-dung into manure for agriculture far more efficiently besides improving the environment. Gobar burnt directly gives 20 per cent less heat energy. For the same quantity of gobar we get 33 per cent more fertilizer compared to direct farm yard manure. The slurry contains 1.5 to 2.0 per cent nitrogen, compared to 0.5 to 0.7 per cent in farm manure. Generating bio-gas is a simple technology which can be easily adopted. It has the potential of transforming the country side by meeting the rural energy requirements locally.

In India also there has been a strong drive since the Sixth Plan to increase the coverage of gobar gas plants (bio-gas units based on cow-dung). There were 15.75 lakh gobar gas units in the country in 1992. Bihar has a rich potential but it has been only nominally utilised. The livestock population inthe State was 358 lakh in 1982, which was about 9% of the total livestock population in the country. The number of gobar gas units in the State was, however, only about 60,000 in 1992. If we could only ensure proper mintenance of gobar gas units, its attraction will greatly increase. The high percentage of non-functioning units (about 25 per cent) has a discouranging effect. Bio-gas units based on human excreta has also tremendous potential. This has been successfully demonstrated by Sulabh Souchalaya Patna. It is possible to establish such units, wherever community latrines are constructed, both in urban and rural areas. Crop residues, or organic wastes and weeds like water hyacinth are also rich source of gas. One hectare of water hyacinth will generate 70,000 cubic metre bio-gas in a year. This is the equivalent of gobar gas which can be obtained from cow-dung of 2,000 cattle in a year. Water hyacinth which covers large tracts in North Bihar and which is considered to be nuisance at present can be gainfully utilised for generation of gas. Suitable technique has to be evolved for extraction of the gas conveniently. The effluent sludge in the case of water hyacinth plants is also a rich manure.

Schemes for utilisation of ground water potential for irrigation facilities, for improvement of cattle wealth, for development of fisheries, for introducing modern methods in agriculture, horticulture, housing for rural homeless, especially scheduled caste, etc., have been in vogue for quite sometime and sufficient experience has been gained for further exrtending them. The villagers can be trained to take up income generating activities.

Village women could be usefully trained in knitting, embroidery work, and pickle making. The rural artisans can be helped to take up trades such as tassar spinning, beedi-making, plate making, from sal leaves, animal skin tanning, weaving, rope-making, cot-making and basket making. There are large number of other schemes which can be adopted by villagers during their idle time for supplementing their income.

As stated earlier there can be no common strategy for rural development. Each region has its specific problems. Its resource potential also differs. Plans for development have to be rooted to ground realities if they are to be relevant and elicit popular response. Our approach to the problems of rural poverty and unemployment has been half hearted. A bolder approach is required to banish poverty. It is better to concentrate our efforts on a few critical items and make larger provision for funds and be sure of achievement. Trying to achieve too many things at the same time and spreading out resources thinly with a weak organisation is not a good strategy. Attention is distracted from the major issues. Development efforts must yield results during our life time. It must be tangible to give satisfaction to the people and provide the feeling of achievement. Allowing problems to persist would lead to distrust and loss of faith in the development programmes of the government.

REFERENCES

1. Report of the Committee to Review the Existing Administrative Arrangements for Rural Development and Poverty Alleviation Programmes (CAARD), Ministry of Agriculture, December, 1985.
2. C.H. Hanumantha Rao - Changes in Rural Poverty in India *IASSI Quarterly*, New Delhi Dec. 1985.
3. R. Nurkse, *Problems of Capital Formation in Underdeveloped Countries*, oxford, 1953.
4. Moonis Raza and Sudesh Nangia, *Atlas of the Child in India*: Concept, 1986.
5. *Wasteland and Development for Fuelwood and Fodder Production;* Forest Research Institute, 1988.
6. *Jawahar Rojgar Yojana: A Quick Study*, Planning Commission, 1992.

7. G.V.K. Rao, *Report on District Planning,* Ministry of Rural Development, 1985.

8. *The State of World's Children,* 1993, UNICEF.

9. *Children and Women in India,* UNICEF.

10. *The Girl Child in Bihar - Recommendations of Symposium,* November, 1989.

11. *World Development Reports,* 1980, 1990, World Bank.

12. *Economic Survey,* Government of India.

6

Making the Economy Broad Based

Urbanisation – A Catalyst for Development

Bihar is the least urbanized of the major States in the country. Urban population in the State is just 13.17%. It is in the company of States such as Sikkim (9.12%), Assam (11.06%), Arunachal Pradesh (12.12%), Himachal Pradesh (8.7%), Orissa (13.43%), mostly hilly States with very sparse population. The all India average is 25.72%. It is not surprising that with every 7 out of 8 Biharis being resident of villages the image which a Bihari conjures is that of an illiterate, ignorant, simple unassuming villager, but of jokes in the metropolitan cities, where they flock in large numbers in search of jobs.

Low level of industrialisation, poor civic services, inadequate housing, difficult communication and lack of public transport has hampered the growth of town and cities in Bihar. Government has been totally indifferent to urban civic services in the State. It is assumed that urbanisation will take care of itself. In fact the experience is to the countrary. If urbanisation does not proceed in a planned manner, there is the risk of urban centres being suffocated for lack of basic services. Naturally growth would be hampered. Capitalism, market economy, industria-lisation all lead to growth of activities concentrated in urban centres. Urbanisation, therefore, appears to proceed hand in hand with industrialisation. Urbanisation thus facilitates the transformation to industrialisation. Industrialisation requires housing, water, sanitation and public transport for workers. The towns must be able to expand to cope with the growing pressure for these services, otherwise they will get choked and discourage new insustries from being located at these places. Urban population in Bihar during 1971-81 grew at 4.37%, higher than the All India average 3.82%. During 1981-91 urban growth rate had slackened to 2.65%, which was lower than the All India average 3.09%. This reflects the growing unattractiveness and inadequacy in Bihar compared to those in other States. Lack of preparedness on the part of the State for growth of business, commerce, industry and other activities would make the situation worse. Orissa has shown greater preparedness in this respect though it was less urbanised than Bihar, when it separated from Bihar, it has now over-taken Bihar.

The inter district distribution of urban population in Bihar indicates that only four districts, East Singhbhum (52.9%), Dhanbad including Bokaro (51.3%), Patna (38%) and Ranchi (33.1%) have greater degree of urbanisation than All India level. There are seven districts which have more urban population than the state average. These are Hazaribagh (18.1%), Munger (16.6%), Singhbhum (15.8%), Giridih (15.4%), Nalanda (14.8%), Deoghar (13.6%) and Gaya (13.3%). Thus, but for a few pockets which are primarily coal and iron ore mining areas, the State is esentially rural and agrarian in character with 85 to 90% of the people being engaged in agriculture.

Conditions have to be created for a shift to non-agricultural occupations and this will naturally involve a structural change in the economy from rural to urban. There is a regular stream of migrants from rural to urban areas for employment and better life. This is the natural trend in keeping with industrialisation and modernisation. The feudal, rural, agrarian set up has to be replaced by urban, industrial society. If we do not facilitate the transformation by advance planning, we will land up in a mess with growth of shanty colonies. Change will take place but quality of life will deteriorate. Urban growth is therefore not to be looked upon as incidental, but as a necessary catalyst for inducing change for better life. Industrialisation and urbanisation are symbiotic.

The neglect of the cities in Bihar, resulting in their degeneration, and lack of urban planning, providing for better basic services as well as expansion of different amenities is acting as a restraint to growth. It has created a situation in which major manufacturing units and commercial and Financial Institutions find it more convenient to operate from outside the State, i.e. in case of Bihar from Calcutta or Lucknow, even if their production activities are located within the State or even if the state constitutes a major market for their products. Thus SAIL, Coal India, D.V.C. Tata, Commercial Banks and financial institutions have their headquarters outside Bihar. All India undertakings do not prefer to have even their regional offices at Patna. This means loss of employment opportunities and income, and since the institutions are located in other States and far away, they become less accessible to the people of the State and also less responsive towards their needs.

Urban centres are the nodal centres for growth. Apart from infrastructure, urban services also play a crucial role in attracting capital. They serve as sites for locating industries, centres for trade and commerce, besides being centres for learning, culture, and administrative centres. Those who have choice to select their place of work, would naturally prefer a place which provides better amenities. Patna, the State capital, with overflowing drains, roads, full of pot-holes, heaps of garbage, cattle roaming freely on the streets, traffic congestion made worse by encreachments, no open space, no place for recreation and sports, apart from the dirt and filth which pose danger for the health of the people, does not serve the cause of the State in attracting entrepreneurs for profitable ventures within the state.

Town planning has to be strictly enforced. Minimum civic services by way of safe water supply, efficient disposal of waste, good roads, cheap public transport and adequate housing has to be ensured for healthy environment and to fulfil the requirements of a modern industrial society. Ignoring this will be a serious omission. It is also essential to enable the people who are working in the towns and cities to perform their jobs more efficiently. The cost of providing civic services is not prohibitive and can be recovered from the users on a quid proquo basis. The inability of the local bodies to recover taxes is primarily due to their laxity. It must be realised that the urban centres contribute as much as 80 to 90% of the revenue of the State. It is a foolish Government that would allow the hen that lays the golden eggs to become sick. Urban votes do not count for much but healthy and clean towns and cities contribute to the efficiency of the work force in urban centres and to the strength of our economy.

There is no conflict between urban and rural growth. The growth of urban areas helps the rural economy. The urban growth centres, especially the small cities and towns, require to be well planned and developed so that industries could be also dispersed in the small cities and towns. This will help the positive impact of development being spread over larger area in the interior, and also prevent concentration of industries in the bigger cities and consequent growth of slums.

Industries for More Jobs and Income:

Industries serve to diversify the economy, open up new avenues for employment. By introducing machines we enhance the productivity of labour and thereby their earning capacity. Labourers are induced to acquire new skills to take advantage of new opportunities. For smooth growth of industries, plentiful and cheap supply of raw materials is necessary. A situation of increasing returns is also necessary i.e. distinct economies emerging as a result of expansion in the scale of operation. A large and growing market is also an important requisite. The other requirements such as availability of finance, and even the skill and management for running these industries can be arranged, though they are no easy tasks.

In a backward agricultural economy with very low per capita income, the market for industrial products is not elastic. People do not have enough income to buy the basic ncessities of life, i.e. food, clothing and housing. Petty and cheap household articles, simple tools for agriculture are all that are in demand. The traditional household industries such as the village potter, blacksmith, carpenter and cobbler meet these needs on a purely local basis. The craftsmen who are engaged in such household occupations are only partly employed, their output and earnings are low. Like the subsistence cultivators, whom they serve, they are also subsistence producers. In the circumstances, the needs for adoption of improved technology or better skills is rarely felt. The village industries cannot, therefore, serve as growth nodules, though they may serve the purpose of providing employment locally and make the villages independent of the cities in catering to their elementry needs.

Correcting Regional Imbalance

The location of basic and heavy industries should be guided by econmic considerations, proximity to raw materials, infrastructure facilities, proximity to market, etc. Political considerations also influence location of such industries. In accordance with Industrial Policy, such industries are mostly in the public sector. It is possible to locate heavy industries in backward regions for correcting regional imbalance. The outlay over such industries is very large, and they immediately generate demand for consumer products, most of which can be locally produced. The demand for intermediate products can be met by development of ancillary industries. But experience has not been very happy. In Bokaro Steel City, situated in desolate tribal area, the local ancillary industries could not grow, because the supplies were monopolised by firms in Calcutta. The backward linkages were not properly assessed and there was no plan to tag the development of local industries with the parent unit and therefore, the opportunities were lost.

In British days, when industrial development in the country was still in its infancy, the Eastern Region was industrially more developed than the rest of the country. The prosperous Jute Industry was located in West Bengal. Bihar also had two major jute factories. The sugar industry was almost entirely located in Bihar and Uttar Pradesh. Almost the entire coal mining was in this region and the first steel plant in the country was located at Jamshedpur. Industrial progress of the country has been quite rapid since independence. But the Eastern States have lagged behind. West Bengal contributed nearly quarter of the industrial production in the country at the time of independence but its share had fallen to 10% in 1981. Total amount sanctioned and disbursed by all the Financial Institutions upto 1981, in Bihar was Rs. 1,548 crores. U.P. received Rs. 6,292 crores. West bengal Rs. 3,617 crores and Orissa Rs.1,913 crores - Bihar's share in total investments by financial institutions in the country was just 2.3%. Bihar's share in the total capital invested in industries was 5.2%, and in net value added was 5%. Uttar Pradesh's share was 10.7% and 9% respectively; West Bengal's 6.4% and 4.3% and Maharashtra's 18.2% and 23%.

Government's efforts to disperse industries to correct regional imbalance is primarily in respect of Small Scale Industries, which are under the control of State Govt. The capacity of a poor and backward State to develop its backward region is much less compared to that of a well to do state. The position is made worse by the poor level of infrastrucutre development in the backward States.

Small Scale Industries

Small Scale Industries have a very large employment potential. Employment potential of heavy industries in comparison, because of capital intensive technology, is much less. Employment in the organised sector has been growing at the rate of 1.3% per annum, and this is entirely due to expansion in the Public Sector, for employment in the organised Private Sector has been falling. Employment in the SSI sector has been growing at the rate of 7% per annum. Nearly 129 Lakh persons are employed in S.S.I. units in the country at present. This expansion of S.S.I. units is an important strategy for aprviding employment. The number of S.S.I. units registered in the country increased from 11.58 Lakhs in 1983-84 to 20.8 Lakhs in 1991-92. In 1992, the total gross output of S.S.I. Sector was Rs.178,700 crores, which was about 35% of the total industrial production in the country. It's share in exports is even more important. Sports goods, processed tobacco, snuff, beedi, lac, finished leather and leather products, drugs and pharmaceuticals, essential oils, rubber and plastic products, processed food, readymade garments, lac, marine products, hides and skins are all S.S.I. products and they constitute nearly 30% of the total exports from the country.

The crucial role of S.S.I. units is clearly evident. They require less capital, as they are less capital intensive. They can make use of local skills and indigenous raw materials. They can serve useful purpose in spreading industrial enterpreneurship. The small scale units can be dispersed and located in backward areas. Because of their small size, small scale units are flexible in products adaptation. Items which are frequently modified according to customer's requirement can be conveniently manufactured by them.

If S.S.I. units are to serve as an engine for growth and to push their sales in international markets, they must improve their efficiency, i.e. improve the quality of their products while keeping their cost in check. It has been observed that even in respect of S.S.I. units, the output capital ratio seems to improve with larger size of operation. This implies that S.S.I. units will have to grow into efficient medium sized firms. Our policy in respect of village and small scale units, especially the former has been dominated by Gandhian thought on the subject. Gandhiji observed, "Mechanisation is good when the hands are too few for the work intended to be accomplished. It is an evil when there are more hands than required for the work, as in the case of India" (Harijan 16.11.1931). But Gandhiji was conscious of the fact that the products of village industries must be competitive enough to have a ready market. He observes. "The villagers should develop such a high degree of skill that articles prepared by them should command a ready market outside. When our villages are fully developed, there will be no dearth in them of capable men and a high degree of skills and artistic talent". (Young India, 12.11.1931). Gandhiji expressed these views more than half a century ago, when the country was ruled by British and therefore he did not consider it necessary to elaborate on how there will be no dearth of men with high degree of skill. Janata Government, during 1977-79, sought to implement Gandhiji's ideas by preserving certain industries exclusively for the cottage and small scale sectors. Thus it was decided that clothing needs of the people would be progressively met through the development of the handloom sector T.S. Papola who made a study of such industries in Uttar Pradesh has very appropriately described the plight of household industries "operating on the very small scale, the household industries are able to turn out a very small volume of production, which despite a reasonably very high value added per unit of out-put, provides only a small income per worker, which in turn restricts the capacity and enthusiasm of entrepreneur households to expand. In order to break this vicious circle, it is necessary to strengthen the units so that they may enlarge the scale of their operations by providing them with capital to meet operational costs and to buy additional tools and equipment, where necessary. As is revealed by the entrepreneurs, the amount of additional capital required are generally small". A logical extension of this programme will involve a gradual shift from household units to a cooperative of rural artisans. Small is beauitiful, but small is small, and tiny household units may not fulfill the aspirations of rural artisans. While stressing employment opportunities, we should also aim at an appropriate technology which is economically viable. Papola further observes, "Even an increase in capital intensity per worker may have to be accepted if that is the only way of providing an adequate level of income to those employed in rural industry. The technology would not only have to be appropriate in relation to the endowment of labour and other resources available in the areas, but also in relation to the specifics of the demand for products, whether from rural or urban areas, so that they must be marketed competitivey at reasonable prices and yield a sufficient income to the producers." "Evidence suggests that small may not be always beautiful, small firms tend to be economically more efficient than large firms only in those industries in which nature of the technology or the characteristics of the market put small firms at an advantage over their large competitors."

Potential for Agro-Processing Industries

There is vast potential for promoting agro-processing industries, as the Indian economy is primarily dependent on agriculture. Though rice and dal mills are traditional industries and are to be found all over the country, there is inadequate development of fruits and vegetable processing units. Bihar produces 10% of the total fruit production in the country and 22% of the vegetable production in the country. The producers are generally small farmers, ignorant of the modern techniques of processing. They are exploited by middlemen, who finance and also market their produce. Bihar produces 80% of the Litchi produced in the country (8 lakh tonnes). It is a major producer of high quality mangoes (9 lakh tonnes). It is the sole producer of Makhana (Water-Chestnuts), an ideal snack and raw-material for pudding when processed. Makhana can bring handsome gains to the farmers, if they can have direct access to the market. U.P. is the largest producer of mangoes in the country. But as mangoes cannot be preserved for long, they cannot exported and transported over long distances. If we have to export our fruit products they have to be in processed stage. West Bengal has emerged as a major producer of pineapple.

It is estimated that nearly 30% of the fruit and vegetables which is produced is lost because of wastage and spoilage. This colossal loss is due to inadequate facilities for storage, processing, preservation and marketing. Lack of such facilities results in undesirable gluts in the markets during the peak harvesting/ripening season.

The fruit and vegetable processing units can be set up under the Cooperatives or even multi-nationals can be invited to take up this job. This will encourage fruit and vegetable cultivation and provide much needed income to the farmers and also provide employment.

The Problem of Sickness

A study made by the Small Industries Development Organisation in Patna, Jasidih and Muzaffarpur in 1986, revealed that nearly 60% of the industrial units at these places were sick. The position has worsened since then. In spite of this high incidence of sickness, more small scale are being registered. In Bihar there were only 5,260 S.S.I units in 1973, which has gone up to over 55,000 and out of this over 17,000 are sick. Apparently industrial sicknesss has not deterred government or the financial institutions from promoting new industrial units; whether they are actually in production is, however, doubtful. According to the S.S.I. Census of 1987-88, the S.S.I. units in Bihar provides employment to 182,000 persons and their total production was worth Rs.878 crores; total fixed investment being Rs. 333 crores and Rs.158 crores being involved as working capital.

The entrepreneurs argue that industrial sickness is due to difficulty in procuring raw matrials, lack of timely financial support and difficulty in marketing their produce, but the basic problem seems to lie somewhere else." The most important factor which is responsible for the rapid spread of industrial sickness in the small sector is inadequate appraisal of projects. In fact sickness has been built into them from the conception stage. Another cause of their failure is their indiscriminate promotion by government agencies. The State Financial Corporation too has financed them indiscriminately without adequate evaluation of the projects. Promotion of industries has become more paying than running them. Projects are cleared on the basis of exaggerated feasibility reports and inflated estimates. When they turn out to be non-viable, additional financial assistance is sought for rehabilitation.

While industrial units are plaugued by sickness, the entrepreneurs prosper. The real losers are the financial institutions, the Govt. and the employees of such industries. The State Financial Corporation lost nearly Rs.400 crores invested in sick and non-operational S.F.C units. The beneficiaries from these dubious investments were the borrowers, some of whom cannot be traced, and the corrupt officials, who acquired pernicious influence. The S.S.I. is at present defunct and unable to perform its vital role.

Encouraging S.S.I. Units

To encourage setting up S.S.I. Industries, all the State Governments have offered liberal incentives. Thus they tend to offset each other and the gains from locating the industry at any place is reduced very much. Basic factors like labour relations, availability of power, raw materials and convenience of marketing continue to have decisive influence. Bihar Government has also not fallen behind in the race. In the latest Industrial Policy of the State announced in April,1993 the concessions have been restricted to industries with investments upto Rs.15 crore only, S.S.I.s have been given special preference. Thus for S.S.I.s with investment upto Rs.75 lakh, capital subsidy at 15% (maximum Rs.7.5 Lakh) has been granted. Besides for preparing feasibility project report subsidy at 0.5% of the cost upto Rs.3 lakh, reimbursement upto 75% of the total fees paid as technical know-how, exemption of stamp duty and registration fees on mortgage bonds upto a maximum of Rs.50,000, 25% subsidy on installation of captive generating sets upto a maximum of Rs.7.5 lakh, etc. and land is also offered on lease on easy instalments. The industrial unit is exempted from payment of sales tax on its produce for the first eight/ten years of its coming into production, and on the raw-materials being used by it. The period depending on whether the units is located in extremely backward or less backward district. Thus the promoter is able to obtain substantial part of the investment 'cost' as subsidy. The rest can be obtained from government financial institutions on easy terms. There is power rebate of 15 paise to 18 paise per unit depending on whether the industrial unit is medium/large or small sized. In the circumstances it is attractive to set-up an industry (provided one has the contacts) but difficult to run it, under competitive market conditions. The rehabilitation subsidies and market guarantees further reinforce this trend. Enhancing the rate of subsidies has come to be accepted as sure means for promoting industries. Actual disbursement of subsidy exceeded Rs.17 crores in 1986-87 and the State was not much behind the industrially developed States. But lately these subsidies have beacome a source of embarrassment as Government has found it difficult to honour its commitments due to lack of budgetary support.

The State Government accords price preference to the products of S.S.I. units located within the State. The Government Departments and the State Public Sector Undertakings have been directed to buy their requirements preferably from the industrial units located within the State The State units are to be preferred even if their prices exceed the lowest quoted prices upto 15%. This big margin of preference in purchases, makes S.S.I. units indifferent to quality and heavily dependent on State Patronage. Such units seldom try to improve their productivity and become competitive.

It is a folly to split the national market on the basis of States, geographical jurisdiction. Many States are too small for economies of scale to be fully realised. A necesary condition for growth of industries is a situation of increasing returns with expansion of operation. Bihar is a big State but it is poor and under developed. It does not offer an attractive market for industrial expansion. The preferential system thus operates in favour of the well to do States, who favour their own units to the exclusion of others. This explains why the more enterprising entrepreneurs from even backward States prefer sites in Bombay, Calcutta and other metropolitan cities for their manufacturing units. The advantage of a big integrated national market, which could promote specialisation and economies of scale are lost due to restriction of the market. The products of the S.S.I. units are sometimes not of desired quality, and their use may undermine operational efficiency of the State undertakings. The sad experience with transformers supplied by S.S.I.units of the State to B.S.E.B. bears testimony to this fact. The nurturing of industries under green house conditions makes such units over dependent on State patronage, so much so that they become sick when government support is withdrawn. In other words government is made to pay for the inefficiency of S.S.I. units, a condition which cannot be said to be conducive for genuine growth.

Utilising Tourism Potential of Bihar

Tourism has become the biggest foreign exchange earner through out the world. In India, nearly two million people are directly or indirectly employed in activities relating to tourism. Tourism promotes better understanding among people and different regions and can become the strongest cementing force in achieving national integration as well as promoting international amity. 1.25 million foreign tourists visited India in 1988. Out of this only 27,000, about 2% visited Bihar. Because of easy accessibility from Calcutta and Varanasi and also because the State lies on the route to Nepal, a favourite destination for the foreign tourists, Bihar can attract larger number of tourists. It is necessary that proper attention is given to the availability of basic amenities at the tourist centres so that Bihar is able to take advantage of the larger flow of tourists to India.

Tourism in Bihar has been a neglected sector. It is the most populous part of the country. The region has historical, archaelogical and natural scenic sites which have great potential from the point of view of tourism. The neglect of tourism in this region has meant not only less arrival of foreign tourists and tourists from other parts of the country, but also poor growth of handicrafts which normally develop around tourist centres. It need not be emphasised that growth of tourism also provides employment opportunities through growth of the informal sector.

The people of this region have suffered as they have very little opportunity for outings. If they decide to go on holiday, it means undertaking a long journey to the distant Himalayas or to the sea-coasts. Not many families can afford this. The result is that people inhabiting this region are deprived of means for relaxation and recreation which greatly adds to the quality of life.

Bihar has most ancient historical and archaelogical sites not only in India but the whole of South Asia. Nalanda and Bodh Gaya qualify to be world heritage sites. There is an ambitious programme to develop the Budhist sites in U.P./Bihar. The Budhist sites in Bihar which have been included are Bodh Gaya, Rajgir, Nalanda and Vaishali. The Project involves an expenditure of Rs.125 crores over the Bihar sector. This project aims primarily at improving the infrastructure facilities, i.e. for better roads connecting these places, better water and power supply at these places, better transport and accomodation facilities at these places. The share of Japanese Assistance is about 1/3rd of the total outlay. This assistance is available only after the expenditure is incurred. Tourism is given very low priority by Bihar. Because of resources constraint the State Government has not been able to show much progress on the Project.

It is doubtful whether the project would confer lasting benefit to the sites. Apart from expenditure on landscaping which is a mere Rs. 2 crores, there is no expenditure on site development. Thus at Bodh Gaya, the Gautam Van Project for which over 20 crores of land were acquired around the Mahabodhi temple 20 years ago, still remains barren tract. This can be suitably landscaped and developed into a zone of serenity where Budhist pilgrims could meditate peacefully in idyllic surrounding. Ministry of Tourism has not been able to decide on a suitable plan as yet. Similarly, Dungeshwari Hills and Sujata Kutir, which are holy and sacred sites for Budhist pilgrims, have not been given any attention and they remain filthy and dreary spots and also very difficult to reach. They should be properly developed in keeping with Budhist sentiments.

The National Park Service, U.S.A. which looks after historical monuments, Nationl Parks and natural scenic sites in U.S.A. were engaged by Ministry of Tourism and the Government of Bihar to suggest a development plan for the major Budhist sites in Bihar. The author was actively associated with the project. The report made useful suggestions for the development of Budhist sites in Bihar. It proposes bye-pass road at Bodh Gaya/Rajgir. The bye-pass road is urgently required to preserve the religious sanctity of the place, and also to enable the Budhist pilgrims coming from all over the world to meditate in silence without being disturbed by the noice of traffic and market place. The market has come up very close to the temple precincts and is spoiling the peace and environment of the temple. The land around the temple has to be acquired and the market and the parking site has to be shifted away from the temple. The P.W.D. I.B. can be utilised for building a Visitors Centre in keeping with the international importance of the site, which would provide for an auditorium for display of films and lectures on different aspects of the place, a gallery for exhibits and a sales counter for handicrafts, pictures, books, mementoes etc.

Similarly at Rajgir, the Kund has to be provided with suitable bathing enclosures for privacy, water has to be suitably stored so that there is regular supply during bathing time. A visitors centre at Rajgir and a Sound and Light show dwelling on the ancient history of the place, would greatly enhance visitors' impressions. At Nalanda we have a beautiful lotus pond around the Huien Tsang Memorial and Pali Institute, which have got silted. These can be restored. It is reported that Huien Tsang Memorial, a beautiful monument built by the Chinese has been handed over to the Open University for its office by the Government. This is unfortunate as it will disturb the serenity of the place.

Apart form the Budhist circuit, there are other beautiful places which can be developed into major attractions. These are the Barabar Caves, Rohtas Fort, Tilaiya Lake, Parasnath Hill, Topchanchi Lake and Valmiki Nagar. Barabar caves built by Emperor Ashok in 3rd Century B.C. has aroused the curiosity of archaelogists all over the World. The dirt road however, acts as a major deterrent. Considering the great tourism potential of the place, providing 10 K.Ms of good metalled road should be no problem. Unfortunately it has escaped attention at all levels. It is only 25 KMs from Gaya and visitors travelling from Patna to Gaya by road can easily cover the place enroute. Both the Barabar caves and Rohtas Fort have been taken over by A.S.I. but they have done very little to develop the sites. Rohtas Fort is on hill top and is cut off due to poor accessibility. It has monuments dating back to Akbar's time and the place is said to be as enchanting as Mandu in Madhya Pradesh. Rohtas Fort is only a few kilometres off from G.T. Road and close to Sasaram, where we have the Sher Shah's tomb.

There are number of large reservoirs in the State Tilaiya, Konar, Panchet, Maithen, Tenughat, Dimna are among the large ones, set in attractive surroundings. The first four are under the central of D.V.C. Maithen has been developed by D.V.C. and Dimna near Jamshedpur is an ideal Picnic spot for the steel city. Tilaiya, very close to the G.T.Road, is the largest in size. It has many small islands. One of them has been provided with a lovely garden and a crocodile farm. A small steamer has been also provided by the D.V.C. for tourists. There is a big guest house on a hillock, close to a deer park, which gives a commanding view of the lake and the impressive river dam. Tilaiya can be developed further as a place for boating and water sports. Topchanchi, further east, only 20 KMs, from Dhanbad, can be similarly developed. It is on the foothills of Parasnath, a holy place for Jains. The feasibility of providing an electric rope way from Topchanchi to Parasnath Hills can be explored. It will be a big boom for the Jain pilgrims and also attract large number of tourists from Calcutta.

Patna is located on the bank of River Ganges. The river has a very wide span near Patna. However, the people of Patna and those visiting Patna do not have convenient access to the bank, as the river bank is mostly occupied by buildings belonging to different institutions. However, the fact that most of the institutions along the river bank are public institutions, provides an opportunity for developing an avenue along the bank, similar to one along Hooghly in Calcutta.

There are three Government bungalows, occupying about 10 to 12 acres of land along the bank, close to the Gandhi Maidan, which can be developed by the State Government into a beautiful recreation centre, with lawns, gardens, restaurant, pavillions etc. The river bank can be developed into a modern ghat, which would provide amenities for those coming for a dip into the holy river or for worship during festivals such as Chhath, Kartik Purnima etc. The visitors can also come here and have a view of the majestic river. Patna has very few attractions. The Gandhi Maidan is heavily polluted. This site would afford the much sought for relaxation to the city inhabitants and tourists.

At Raxaul, the Indian Embassy had a Counsellate some time ago. It has a very big orchard, nearly 10 to 15 acres in size and an old dak-bungalow. This site on the Indo-Nepal Boarder can be handed over to I.T.D.C. or any private Hotel Group. A luxuty hotel at this site would be a great attraction for people travelling by road from India to Kathmandu. Raxaul, incidentially, has a very good metalled landing ground also, which at present is under the control of the Defence Ministry.

Valmikinagar on Bihar, U.P., Nepal Border, located by the side of the barrage on River Gandak is an enchanting place located in the midst of forests. The cool and refreshing atmosphere and the sight of crystal clear water gushing down the hills is an unforgettable experience. However, there is no accomodation for tourists. Land for providing accommodation facilities is no problem, as most of the land by the side of the river Gandak is owned by the State Irrigation Department.

If the tourism potential is utilised to the full, it will provide substantial income and employment opportunities through opening of roadside motels, provision of transport facilities, star hotels and demand for local handicrafts. The potential should not be under-estimated. Even though India is not a very popular destination for foreign tourists, ranking lower than Sri Lanka, earnings of foreign exchange from tourism is next only to earnings from exports of gems and jewellery.

REFERENCES

1. T.S.Papola, *Rural Industrialisation*, Himalaya Publishing House, 1982, pp. 10-11.
2. *World Development Report*, 1987, p. 130 (Box 7-8).
3. Vasant Desai, *Problems and Prospects of S.S.I. in India*, Himalaya Publishing House, 1983.
4. *Consultancy Capabilities in the State of Bihar*, Department of Scientific and Industrial Research, February, 1993.
5. *Report of the National Commission on Urbanisation*, Government of India, August, 1988.
6. *World Development Reports* 1979, 1981, World Bank.

7

Population Control

India is the most populous country after China. But China has been able to control its population growth and reduce it to 1.2% per annum, in India it continues to grow at nearly 2% per annum. At this rate India will end up as the most populous country in the world by 2030 A.D. Over population is the greatest retarding factor. The impact of over population is felt most in the Gangetic plains. North Bihar is emerging as the most densely populated region in the world. The impact of over population on development efforts in Bihar carries alarming message. The present chapter intends to formulate a population policy keeping the situation of Bihar in view.

Bihar's population according to the latest census is over 86 millions. It is at present close 90 millions. The decennial growth of population in the State during 1941-51 was 25% lower, than the growth of the population in the country. Population more than doubled from 3.88 crore in 1951 to 8.6 crore in 1991. The density of population in North Bihar at 761 is the highest in the country. The density of population of West Bengal is 766 but it includes the huge metropolis, Calcutta, with a population of nearly 11 millions i.e. 1/6th of the population of the State. The population of Saran,Tirhut and Mithila divisions with less than 32,000 Sq.KMs was recorded at 27.33 millions in 1991, which was more than that of Canada, 26.5 millions; and more than one and half times than that of Australia, 17.1 millions. Canada is more than three times the size of India and Australia is more than twice the size of India.

It is indeed an alarming situation. The main demographic characteristics of the State are given in Table 7.4. Regions in which density has reached the thousand mark are in a critical stage. A density of 1000 per Sq.KMs means that there are four persons for every acre. Bihar has also to support 208 lac cattle and buffaloes, total livestock being 309 lac according to the cattle census taken in 1982. With hills, rivers, roads actual usable area would not be more than half. Thus the effective density is nearly 10 per acre which means that people will come in each other's way and land and nature would be over exploited, leading to its degradation. No doubt North Bihar is heading towards a great crisis, a demographic calamity of unprecedented character. Over-population is one of the main causes of poverty and is responsible for rising incidence of child labour and illiteracy among labouring classes. It creates grave problems, environmental degradation, insanitation, disease, unemployment, landlessness, crime and discontent. The invisible forces of nature will sooner or later restore the balance. But that will be very tortuous.

Kerala recorded the highest density of population in 1981, 655. But Kerala turned the corner, and between 1981-1991 population in Kerala grew by 13.98% only, the lowest in the country. India's population grew by 23.5% and Bihar's population at 23.49%. The fall in growth rate of Kerala's population is attributed to high percentage of female literacy and education. Female literacy in Kerala is nearly 87% compared to only 23% in Bihar. In normal course it would take atleast two decades before Bihar can attain Kerala's level of literacy and by that time Bihar's population according to present trends would have increased to 120 millions. Can we afford to wait till then, Keralites because of their educational attainments spread out throughout the country in search of jobs and relieved the pressure within the State. The same does not hold good for Bihar. Surplus agricultural labour struggles to find gainful employment. The seasonal migrants from the State are subjected to attrocities in Punjab, Haryana and other distant places. Even within the State, Jharkhand has closed the door to them.

Bihar's per-capita income is only slightly more than half of All-India average. Bihar produced only 110 lac tonnes of foodgrains in 1991, when its requirement is about 157 lac tonnes

@ 1/2 kg per head per day. With increasing pressure of population on land, the land holdings have become smaller and the plots have been split into tiny plots of ridiculous size. At present nearly 80% of the holdings are held by marginal farmers with average area of less than 1 acre. It is impossible to carry scientific cultivation on such uneconomic and tiny holdings. The message is clear. We cannot allow matters to drift. There has to be drastic control over population-growth. We have to stabilise it and if possible at its present size, around 90 millions. Forty per cent of the population are below poverty line and the State will be hard pressed with the available rescources to provide enough food and satisfactory shelter, schooling, health facilities and other basic amenities of life. If matters are allowed to drift, food production will have to be doubled i.e. raised to 220 lac tonnes in 20 years to feed a population of 120 millions. This looks impossible. For the last decade or so the economy is stagnant and during the last two or three years the economy has shown a declining trend. Outside assistance either from the Indian Union or abroad is unlikely. North Bihar will thus emerge as the most poverty stricken region in the world with malnutrition, pestilence, and appalling living conditions, holding grim prospects for the future. Already there is increasing incidence of forcible harvesting of crops and land grabbing leading to fertile land remaining fallow in retaliation by land owners.

Our approach to population control has been very diffident. We have preferred to describe this programme as family welfare or family planning. Such coyness in our approach is not conducive in combating a problem which threatens to blighten the future of over 120 millions people struggling to make a living in the Gangetic plains in Bihar and U.P. The stress at present is on a voluntary acceptance of the programme, carrying the message of the programme through mass media to the remotest village and household. The objective is to educate the people and enlist their support in fulfilling the objective of "two-child" norm for all families. But then this programme is not backed up by making family planning aids easily accessible. There is ignorance, prejudice and there are also social and religious taboos which prevent universal voluntary acceptance of the programme. The individual may not realise the consequences of a large family; and in case of poor families a large family may confer benefits as the additions to the family are looked upon as additional hands which can also support the family, totally oblivious of its dire consequences. In a civillized society we cannot allow human beings relegated to the status of animals. Nor can individuals be allowed to act irresponsibly in the name of freedom when their conduct zeoparadises the public welfare or national objectives. It is therefore, necessary to have a consensus of all political parties, religious and ethnic groups and of all sections of the community on population control. This is necessary so that no political party takes advantage of this in elections. Dissenters will have to accede to the majority view. Population control in the present situation is in the people's interest and in the national interest. If the programme is to succeed it has to be universally accepted. There has to be deterrents for dissenters.

We assume that the average number of children per family consists of three children. There is no actual assessment of the size of the average family. It is quite probable that in the populous regions and in regions where population is growing rapidly, the average number of children per family is more than "three" and "four" is a more realistic figure. This means that to achieve even the three child norm universal acceptance of family planing is necessary. Can the two-child norm enable us to stabililze the population at present level? Theoretically yes, because if we do not procreate more children than our existing number, over a period of time the population will be stablised. But when will this stability be achieved and at what level? Not much serious thought has been given to these aspects of the problem.

According to estimates of Health Ministry by the end of present century, birth rate of 21 will be achieved with three child norm, birth rate of 17 with two child norm and birth rate of 9 with one chiid norm. The sample Registration System has estimated the birth rate in Bihar to be 30.5, death rate 9.8 and infant mortality rate 69, compared to 29.3, 9.8 and 80 respectively for all-India. Thus with one child norm, the population will be more or less stablised.

It has to be appreciated that to achieve the "three-child" "two-child" or "one-child" norm same effort will be required. The expenses will be the same. Solution lies in universal coverage.

Partial coverage would lead to infructuous expenditure, as has been our experience so far, for those who really need to be covered may remain out of the net. China has therefore adopted a very realistic approach in adopting the one child norm. The author was recently in China. The one child norm has been accepted by the people and there is no resentment. Women enjoy equal status as men and majority of them are working women. One child has liberated the women and induced them to work for greater well being of the family. The Indian society is a democratic society and not a regimented one like China. Besides level of literacy and awareness in China is also much higher than in India. The Indian population has to be mentally and attitudinally prepared to accept the one child norm. It is therefore, proposed that we have a campaign for five years during which married couples should not have children. There should be really no serious objection to such a programme. But there will be a positive gain as it will prepare the population to accept the one child norm and it will also help us to identify the difficulties and problem "groups" and areas. The objections to the programme could be dealt more carefully and sensitively. What are the implications of such a five year no birth programme for the State of Bihar. According to the estimates of the Health Deptt. Govt. of Bihar, the number of infants below the age of "one" in 26 lakhs. Which means nearly one hundred twenty five lakhs infants will not be there. At the same time 50 lakhs deaths would have occurned. Mothers would be relieved of the burden of looking after infants, and they will be able to work for more income. We can take up a vigorous programme for educating women and female literacy during the period to motivate them. If the benefits are there to see, it will be much easier to have mass support for the programme. This will also enable us to achieve our objective of stabalising the population at current level and make up for the slippages.

The existing organisation with the State Government can undertake the family planning programme providing full coverage to the eligible couples without much difficulty. The target for sterilization in 1992-93 for Bihar was 5 lac and for IUD, C.C. & O.P. i.e. other methods, 1.66 lac. Thus only 6.66 lac couples were being covered which means that it will take nearly 17 years to fully cover the population at this rate. Even these modest targets are not achieved. 1989-90 was comparatively a satisfactory year, but still the coverage was only 4.9 lac persons and with this lackadaisical approach the problem will certainly get out of control.

The State Health Deptt. is confident that there are enough doctors/para-medical and otherfield staff to cope with the task. Additional expenditure would be by way of supplying family planning aids as per requirement and making them conveniently accessible to all the eligible couples. It is estimated that nearly 1,13,00,000 eligible couples in the State are unprotected. Allowing for margin of error, we can assume that about 120 lakh women have to fully protected to make the family planning programme really effective. It is also estimated that 70% of these couples have more than two children. For such couples, both termination and spacing methods have to be adopted, the termination method i.e. use of Intra Uterine Devices or sterilisation being used in case of recalcitrant couples or where the couples are not confident of the use of spacing methods. The remaining 30% and the newly married couples will have the option of adopting the spacing methods, i.e. oral pills or contraceptives. The cost of Copper-T is Rupees 80, cost of oral pills approximately Rupees 60 per annum and the cost of sterilisation Rupees 50, excluding the establishment cost. The average cost can be taken as Rupees 60 per couple. For 120 lac couples the total cost would be Rupees 72 crores. Even if the expenditure is Rupees 100 crores, it is not prohibitive and can be well absorbed by the State Government by pruning down expenditure on several infructuous schemes. The World Bank and other international institutions would be only too willing to lend financial assistance for the programme.

It is observed that 75% of the births in Bihar take place during the months of July to October. This implies that if we concentrate our effort during the corresponding period of conception, i.e. between October to January we can achieve better results at less cost. The pattern and trend of births could be further studied in depth and the programme suitably modified to make it more effective.

The following tables prepared on the basis of information furnished by the Health Department give an interesting insight regarding acceptability of the programme at present:

Table-7.1

Religion/ Caste	*Share in total population %*	*Share in sterlisation %*	*Share in I.U.D. %*
Hindu	60.2	66.2	67.1
Muslim	14.0	3.6	7.1
S.C.	14.5	11.3	12.9
S.T.	8.3	7.4	7.4
Christian	1.06	1.6	2.9
Others i.e. those who did not state their religion.		9.8	2.4

Table-7.2 Distribution of F.P. Cases According to Wife's Age

Age Group	*Share in sterlisation %*	*Share in I.U.D. %*
15-19	–	8.5
20-24	11.3	30.2
25-29	27.2	30.4
30-34	32.6	29.6
35-39	15.9	7.3
40-44	3.6	0.9
Age not recorded	9.4	2.1
	100.00	100.0

Table-7.3 Distribution of F.P. cases according to size of family

No. of children	*Share of sterlisation.*	*Share in I.U.D.*
Nill	–	5.2
1	0.2	25.2
2	17.5	35.5
3	33.0	21.5
4	26.0	7.2
5 & more	13.8	3.3
Mother could not recollect no. of children.	9.5	2.1
	100.0	100.0

The programme is less acceptable to Muslims, Scheduled Castes and Scheduled Tibes. These groups have to be 'motivated' and special attention directed towards them. The destitute and deprived are hardly concerned about the size of their family. 'Reservation' may have also instilled a sense of complacency. In Indonesia, predominantly a Muslim country, family planning has ben greatly successful. In India, too, we may expect a turnover.

Table 7.2 and 7.3 indicates that sterlisation becomes popular with married women only after they attain 25 years and after they have 3 children. There are very few opting for sterlisation after only one child. The objective of having one child family will not be easy to achieve in the beginning. There has to be mass movement for creating awareness among young couples and by educating newly married women about the urgent necessity of resorting to family planning. The table also indicates that the use of I.U.D. picks up after one child and is popular in the age group 20-24. This may be taken as preference for having small families limited to one or two child. The problem is therefore not unsurmountable. With attentive extension staff and regular counselling resistance can be overcome. It has been witnessed that there is positive response to family planning programme even among rural illiterate women.

Compulsion has to be used because nobody has the right to burden the society with un-productive, un-healthy and handicapped offspring. It is unfair and cruel for the offspring. Young people should be discouraged from marrying till they are economically independent. Childless couples should be similarly discouraged from entering into fresh wedlock, instead they should be encouraged to adopt orphans or forsaken babies. For Government employees and employees in organised private sector there should be family planing counselling cells to assist them. Those having larger family than the accepted norm should be deprived of the benefit of 'reservation' and other concessions granted by the State. Such an announcement either at the level of Central or State Government would have greater publicity, and would convey the message far more emphatically then all the money spent on advertising the "population-clock." This will also serve as an effective check on the 'creamy' sections of the reserved categories, who tend to monopolise the benefits meant for the group as a whole. We can withhold increments in salary or even promotion to those who defy the norm. Abortion should be liberalised and facilities for abortion made more safe and convenient. Of course abortion of foetus should be allowed only within early stage of preganancy, so that health of mother is not affected. Inheritance law may be amended so that landed property can be inherited in case of holdings less than one hectare only by one child. These are some of the deterrents that can be considered.

The fundamental approach, namely universal coverage of eligible couples cannot be compromised. We cannot leave birth to chance. Even if we succeed in reducing the birth rate by 50%, it would mean we wiil have 12 lac less babies to look after. The expenses over an infant cannot be less than Rs.500 per child and its mother in a year. Thus the society will be relieved of the burden of Rs.60 crores on new births and care of infants. If there are no births, 25 lac births will be prevented and it will mean saving of Rs.125 crores. The expenditure on family planning (on full coverage basis) has thus direct impact without time lag. With fewer number of births it will be possible to have better pre and post delivery care, which will help us in bringing down incidence of mortality among infants. I.M.R. also influences the attitude of couples to the number of children they wish to have. A child has to be looked after not only in its year of birth, but investments in child continue till such time he becomes productive member of the society. There is considerable expenditure over schooling, also. Besides the frustrations and social tensions caused by unemployment and unfulfilled aspirations and other consequences referred to in the opening paragraphs cannot be measured in monetary terms. Over a period of 18 to 20 years the society spends nearly Rs.10,000 on an average to rear the young and prepare them for productive employment. Thus prevention of 12 lac births per annum means a saving of Rs.1200 crores to the society. Thus the economic and social gains of the programme far outweigh the expenses.

The proposed programme does not minimise the role of female education, age at marriage, etc. in checking birth rate. Female literacy in Bihar is only 23.1% compared to All India level, 39.4%. Similarly mean age at marriage for girls in Bihar is 16.5 years compared to 18.3 years for All-India. The preference for male child has to be overcome by eliminating the discrimination against female sex and granting them equal status. The one child norm will become practical only if the preference for male child is prevented from asserting itself. Amniocentesis, i.e. test, for detecting the sex of un-born child within a few months of conception, has to be banned to prevent abortion of female foetus. This is necessary otherwise there will be serious imbalance in female-male ratio. These programmes will have to be vigorously pursued so that they provide effective support to the family planning programme. We have legislation fixing the minimum age for marriage for men at 21 years and women at 18 years. This has to be strictly enforced. Female education, especially in regard to their crucial role and influence which they exercise in determining the size of the family has to be emphatically brought home. So far we have been trying to achieve acceptability through vigorous publicity campaign. The publicity programme has created awareness, but we have failed in action. The loop holes have to be plugged to ensure the desired result.

Research and development for evolving more convenient and effective means of family planning has to be encouraged and suitable rewards and incentives provided to those engaged in the task. Thus the introduction of Saheli, an oral contraceptive which requires to be taken only once a week will be of much assistance. Research to evolve pill for males or vaccine which would induce temporary sterility are in progress and when available will greatly facilitate the programme. Suggestions for inventing some chemical which could be added to salt or water, whose consumption would reduce fetility are welcome. But in respect of all such medicines, seeking to induce sterility or reduce fertility, it has to be ensured, that there are no side effects, which effect the health or life of the people.

It is rightly said that family planning programme should become a mass movement. Apart from consensus of all political parties, religious and ethnic groups and stratas of society, what is required is a dedicated band of workers, social as well as medical practitioners who can take up this challenge on a mass scale. Voluntary organisations and womens' organisations will have to spearhead the campaign. The panchayats will have to be involved actively. Private doctors can be also persuaded to fix their own targets. Mr. Bhairav Singh Sekhawat, Chief Minister of Rajasthan is to be commended for his brave stand that only individuals having two children would be eligible for contesting elections to Panchayats in the state. Those at the helm of affairs must take the lead and set the trend.

Bihar's burgeoning population has reached the stage of oversaturation. There can be no doubt about this as far as the Gangetic plains are concerned, especially in North Bihar. Development programmes are being baulked. The poverty in North Bihar, unemployment, dependence of the ignorant and weak on the strong, has led to a situation in which the development schemes are becoming in-fructuous as the benefits from the scheme are being grabbed by contractors, local leaders and officials. Poverty and unemployment has become pervasive. The situation is really desperate. It is improbable that development efforts in such a situation would have the desired impact.

It is strange that not much concern is being shown by our leaders at present to the problem of population control. The present day leadership has to realise the grave threat to our future and take up the cause in right earnest. It is the most important issue of our times which affects all of us and has far reaching consequences on the quality of our life and for the future development of the State.

It is surprising that we do not have a population policy, clearly spelling out the objectives and the strategy for containing it. Our approach so far has been to popularise family planning. This has helped us little. A bold approach is required, aiming to restrict the family to one or two child, depending on our objectives, with total commitment involving both Government and people's organisations, and with strong deterrents.

Table-7.4 Demographic Profile of Bihar (1981 Census)

		1981 Census	Remarks
1. Estimated number of couples with wives in the age-group (15-44) years per thousand (1000) population	Bihar	180	
	Max (Madhubani)	195	
	Mini (Singhbhum)	156	

2. Classification of couples according to number of children:-

No. of Children	*Bihar*	*Maximum*	*Minimum*
0	27,64,459	1,75,877 (Saharsa)	34,680 (Nawada)
1	21,73,533	1,24,816 (S.Pargna)	32,710 "
2	23,07,592	1,22,336 (")	34,460 "
3.	22,79,666	1,12,568 (")	38,155 (Katihar)
4+	64,92,067	3,28,465 (Munger)	1,13,885 (Nawada)

3. *Percentage of un-married females to total females in the age group (15-44)*

Bihar	Maximum	minimum
16.00	17.4 (Singhbhum)	14.7 (Nawada)

4. (a) *Estimate of Birth Rate/Death Rate/Natural Growth Rate*

	C B R*	C D R*	N G R* %
Bihar	36.87	16.42	2.04* %
Maximum	40.61 (Saharsa)	26.13 (Nawada)	2.62 (Dhanbad)
Minimum	32.48 (Singhbhum)	8.66 (Dhanbad)	1.37 (Nawada)

* CBR -Crude B.R.
* CDR -Crude D.R.
* NGR -Natural G.R.%

	Bihar	Max	Min
4. (b) Infant Mortality Rate (1989).	91	129 (Muzaffarpur)	59 (Siwan)
4. (c) Expectation of life at birth.	50.5	59 (Dhanbad)	45.8 (Munger)

5. *Different Types of Fertility Rates*

Items	*Bihar*	*Maximum*	*Minimum*
GFR (General Fertility Rate)	160.0	168.3 (Palamau)	113.3 (Singhbhum)
GMFR (General Marital Fertility Rate)	182.0	190.1 (Katihar)	140.3 (Madhubani)
TFR (Total Fertility Rate).	5.20	5.86 (Palamau)	4.24 (Singhbhum)
TMFR (Total Marital Fertility Rate)	5.7	6.7 (Palamau)	5.1 (Madhubani)
GRR (Gross Reproduction Rate).	2.536	2.829 (Sahaesa)	1.902 (S.Parganas)

6. *Percentage of couples effectively protected as on 31 .3 .89*

Year	*Bihar*	*Maximum*	*Minimum*
1984	16.2	28.9 (Ranchi)	11.3 (Rohtas)
1987	20.6	31.4 (Dhanbad)	11.7(Khagaria)
1989	26.72	43.43 (Patna)	17.77 (Siwan)

7. *Health Manpower Availability in Bihar (1984)*

Items	*Bihar*	*Maximu;m*	*Minimum*
Physician density per lakh population.	12.66	27.69 (Patna)	4.81 (Vaaishali)
No. of Nurses per Doctor.	0.46	0.99 (Singhbhum)	0.04 (Siwan)
ANM density per lakh population.	9.29	15.45 (E.Champaran)	0.39 (Siwan)
Male worker density per lakh population	21.3	35.6 (Ranchi)	10.0 (Nalanda)
LHV density per Lakh population.	1.5	3.7 (Munger)	0.6 (Muzaffarpur)
Supervisor density per lakh population.	2.5	4.5 (Hazaribagh)	1.4 (Samastipur)

District Profile of Bihar

Source - PRC Mimeograph Series No. 120
Population Research Centre Deptt. of Statistics Patna University, Patna.

REFERENCES

1. *Annual Report*, Ministry of Health & Family Welfare, Government of India.

2. *Annual Report*, Programme and Implementation Department, Government of India.

3. *Provisional Population Totals*, 1991, Director of Census Operations, Bihar.

4. *Family Welfare Programme in the State of Bihar*, National Institute of Health and Family Welfare Delhi.

5. Census of India - Series 1, Paper 2 of 1992, *Brief Analysis of Primary Census Abstract*.

8

Power: The Critical Input

The importance of electric power to the economy cannot be underestimated. Just as modern transport is totally dependent upon diesel/petrol, electric power is basic to modern industries. Underutilisation of capacity in industry, other than due to short-fall in demand is attributed largely to irregular supply of power. Idle capacity is one of the principal reasons for high capital-output ratio. The close correlation between per capita consumption of power and per capita income indicates the vital role of power to economic development. States with higher per capita incomes, Punjab, Haryana, Gujarat and Maharashtra are also the States with higher per capita consumption of power in the same order. The level of power availability determines the level of industrial activity. Intensive agriculture has also come to depend more and more on availability of power.

The State of Bihar with its low installed capacity, low plant load factor, and undependable supply of power affords an interesting study of a region grappling with the problems of development with chronic shortage of power. Non-availability of power has led to suppression of demand for power. Demand forecasts are based on projections of existing load and therefore underestimate the real requirement. Under planning of power availability, therefore operates as a limit to development efforts. The great potential for ground water irrigation and requirement for pumps in North Bihar as well as in South Bihar cannot be denied. Because of non-availability of power there are not many applications for power connections for new motor pumps. This does not mean that there is no demand for motor pumps for groundwater irrigation. Due to scarcity of power and erratic supply, people have perforce opted for diesel pumps. Small and marginal farmers hire diesel pumps for irrigation at the cost of nearly Rs. 25/- per hour. The bill for operating an electric pump will be less than Rs. 100/- per month. This indicates the heavy burden, which has been imposed over farmers by non-availability of power.

The average per capita consumption of power in Bihar was higher than the All India average up to 1962. But in 1989, per capita consumption of power in Bihar was only 110 units compared to the national average of 216 units. Power availability is concentrated in Chotanagpur where per capita consumption is 315 units compared to only 26 units in North Bihar and 77 units in South Bihar.

The total connected load in Bihar as on 31.3..1989 was 2342 MW against the installed capacity of 1548 MW. The connected load covered 82 MW of traction load, 620 MW of rural loads and 1090 MW of industrial loads. The installed capacity of 1548 MW included 1319 MW of thermal power and 149 MW of hydro power. The latter is designed to meet only peak loads. It is true that the entire load does not require to the served at the same time, still the gap is too wide to permit prudent management, especially when the Plant Load Factor (PLF) in Bihar has remained between 30 to 35 per cent. Between 1990-92 it slumped to less than 25% . It is rather, difficult to assess the demand for power correctly, but on the basis of the existing load the shortage for the B.S.E.B. system is estimated around 40 per cent. Naturally load shedding has to be imposed on a regular basis to balance demand with supply. The power cuts are seldom based on any rational system of power allocation. Agriculture is the worst sufferer as it brings least revenue. The industries which maintain better liaison with B.S.E.B. are favoured. Even if P.L.F. were to improve, the fact remains that installed capacity is very inadequate, considering the size of the State and the potential demand for power. The per capita installed capacity in Bihar is only 16.6 watts, which is the lowest in the country, compared to 146 watts in Punjab, 72 watts in Maharashtra and 58 watts in Andhra Pradesh. Orissa and Uttar Pradesh have per capita installed capacity which is twice as much in Bihar. Obviously less resources have gone into building up the power base in Bihar. Up to 30.11.94 the installed capacity in Bihar was 1765 MW compared to 6074 MW in U.P., 3526 MW in West Bengal, 1952 MW in Orissa and 2241 MW under D.V.C. Because of the incapacity to generate enough power, which will continue in near future, Bihar has landed itself in a helpless situation.

Some fifteen years ago West Bengal and U.P. faced a similar situation. Load shedding in Calcutta was very frequent causing serious concern for industries located in the State. Most parts of U.P. remained plunged in darkness U.P. primarily through investment in Central sector, but West Bengal largely on its own efforts emerged from the crisis successfully. Orissa's position was no better but through planned investment in power they are in comfortable position. Even the N.E. States have turned the corner.

Table 8.1 indicates the share of power and irrigation in total plan allocations for Bihar and All India since the First Plan. Since the Sixth Plan power has been given lower priority. It is surprising, considering the fact that the State has been experiencing severe power shortage since 1980. The State opted for more investments in irrigation, the outlay for irrigation being nearly 50% more than power since the Sixth Plan. Bihar's outlay on power during the Eighth Plan at Rs. 2,120 crore is much less than that of Orissa 2,638 crore, W.B. 3,016 crore and Utter Pradesh 6,974 crore. In Bihar because of serious resource crunch not more than 50% of the proposed outlay will be invested. The implications are ominous.

Table. 8.1. Share of Power and Irrigation in Plan Outlay

(in Rs. Crores)

	Power		*Irrigation & Flood Control*	
	All-India	*Bihar*	*All-India*	*Bihar*
First Plan	149 (7.6)	9.46 (12.9)	434 (22.2)	12.94 (17.66)
Second Plan	452 (9.7)	31.14 (17.5)	430 (9.2)	26.98 (15.2)
Third Plan	1252 (14.6)	94.05 (28.6)	675 (7.8)	81.77 (24.7)
Forth Plan	2932 (17.8)	135.77 (28.0)	3877 (7.4)	145.4 (30.0)

Fifth Plan	7400 (18.6)	248.3 (27.2)	1354 (8.8)	270.6 (29.6)
Sixth Plan	31060 (28.3)	601.57 (19.5)	10925 (10.0)	823.16 (26.6)
Seventh Plan	37895 (20)	1068 (17.7)	16590 (8.8)	1861 (30.68)
Eighth Plan (Proposed)	79588 (18.3)	2146 (16.5)	32525 (7.5)	3270 (25.2)

Note: Figure in Brackets Indicate Per centage In Plan outlay.

The Damoder Valley Corporation is also entrusted with the responsibility of meeting the power requirements in the Damoder Valley. The higher generation by D.V.C. has largely gone to meet the growing requirements of the Central Government undertakings in the valley, namely, B.C.C.L, C.C.L. Bokaro Steel limited, H.E.C. Railways, etc. The general consumer has been left high and dry. The State's share in Chukha Hydel project and Farakka Super Thermal Project is 32 MW and 35 MW respectively. Fortunately since other states are not drawing their assigned quota from N.T.P.C., Bihar is able to draw more than its share and meet its shortage to a great extent.

The table brings into sharp relief the decline in allocation for power in Bihar from 1979-80 onwards. This is in contrast to the steadily increasing allocation for power at the All India level. On the other hand Bihar Government has been making more allocation for irrigation than for power since the Forth Plan; allocations for irrigation in Seventh Plan were nearly 60 per cent more than power. There does not appear to be any conscious decision for giving lower priority to power. It is surprising that the Planning Commission nor the State Government have tried to correct this imbalance.

Because of lower priority and investment in power sector, serious power shortages are likely to emerge during Eighth Plan and thereafter. The allocations for power have naturally to be stepped up substantially if the situation is to be saved. There has been no increase in installed capacity since 1987. Much advance planning is required. Experience has been that power projects in Bihar have taken unduly long time to be completed. Muzaffarpur Thermal Power project was approved in 1978, but unit No. 1 was commissioned in 1984, and the second unit could be commissioned during 1986-87 only. Such time overruns involve substantial cost overruns as well. Tenughat Thermal Power Project has not been put on commercial operation even after more than 15 years. Since 1994, unit-I of the project is ready for generation, but because of lack of operational staff is lying idle. It is indeed a shame.. If sufficient Funds had been provided and the project pursued, it could have been commissioned by the end of the Seventh Plan. As matters stand the project may be operational only by the end of 1995. Meantime the estimated cost has gone up from Rs. 175.13 crore to Rs. 1,400 crore,i.e. by nearly 8 times. The total expenditure incurred over the project so far has crossed Rs. 1,000 crore.

The first super thermal power station to be set up in the eastern region by N.T.P.C. was at Farakka. Its unit was commissioned in January 1986 only. A super thermal power station (IXth by N.T.P.C.) was set up at Kahalgaon with ultimate installed capacity of 1840 MW to be constructed in two phases of 4x210 MW and 2x500 MW. The first phase of Kahalgaon would be completed by 1995, as projected. The State's share in power from Kahalgaon would be 40%. The demand for power in the state is not growing and load is not picking up because of major gaps in the transmission and distribution system. The latter needs to be strengthened urgently, if Bihar is to take advantage of the proposed expansion in generation by N.T.P.C. Bacause of lack of demand, N.T.P.C. has staggered its programme of expansion of power generation, a paradoxical situation considering the great scarcity for power in the state. The rural electrification programme is at a standstill for the last ten years. Nearly one third of the state is still to be covered under the programme; and when this will be achieved is uncertain. With power supply to agriculture being irregular, the expected increase in agricultural productivity has not occured. If agriculture was provided power as required. the load will immediately jump up by 200 to 300 MW.

The non-execution of Koel Karo H.E.P. (710 MW) has thrown the entire power planning in Bihar in disarray. As a result there is much diffidence in pressing for other Hydro-Electric projects in Chotanagpur, e.g. Sankh which can generate upto 580 MW. Koel Karo would have provided the much needed Peak-load power and restored the thermal hydro balance.

It is rather surprising that B.S.E.B. continues to press for fanciful schemes like Patna Thermal Power Station (2 units of 70

MW each) for meeting the power needs for the State capital, even after the units at Muzaffarpur have been commissioned and there is not sufficient load in North Bihar. With our previous experience of severe bottlenecks in coal supply to Barauni and Muzaffarpur Power Units, it is expected that B.S.E.B. will be wiser. Locating thermal power plants in rich agricultural area should be avoided, because of serious problems of land acquisition and atmospheric pollution. Units of small for generation are also technologically less efficient.

The Plant Load Factor of Thermal Units in the eastern region has been consistently lower than the All India average. All-India P.L.F. in 1987-88 was 56.5 per cent whereas it was 33 per cent for Bihar, 32 per cent for Orissa, 47 per cent for Uttar Pradesh, 52 per cent for West Bengal and 40 per cent for D.V.C. The N.T.P.C. units achieved P.L.F. of over 70 per cent, demonstrating that even under Indiaa conditions it is possible to attain high levels of operational efficiency.

The All India P.L.F. in 1993-94 was 61.5% the highest achieved so far; whereas in Bihar it had slumped to less than 20%, the lowest so far. Though at All India level, new land marks of efficiency were being reached, there was no end to B.S.E.B.'s mismanagement and woes. The low plant load factor has been attributed to several factors, poor management, technical inefficiency, poor maintenance and high ash content of coal. The other issues are rather controversial and opinion has been sharply divided. Coal India repudiates the charge that the coal supplied to the power stations is highly mixed with shale and contains big lumps which damage the conveyor belts and crusher of the coal handling system of the thermal plants. Attempt has been made to prescribe minimum standards of quality for coal supplies, but in view of the great demand for coal and its urgent need, quality control has been difficult to enforce. Open cast mining neccessarily involves higher admixture of shale.

There is also much pilferage of coal in transit, both by rail and road. Recent enquiry at M.T.P.S. revealed that there was short supply of coal to the extent of Rs.5.40 crores between February'94 to March'95. This was an understatement for generation by M.P.T.S. during 94-95 showed consumption of coal at 1.15kg per unit. The national average is only 0.7Kg. Even if we take it at 0.9Kg, coal of the value of over Rs.5 crores remains unaccounted. Coal pilfered from supplies for M.P.T.S meets the requirements of brick klins, way side restaurants and even Muzaffarpur town. This lot has been going on for years in collusion with B.S.E.B. staff, but administration has remained unconcerned. The wegh bridge has not been commissioned even after 10 years, clearly indicating that the theft is part of a well organised plan. This high fuel cost due to pilferage, short supply of coal, as well as inferior quality contributes to the high cost of generation, which the Government and public have ultimately to bear. Most of the supply of coal to Patratu and Bokaro and Chandrapura, (D.V.C.Units) is by road, as they are located in close proximity of coal mines. Road transport inspite of the short distances becomes extremely difficult during monsoon. Initially, when the smaller units only had been commissioned at Patratu, the roads could cope with the pressure. But now with as many as ten units in Patratu and installed capacity having gone upto 840 MW, and the volume of coal movement also having gone up several times, the roads are not good enough to cope with the pressure. It will take some time for the roads to be rebuilt according to the required specifications, meantime the power stations run under the constant threat of supplies being exhausted. There are good reasons to believe that the under such a crisis, the units have to be run at less than optimal efficiency, for fear of closing the units for lack of supply of coal. The latter is an ignominy which no manager of the plant will like to face. Failure to arrange adequate supply of coal is considered to be an unpardonable failure on part of the management.

The transmission and distribution losses in the State are very high. In fixation of tariff by the B.S.E.B. it is assumed at 20%. Technically it should not be more than 12%. Over the years the loss on these counts has increased. The Board has not shown much concern for reducing it within acceptable limits. The 7th and 8th units at Patratu belong to the first batch of 110 MW units set up by BHEL in the country. The 210 MW units give streadier performance. Though N.T.P.C. has commissioned 500 MW units (Singrauli and Korba), Bihar's first 210 MW set at Tenughat will be functional hepefully only in 1997, since 1995 we are anxiously waiting. Even for 110 MW units at Muzaffarpur there is shortage of trained staff. The technological backwardness as well as lack of training and confidence in the staff to operate the bigger sophisticated units has also affected efficiency. There has to be careful matching between installed capacity, training of staff to run new units efficiently, building up the infraststructure to arrange unhindered supply of inputs (coal, oil, spares, etc.) and strengthening of delivery system (transmission and distribution of power) to derive the maximum advantage from additional capacity.

Bihar is the only State which has created a separate Hydro-Electrical Corporation for development of hydro-power. The corporation has been sanctioned Rs.150 crores so far to execute small sized hydro-electric projects located on Sone canal, north Koel and eastern Gandak. These projects were expected to be commissioned in 1988-89 and generate 49MW. As extra budgetary support could not be found, shortage of funds became a convenient excuse for postponding completion of the projects. In view of the acute shortage, investment in hydro-electric projects would have been justifiable if the additional generating capacity could be availed of quickly. These small hydro-electric projects are as capital intensive as thermal power units, besides involving acquisition of rich cultivable land. Thus they are not as attractive as they are made out to be. The Hydro-Elctric Corporation has become a parallel organisation heavily dependent upon deputationists from B.S.E.B., which is itself short of technical staff. The corporation competes with B.S.E.B. for scarce funds for budgetary support. B.H.P.C. has been able to add only 12 MW to generation capacity. It is a white elephant and is very lax in enforicng financial discipline.

There has been growth in consumption of power by the agricultural sector in Bihar. In 1986, it consumed nearly 20 per cent of the power supply. This is likely to grow as rural electrification covers more villages. Power is provided to agriculture at 50 paise per unit, which is less than half the prevailing average rate. The benefits of subsidised rate can be had only if more power over and above the use for industrial purposes is available for consumption by agriculturists. Compartive figures for 1988-89 indicate that consumption of electricity for agriculture in Bihar was only 19.1%, in Uttar Pradesh 38.4%, in Maharashtra 20.1%, and 39.8% in Punjab.

The gaps in the transmission and distribution system of the B.S.E.B. pose serious constraints, whenever generation crosses

700 MW level which, is of course rare, the system is unable to absorb power. Naturally the extrapower is passed on to the neighbouring system, U.P.& D.V.C. The below capacity operation of the system has led to under-development of transmission and distribution lines. Benefits of higher power generation are not available to the areas lying in the interior, because of large scale theft of conductors. Not much attention is given to the guarding or maintenace of these lines either, for electricity does not pass through them most of the time. The annual theft of conductors of 33 KV, and low tension 440 volt lines is estimated to be nearly 7000 kilometres. The distribution system in the cities is inadequate to cope with the growing demand for power. The transformers are over-loaded leading to frequent break-downs. About 500 transformers need to be replaced annually. The maintenance cost because of such large scale thefts of conductors and replacement of demaged transformers comes to about Rs. 5 to 6 crores per annum. This is not fully provided for in the B.S.E.B. budget and replacement is taken up only when popular pressure builds up, by diversion from capital provisions.

The power system in Bihar, due to erratic and unstable generation of power, with the level of generation fluctuating between 600 MW to 300 MW, it gose down to 100 MW even has had a restraining effect on all sectors which are dependent on power. It has frustrated plans to industrialise and diversify the economy. Concerted efforts are therefore required to reduce power shortage and ensure greater availability of power, by improving P.L.F. and creating additional capacity.

Bihar at present is heavily dependent on outside power. Internal generation accounts for one-third of total supply. But to ensure that this supply is dependable, we have to ensure prompt payment. The revenue collections, however, reveal that only 40% of the power that is received is being billed to consumers, and out of this realisations are on the average 60% . Thus 3/4th of the total supply earns no revenue. The B.S.E.B. has to tighten its collections and prevent theft of power through establishment of electronic metres and taking strong penal action against those involved in theft of power. Otherwise it will be difficult to meet our obligations to N.T.P.C. / D.V.C. The state can not be made to bear the burden of inefficiency and corruption in B.S.E.B.

The inability to invest in power projects including essential maintenance of existing units and their renovation; and large scale pilferage/theft in sale of power that is mainly responsible for the present mess. The State Government dose not have the 'resources' to invest in power, which costs nearly Rs. 3 to 4 crores per MW of additional generation capacity at present. There is no option but to involve the private sector in future expansion programmes. Tenughat phase-II, becouse of the existing infrastructure and its ideal location, will offer no problem in attracting bidders. But the same cannot be said of Kanti phase-II lacoted in mafiabelt in North Bihar. Chandil was offered to Mr. R.P. Goenka, but he dilly-dallied with the proposal. Involvement of private parties necessarily involves guaranteeing a return of 16% on the capital invested. Government had envisaged a return of only 3% on power projects in the public sector, and even this was not insisted upon. With private sector participation cost of power to the consumers will nearly double, but this should not be a deterrent. Power is so scarce at present, and the benefit from assured and dependable supply of power so large that this does not pose any real problem. Of course 'industry' and other major consumers should face the challenge of using electricity more efficiently than at present.

9

Investing in Human Beings

"If you plan for a year, plant a seed. If for ten years, plant a tree. If for a hundred years, teach the people. When you sow a seed once, you will reap a single harvest. When you teach the people, you will reap a hundred harvests."

— Kuan-Tzu, 551-499 B.C.

"I do not call him a Brahman, merely because he is born of a womb or spring from a Brahman mother .... He whose knowledge is deep, he who is wise, he who is skilled in the right and wrong way, he who has reached the highest goal, him I call a Brahman."

— Gautam Buddha, *Dhamapadda Verses* 396, 403.

Developing Human Capability

Development is generally associated with more intensive utilisation of material resources. Though labour has been accepted as a factor of production, only recently it has been recognised that skilled and educated labour can make significant difference to production. The productive capacity of the population depends on its physical strength, skills, and its motivations. This can be developed through appropriate health, and education measures. According to Nobel Prize Laureate, Theodore W. Schultz, human capital is decisive in improving the welfare of the people. Human resources constitute the ultimate basis for wealth of nations. Capital and natural resources are passive factors of production, but human beings are active agents. They 'save' for investment, exploit natural resources and build up social, economic and political organizations to carry forward the task of national development.

Human development has lately come to be recognised as an important goal of economic development. This means that mere increase in material welfare or per capita income is not enough, unless it is accompanied by better health for enjoyment of life and better educational attainments which would result in enlargement of human choices. The physical well being, health of the population is dependent on access to safe water, sanitation and better nourishment. Knowledge through education empowers individuals and motivates him to strive for better standards of living. U.N.D.P. since 1990, has been evaluating countries on the basis of their levels of human development. The Human Development Report has ranked countries on the basis of their human development indices. Though India has been ranked 12 places higher than on the basis of per capita income, it is ranked lower than China, Mauritius, Sri Lanka, Pakistan and even Myanmar. Indias' poor ranking is on account of high incidence of illiteracy, poor standards of sanitation, malnourishment of children, inferior status of women and high incidence of poverty. Future policy should be directed towards tackling these sensitive problems for improving the quality of life.

The value of development of human resources is acknowledged by the Seventh Plan. "Human Resources are a country's most precious endowment. The success of a plan depends on the extent to which resources are developed in terms of education, skills, health and well being."[1] On education, the plan observes, "Trained and educated on sound lines, a large population can itself become an asset in accelerating economic growth and in ensuring social change in desired directions. Education develops basic skills and abilities and fosters a value system conducive to, and in support of, national development goals both long term and immediate."[2] By improving people's ability to acquire and use information, education deepens their understanding. By improving people's confidence and their ability to create and innovate, it multiplies their opportunities for personal and social achievement.

It is obvious that with pre-independence stock of human resources we would not be able to perform our present day activities. Similarly, to meet the future growth requirements, besides strengthening of infrastructure and building up of industrial capacity as well as improvement of modern agriculture practices, we need to add to our strength of qualified and skilled people to take care of the growing needs. Meeting the man power requirements or human capital formation thus resembles capital formation in material resources. But there is a fundamental difference. Investment in material resources may give yield lower than the economic return and to this extent resources may be alleged to have been misallocated. On the other hand, wrongly trained or ill-trained human beings cannot be eliminated. They tend to perpetuate themselves and they tend not only to distort but even disrupt the economy.

The standards prevalent in a society are set not by the well-to-do- and progressive sections, but by the attitudes and habits of persons who are numerically dominant i.e., by the common nass. In case of hygienic standards this is apparent. This phenomenon can be observed in other activities as well. Public property is wantonly misused and damaged by ununderstanding public. There is little concern for cleanliness. Popular response for any public venture is minimal in an ignorant society and the risk of their being misled by vested interest is also very much.

Unless there is respect for authority, concern for public assets and preservation of environment, desire for better life and involvement in programmes for development, in brief, the masses are educated and made to realise the implications of their actions, our actions would be devoid of zeal and achievement would be difficult.

Educating the People

It is important to maintain a proper balance between material capital formation and human capital. Shortage of human skills, such as engineers, technicians, doctors, managers, or even teachers can create serious bottlenecks in realizing the targetted physical growth. Further, education and training programmes for creating additional manpower must be carefully planned so that we are able to match the requirements in different sectors and there are no surpluses or shortages. Thus in respect of education policy, the emphasis we attach to primary, secondary, higher, vocational, scientific and technical or professional education has a decisive impact. We are committed to provide free universal primary education. The Constitution aimed at attainning this goal by 1960 only. Considering the high level of drop-outs it is unlikely that we will achieve this goal even by the end of the present century. The retention level in Bihar in 1990, for classes I to V was 33.6 per cent and only 21 per cent for classes VI to VIII. For All India, retention level at the primary stage was estimated at 53 per cent. It is difficult to have data of drops outs. Information regarding drop outs is not being maintained at the District or State level in Bihar. Our inability to reduce drop-outs seriously hinders our drive against illiteracy. For better monitoring of literacy drive we must have system for reporting those who receive minimum education for atleast 3 years, apart from enrolment figures. The primary schools have to be made more attractive. Mid-day meals to children considerably enhances the attraction of schools to children and also improves their performance in studies at school.

The population of literates in India recorded in last census for those aged 7 years and above was 52 per cent. This is a significant gain since 1951, when literacy was only 16.7 per cent. The figures are, however, not comparable as the minimum age for enumeration of illiterates has been raised from 5 to 7 years since 1981 census. But the population boom has thwarted our efforts, and number of illiterates during the same period has increased from 30 crores to 35 crores.

It is estimated that nearly half of the population in the age group 6-14 do not receive any education at the All-India level. Table 9.1 gives the level of literacy and education in Bihar at present. In 1990-91, there were 53,252 primary schools in Bihar with 85.65 lac students and 13, 170 middle schools with 21.21 lac students. There were 4,097 high schools with 12.97 lac students. Thus the total number of students in class I to VIII was about 107 lac which is nearly 54% of the estimated population in the age group 6-14 and 17.5% of the population above 6. The adult literacy programme claims to have made literate 50 lac persons between 1980-1990, i.e. just 5 lac per annum on average. We must strengthen our primary schools and prevent drop outs if the drive against illiteracy is to succeed. The drive against illiteracy will have to become people's programme. Government on its own cannot tackle this massive problem.

Table - 9.1 Spread of Literacy and Education in Bihar (1990)

	No. of Institutions	*No. of Teachers*	*Enrolment in (000)*	
Primary Schools	53252	117600	8565	B–5723 G–2842
Middle Schools	13170	98400	2121	B–1560 G– 561
Secondary/Higher Secondary Schools	4097	47100	1297	B–1044 G– 253
General Education colleges	557			
Professional Education	31		495	B–401
Universities	11			G–95

Drop out Rate (1987-88) in percent

		Bihar	*All India*
Class I to V	Boys	63.88	43.35
	Girls	68.93	49.42
	Total	65.63	46.97
Class I to VIII	Boys	76.77	58.80
	Girls	84.19	67.55
	Total	79.08	62.29
Class I to X	Total	85.17	75.36

Adult Literacy–Bihar

Year		*No made Literate*
1987-88	-	698250
1988-89	-	698250
1989-90	-	698250
1990-91	-	875001

Total made Literates from 1980-81 to 1990-91 - 4967562

Expenditure on Education: Bihar

Year	*Expenditure (in Rs. Crores)*	*Per Capita Expenditure (in Rs)*
1970-71	48	8.6
1980-81	236	33.8
1990-91	1228	142.3

Source-- Statistics Relating to Indian Economy 1992

To make our democracy purposeful and to have popular participation in our development programmes, universal primary education and higher literacy level is an important social objective which must be attained at the earliest. Primary education has a critical role. The number of Primary schools in the country increased from 2,10,000 in 1950-51 to 5,50,700 in 1989-90, enrolment having gone up from 19.1 million to 93.3 million during the same period. The pace of growth has slackened in recent times, because the additional intake is from the very poor and ignorant classes, who do not attach much value to education, as their children contribute to family income through their labour. The increase has been more in case of middle schools. The number of middle schools increased from 13,600 to 1,43,747, enrolment having gone up from 3.1 million to 32.2 million during the same period. In case of high schools, the expansion has been even larger. The number of high schools increased from 7,288 to 76,119: enrolment having gone up from nearly 1.5 million to nearly 20 million. Thus primary education, which provides the base for school education did not expand at the same pace as secondary or higher education. This neglect of primary education has weakened our drive against illiteracy and has also led to decline in the quality of students at higher levels of education.

Additional enrolment in class-I to VIII in Bihar during 1985-90, was only 7.18 lac which was less than 8.70 lac in Orissa and much less than W.B. 20.35 lac. Other States with low literacy performed much better Madhya Pradesh reported achievement of 25 lac and U.P. 22.15 lac. Bihar's population is more than two and half times of Orissa and 30% more than Madhya Pradesh. Bihar's situation is indeed alarming. The Eighth Plan target of 105 lac is beyond the States' capacity, and it is improbable that we would be able to make up for the back log even in the next two decades.

This phenomenal increase in the number of schools is illusory for 40 per cent of the schools do not have pucca building or even blackboaards. Over 18 per cent of the primary and middle schools in Bihar, over 16 per cent in U.P. and over 12 per cent in Orissa do not have any buildings, pucca or katcha. Thirty five per cent of the schools have only one teacher, 20 per cent of the villages still do not have any primary school and their children have to walk to the primary school, some 2 to 3 Kms. away. Seventy per cent of the primary and middle schools do not have any library facility, 54 per cent do not have play grounds and 60 per cent do not have drinking water facilities. In rural areas 89 per cent of primary schools, 70 per cent middle schools, 27 per cent secondary schools and 10 per cent of the higher secondary schools do not have urinals or latrines. Over 90 per cent of the budget outlay on primary and middle schools is over salary and administrative expenses, leaving very little for construction or repair of buildings, teaching aids, furniture, books or recreation. The share of primary and middle education in total outlay over education, has been going down. It is because of this decay of Government Schools that there has been proliferation of private schools charging high fees. Running primary schools has become one of the most lucrative business in towns and cities.

Considering the vast size of the problem, it would have been advisable to leave the responsibility for staffing and running of primary and middle schools to local bodies, the village Panchayats, voluntary organisations, etc., with State assistance being directed towards meeting non-recurring expenses, such as construction and repair of buildings, teaching aids, libraries, recreation facilities, etc. The local bodies may find it extremely difficult to maintain teachers on their present high salaries sanctioned by Government. The documents on "Education Policy", prepared by the Government of India laments the fact that expenditure by non-official agencies in education has come down to a mere 2 to 3 per cent, whereas it used to be as much as 25 per cent in pre-independence days. This is the result of our policy of bringing education fully under the State control.

The teachers are now much better paid, but the quality of teaching has deteriorated. It will be very difficult to reverse the present policy but it is abundantly clear that our present policy is inadequate to meet our present day challenges. Absenteeism among teachers has become a serious problem. They have become highly politicised and have resorted to strikes, more frequently than even trade unions, to press for better emoluments. The expectation that with better paid teachers, quality of teaching and discipline in schools would improve has been belied.

There is a vast pool of educated unemployed in rural areas.

They could be utilised on part time basis for teaching. Such an arrangement would help in identifying good teachers and absorbing the selected ones on permanent basis subsequently. Apart from the core staff, who may be required to combine administrative with teaching work, it may not be necesssary to retain such large staff on permanent basis. Decentralised and localised control of schools is necessary for better supervision. Local contributions would also reduce the financial burden on Government. Parents are much concerned about providing better education to their children. It is for this that reason there has been large proliferation of private schools even in rural areas. Local control would create greater interest in improving the teaching standards. Similarly, it may be worthwhile to recruit only lady teachers in primary schools. This would give a boost to female education and involve women more actively in public life. Such a shift in policy would be naturally resisted by vested interests. But there is no choice. Even the Seventh Plan accepted that "Part-time teachers or helper teachers on fixed salary, selected from among locally available educated men and women will be utilised to augment teaching resources and also improve relevance and cost effectiveness of elementary education"[3].

The expansion of University Education has been far more rapid than school education. The number of Arts, Science and Commerce College increased form 548 in 1950-51 to 4,755 in 1989-90. Besides, there were 278 Engineering Colleges, 117 Medical Colleges and 425 Polytechnics in the country in 1989-90. The number of Universities has increased from 28 to 190 and their intake has gone up by twenty times from just 1,74,000 in 1950-51 to nearly 4 million in 1989-90, of this 1,82,000 were engineering students and 79,000 were medicos. This is still less than 5 per cent of the population in the relevant age-group, which suggests there will be further increase in the number of students seeking admission in the Universities.

It is argued that educational standards would improve if more funds were allocated to education. The plan allocations and per capita expenditure on education is said to be low. The proposed outlay on education in Eighth Plan is 4.5% of the total outlay. The outlay on education was only 4% of the total outlay under the Seventh Plan. It declined from 6.9% in Second Plan to just 2.8% in Sixth Plan. But plan expenditure is only a small part of the total expenditure on education. Eighty five per cent of the total expenditure on education is under non-plan. The share of education in the combined revenue and capital expenditure of the Centre and States is more than defence and also exceeds total expenditure on infrastructure development sectors of power, irrigation and transport. As such better management of expenditure on education is required. Bulk of the plan expenditure on education is being used for strengthening of staff and administration. The table (Table-9.2) summaries some of the main aspects of expenditure on education, in respect of some of the major States for purposes of comparision.

The table gives the expenditure, which is being directly incurred by the State Education Departments. Substantial funds under Jawahar Rojgar Yojna and also under District Plans are being spent over construction of school buildings, with the objective of providing essential services, Bihar spends larger share of its budget on education than any other State except Kerala. Considering that per capita income in Bihar is very low, people of Bihar have to make greater sacrifice to meet this high burden. Since 80 to 90% of the expenditure is on salaries, the beneficiarieis of this munificence are the teachers. The initiative for reform in the educational system should come from the teachers themselves. The neglect of elementary education implies that we are trying to build a super-structure on a weak base. We should aim at improving the teaching standards at the lower levels and limit the number of those seeking admission in higher educational institutions. It will be very difficult to maintain standards at the University if the standaards of school education continue to stagnate. A few elite schools would not help in improving the general standards. Such elite schools take care of only a privileged few. It will be difficult to restrict entry to these schools on the basis of merit only, for past experience indicates that those with influence will manoeuvre to secure place for their wards. On the other hand, it will widen the gulf between the elite and the have-nots. Bihar Government has constructed a hostel for the Sainik School, Tilaya at the cost of Rs.2.2 crores. The intake of the school per annum is less than 200. This extravagance is certainly at the cost of schools meant for the general public, large number of which are without class rooms.

Table - 9.2. Espenditure on Education for selected states

State	Expenditure on Education Rev. and Capital accounts Combined. Rs crores (90-91)	Per capita Expenditure (In Rs.) 90-91	Percentage of literacy -91	Percentage of Expenditure on Education to total Budget. (84-85)
Bihar	1228	142.3	38.5	28.9
Orissa	539	171.1	48.5	22.1
U.P.	2141	154.3	41.7	21.3
Kerala	779	268.6	90.6	34.5
Maharastra	1749	222.2	63.0	20.6
West Bengal	1481	217.9	57.7	26.1
Punjab	566	280.6	57.1	25.0
All India	16066	190.4	52.1	23.6

Source- Bihar Statistics 1992, Centre for Monitoring India Economy

Governmnet's policy in respect of supply of education is primarily dictated by the demand for education. People's demand for education is not related to the economics of education. The State's need for education is limited to its needs for high skilled man power requirements, such as engineers, doctor, lawyers, managers, administrators, technicians, etc. If we produce more than what we can gainfully employ, it results in over-qualified persons being engaged on jobs meant for less qualified persons; or highly trained staff remaining unemployed. This is a tremendous waste of resources and has a demoralising effect on the affected persons. This discontent has a destablisilng effect on society. Besides by over crowding our higher institutions of learning we only create conditions for fall in standards. we cannot run industries or institutions at top effeciency with ill-qualified people.

Learning for the sake of leaarning can be the objective for only devoted scholars. For the vast majority, education is only a means for finding a suitable job. Thus social and political pressures for education are governed by economic motivations. Un-employment is least among the highly educated and skilled and therefore, there is greater demand for higher and technical education. Education is not only a means for economic advancement but for social advancement as well, and in a heirarchical society, there is demand for higher education, also, for improving one's status in society. In a situation where jobs are scarce, individuals seek higher education, which is more than what they really need, or are capable of, in order to improve their prospects for employment. The combined effect of all these influences is that there is a great upsurge of demand for higher education and pressure for limited jobs. It will be unpopular for a democratic government to restrict educational opportunities. Since there is not enough seats in government colleges, there is mushroom growth of private colleges. Government is not able to prevent this in face of great popular pressure. This unregulated growth has not only led to fall in standards but has also added to the size of the educated unemployed.

In view of the widening gap between the number of educated youth seeking jobs commensurate with their abilities and the capacity of the economy to absorb them, the minimum educational qualifications prescribed for entry into government service need to be revised. For skilled jobs we have to insist on vocational qualifications to encourage youngmen to join vocational institutions. There is no reason why we should employ illiterate persons against class IV jobs, such as peons. khalasis, chowkidars, etc. when large number of Matriculates go begging for jobs. Similaarly, the minimum qualifications for class III jobs in government service have to be revised to enable more qualified and competent persons to enter government service. The entry/eligibility qualifications were fixed by the British when there was less number of educated youth and there was also no problem of educated unemployed. Since government is encouraging people to go in for higher education by charging nominal fees, and opening more and more of such institutions, it is obligatory that we take care of such persons. This will be also in keeping with the government policy to provide promotional opportunities from lower ranks to higher ranks. At present entry qualifications are so low, that at times it is embarassing for government to promote persons merely on the length of their service, when they are otherwise not fit for superior charge. Similarly it is not advisable to extend the age of superannuation when younger and qualified people are waiting for employment.

Professional Education

Since admission to technical and professional institutions is by competitive selection, coaching institutions too, have sprung up in large numbers. These coaching institutions are run by University Professors and Lecturers. This is at the cost of teaching in the colleges. Classes are not taken regularly and course of study is seldom completed. This private practice by lecturing in coaching institutions by science and technical teachers in employment of Universities is a dangerous trend and threatens to ruin the entire system of regular instruction. The poor students have been forced to come out in the open and oppose this practice of coaching in Bihar by offering Dharna to draw public attention to this malaise afflicting our higher institutions. Government intervention is called for urgently to salvage the situation.

The demand for technical and medical education as well as professional education has led to the establishment of institutions which admit students on the basis of exorbitant capitation

Table - 9.3 Spread of Higher Education in Selected States

Name of Institutions	*Bihar*	*Orissa*	*U.P.*	*W.B.*	*Kerala*	*Maha-ashtra*	*Punjab*	*All India*
Art, Science & Commerce Colleges	312	139	401	264	130	514	166	4005
Engineering & Technical Colleges	6	3	3	9	6	49	3	198
Medical Colleges	10	3	7	10	5	17	5	117
Polytechnics	16	4	48	46	23	50	10	389
Enrolment								
M.A., M.Sc., M.Com	13635	6946	88421	21792	9414	32700	7377	
B.Com	201866	40025	299900	196558	102572	277000	92215	
B.Engg.	6697	2154	12653	7418	8415	18500	1728	
B.Ed.	6225	2168	15203	8645	2899	9106	3384	
M.B.B.S.	4396	1840	6728	5099	4430	10100	2346	
Polytechnics	4734	–	19399	18333	9014	16000	3934	
Indian Arts & Crafts Schools	1289	4790	27715	9930	24535	70000	16831	

Source: Selected Educational Statistics, 1984-85, Ministry of Human Resources Development, 1986.

fees. This is certainly discriminating as it deprives the meritorious students and enables wards of rich to receive professional education, which they may be otherwise ill equipped to receive. This has enabled unscrupulous politicians to make money at the cost of desparate parents. The unbounded aspirations of parents for their sons and daughters, the craving for better and more education to improve one's prospects in the job-market, has led to the present day chaotic situation in which poor guardians are forced to spend far more on education of their children than they can afford. The society is thus spending much more on education than is generally assumed, but this sizeable expenditure does not result in improvement of the system. The abuses referred to above, results in the money being siphoned off by promoters of mushroom institutions and teachers, who have no concern for academic standards and who exploit the situation for their own pecuniary gain. It is surprising that political leadership, intelligentsia and administration have been a mute a spectator to this rot.

The incidence of educated unemployment is maximum among general graduates and least amogst technically qualified persons. Table (9.3) shows the educational structure in some selected States in 1984-85 for comparison. The enrolment in polytechnics and Industrial Arts and Crafts Schools in Bihar is very samll. Uttar Pradesh and West Bengal have also high weightage of generalists, but they are giving more preference to technical and professional courses. Kerala, Maharashtra and Punjab are more pragmatic and they have given high weightage to technical schools.

Since 1985, there has been tremendous expansion in technical education in the country. In Bihar, however, there has been practically no change in the out-turn of technically qualified men and women during the period. At present, we have over 350 institutions at the degree level and 1,200 institutions at the diploma level in the country, with an annual intake of nearly 75,000 and 120,000 students, respectively. Bihar's share in the intake into degree courses is less than 2.2%, and for diploma courses 2.1%, even though the number passing the matriculation examination in the State is over 8% of the total number in the country and over 6.6% of those passing the 12th level science stream in the country. Naturally, there is a great pressure for admission into technical institutions. There are nearly 25 applicants for every seat in Bihar. Rich parents and those with black money, unmindful of the expenses, send their ward to private technical colleges in Maharashtra, Karnataka and other distant States. State Government's policy of not allowing any private engineering college, (exception has been made in the case of minority institutions) thus makes technical education for the students of the State very expensive and difficult.

The diffidence of the State Government is due to growing unemployment among engineers graduating from the State and sad experience in the past, when unscrupulous politicians made this a commercial venture, by establishing sham institutions with the intention of defrauding unsuspecting guardians. It is true that 50% of the engineering graduates from the State find employment outside the State. In case of diploma holders also 25% are absorbed outside the State. Because of poor quality of instruction, engineering graduates from Bihar are not able to compete with students from other states. As Bihar is facing stagnation; and industrialisation is concentrated in Western and Northern India, students from Bihar are compelled to seek employment outside the State. In the circumstances, it is necessary that we maintain high standards. If there is expansion, it should be through institutions that are committed to quality as well. It should be in new disciplines, in which the employment prospects are very good. There has to be close rapport with industries, so that the training is relevant to the requirements of industry. Otherwise, we will only add to the difficulties of the technical students from the State, who will continue to be unwanted.

Better Health and Family Welfare

Poverty is the major cause for malnutrition, which reduces man's resistance to disease, the morbidity in turn leads to physical and mental lethargy, which further reduces man's earning capacity. Thus ill-health is a cause of poverty and poverty contributes to ill-health. Social and economic planning, therefore, are not competitive but should be viewed as being complementary to each other. Health care by enhancing population's physical fitness directly contributes to the developmental process. Better health improves the capability of the population and thereby enables the population to enjoy life more. Life expectancy at birth

Table. 9.4. Level of Health Services Comparative Situation for some States No. per 100,000 Population in 1991.

States	*Hospitals*	*Beds*	*PHCS*	*Doctors*	*Nurses*	*Rev. Exp on Health Rs. Crore 92-93*	*% of total expend.*	*Exp. on Health per capita 92-93*	*Couple Pr tection Rate % 19*
	1	*2*	*3*	*4*	*5*	*6*	*7*	*8*	*9*
Andhra Pradesh	1.75	64.54	2.64	50	23	465	5.63	69	44.1
Assam	1.20	56.98	2.23	47	10	143	6.00	80	28.2
Bihar	0.35	32.70	3.33	31	10	457	6.89	59	26.0
Gujrat	4.34	145.76	3.24	53	59	334	5.21	80	57.8
Kerala	7.02	263.20	4.27	57	78	230	7.44	122	55.6
Madhya Pradesh	0.61	38.27	2.33	17	88	337	5.55	63	40.3
Maharashtra	2.67	144.64	3.41	63	49	616	4.67	78	56.2
Orissa	0.91	44.64	3.75	35	50	172	5.00	64	41.0
Punjab	1.14	101.8	14.35	135	116	198	5.33	105	75.8
Rajasthan	0.49	44.1	3.91	32	22	332	6.97	93	29.0
Tamilnadu	0.73	88.2	1.17	82	61	489	6.59	101	57.3
Uttar Pradesh	0.53	38.2	3.27	24	9	738	5.38	52	35.5
West Bengal	0.61	80.1	3.13	61	25	428	6.58	72	33.7
All-India	1.32	78.7	3.55	47	37	6204	2.63	85	44.1

Source– (1) Health Information of India, M.O.H. F.W. G.O.I.
(2) Combined Revenue & Dinance Accounts, Comptroller and Auditor General of India.

in India has gone up from 27.4 years in pre-independence days to 55.9% years in 1991. It is indeed a remarkable achievement. Other things remaining the same, if a man lives longer he is certainly better off. Longevity implies that investments to improve the knowledge and skills of the population are even more worthwhile.

Table 9.4 highlights some of the main features relating to health and family welfare services in the country. The table clearly indicates the poor development of infrastructure for health services in Bihar. Not surprisingly, the State constitutes the biggest market for medicines in the country after Maharashtra. Bihar's expenditure on health programmes is much below the All India average. A committee of doctors which enquired into the State of affairs in Bihar Hospitals reported that except for Patna Medical College Hospital, which was over crowded, the rate of occupancy in other Medical College Hospitals was very low, 66% in Ranchi Medical College Hospital, 25% in Darbhanga Medical College Hospital, 33% in Gaya Medical College Hospital and 50% in Nalanda Medical College Hospital. This is surprising considering the very large number of patients and the rush of patients in private nursing homes. The committee felt this was because the patients were reluctant to go to the government hospitals because of unhygeinic conditions and apathetic attitude of hospital staff.

There is need for close monitoring of expenditure on health service and the quality of services being renderd to the patients to ensure that the resources provided by the Government are properly utilised. There are complaints of X-ray machines and other expensive essential equipments, apart from infrastructure facilities created at much cost, remaining unutilized for years. Sub-standard medicines are supplied. Doctors seldom attend health centres in rural areas, thereby depriving the public the benefit of these health centres. Neglect of hospitals is largely due to private practice by doctors. Private practice can prosper only when Government hospitals become unacceptable. If Government doctors are allowed private practice, they have a vested interest in not improving the quality of service in the Government hospitals. The system makes them apathetic and callous to the needs of the ailing patients visiting the hospitals. Higher allowance for diet, medicines, equipments, etc., will help in improving matters, but if the doctors responsible for the service lack the motivation and do not take interest, the additional provisions will not have the desired effect. Ban on private practice of doctors engaged in Government hospitals is a necessary condition for improvement of medical services in Government hospitals. Lure of private practice has prevented doctors from going to rural areas, as the cities where the patients come for treatment offer far better prospects for private practice. Imposition of ban on private practice by doctors employed in Government hospitals would induce larger number of doctors to set up clinic in rural areas. The ban imposed by Bihar Government on private practice is an eye-wash. The Government has shown no will to enforce it. Doctors have made it only an excuse for charging higher fees for their services. The poor patients suffer more than before.

Considering the high incidence of poverty and low per capita income of the population, our aim should be to make the health services cheap and within the reach of the common man. They have to be also close to the users. Specialised hospitals for treatment of certain diseases are not only expensive but also take a long time to set up. Such specialised services are generally availed by well to do people and are beyond the reach of the common man.

Health Centres widely dispersed over rural areas, offering quick treatment, would be of greater service to the rural people. The requirement by Government that fresh medical graduates should spend atleast a few years in rural areas offers no solution since their number is small. The only practical solution is to create a cadre of rural medical practitioners, on the basis of condensed medical course suited to the requirements, similar to the bare foot doctors in China.

Brian Abel Smith rightly points out "The most important health message relates to the basic aspects of life, an adequate diet, safe water supplies, safe disposal of excreta, personal hygiene, and the control of vectors and rodents"[4]. In all these areas the community can do much for itself. It is true that the community cannot easily change their beliefs, customs or habits. This can be achieved only through educating the public. More than money, this requires right type of leadership and political commitment. The common man because of bother and expenses involved generally resigns himself to fate and accepts disease stoically. Prevention and control of disease is more important in our poverty ridden society. Because of unhygenic living habits in Bihar, Kalazar and Malaria have emerged as major threats.

Bihar is rather fortunate as far as availability of drinking water is concerned. By the end of Seventh Plan, all the villages nearly 67,500 in all, had been provided atleast one source of safe drinking water. Against the All India norm of providing atleast one source of water for 250 persons, the average in the State works out to 60 only. Nearly 75% of the urban population is served with piped water supply. However, not much attention has been given to the safety of water for health. Jaundice, a water-borne disease, is widely rampant even in the State capital.

The position in respect of sanitation, however, is very shocking. Only 25% of the urban population in India is covered by sewerage facilities. Though there is an ambitious programme to extend the coverage of low cost sanitation facilities, sewage facilities remain confined to only select urban areas. In rural areas, less than 4% of the rural population is covered by sanitation facilities. Waste water is discharged into village lanes. It will be worthwhile constructing village drains from funds provided under J.R.Y.

Pregnant women and children are the most vulnerable group and their health is of much consequence to the well being of the society. Mother's good health strongly influences the early physical and mental development of her babies. "There are some developing countries where only a third of the children conceived are born and live to the age of 5. Apart from the tragedy of this loss to the parents, a child that does not survice to adulthood draws on family and national resources without making more than a negligible contribution to the country's or the family's economy. It is wasteful reproduction. The loss of working time of the mother in caring for the child is a loss with no economic or social gain. If the survival rates of foetus and child were raised to those of more developed countries, the same future adult population could be raised with much lower use of resources, leaving women with the time and energy to make a wider contribution to the economic and social well being of their families"[5]. Expenditure on the health of mothers and children contributes to higher labour productivity by preventing wasteful physical, mental and social potential of stunted growth.

Infant mortality can be fairly reliable index for determining the extent of poverty and hunger in a community. Data on infant mortality are, however, not reliable because of the wide gaps in information. The infant mortality rate for India has been provisionally estimated at 73 per 1000 in 1994, by Sample Registration System. Kerala has the lowest IMOR of 16. Orissa has the highest IMOR of 103, U.P. 88 and West Bengal 61. Bihar surprisingly has the lowest IMOR in the region, only 66. IMOR is more among faemles, due to neglect of female infants. As expected IMOR in case of children of literate mothers is nearly 30% less compared to illiterate mothers, and twice as much in rural areas compared to urban areas. The latter is obvious due to inadequate availability of health facilities in rural areas. Life expectancy, too, in Bihar at 57.5 years is almost the same as the national average, 58.7 years; and is more than U.P. (55.4), Madhya Pradesh (53.4), Assam (54.1) and Rajasthan (56.3). This would indicate that Bihar's population has shown more resilience in poverty than their neighbourers. The high population growth rate in Bihar 2.1%, high gross reproduction rate 2.72 (compared to 2.20 for All-India), low female literacy 23.1% and low couple protection rate 26% (44.2% for the rest of the country) constitute a vicious circle and the indications are that the population would continue to increase, threatening to drag us further into poverty, unless conscious efforts are made to control the size of the family and population growth.

Evaluation by the Author

Author conducted an evaluation study, with financial support from UNICEF in 1994-95, to ascertain the current status of maternity and child health programmes in rural areas of Bihar. Fifteen districts, Bhagalpur, Garhwa, Supaul, W. Champaran, Gopalganj, Deoghar, W. Singhbhum, Palamau, Ranchi, Saharsa, Muzaffarpur, Patna, Gaya Rohtas and Samastipur were covered by the survey. 15 villages in each district were selected on a random basis. In all 225 villages, 10,028 families, 66,766 family members, including 13,013 children below 5 years and 5,066 children in the age group 12-23 months, 11,065 boys and girls in the age group, 5-11 years and 2,209 pregnant members were covered by the survey.

The findings were quite revealing. One-third of the villages have access to medicine shops in close vicinity. Eighty one per cent of the villagers were consuming iodised salt. There were 9,004 sources of drinking water for 10,028 families; but nearly 30% of the hand tube wells, which was source for 70% of the families, were non-functional. In contrast only 8% of the families were having latrine facilities.

Forty five per cent of the children below 5 years had mean arm circumference less than 12.5 cms., i.e. they were either malnourished or undernourished. Only one third of 20% of the children, who were afflicted by diarrhoea, within 2 months of investigation, were given oral re-hydration therapy; 47% were not immunised. Only 2/3rd of the boys and half of the girls in the age-group, 5-7 years, were enrolled in school, but out of this 25% of the boys and 50% of the girls dropped out.

Though women had sufficient knowledge of family planning and also apreciated its need, the impact of family planning programme was minimal. Of the 2,207 pregnant women, over 90% had not used any family planning aids; only 17 had taken oral pills and 18 couples had used condoms. The investigators came across merely 5 cases of I.U.D., 33 cases of tubectomies and just one case of vasectomy. Nearly 75% of the married women became mothers while they were still in their teens and physically not fully developed to bear healthy children. Only 11% of the deliveries were by trained nurses or doctors.

The findings are indeed very disconcerting and raise grave doubts over the state's commitment to achieve universal literacy, fulfill the minimum health requirements of women and children or control population growth. The main reason for this dismal situation is neglect of these programmes by the State Government. During Eighth Plan period, central grants meant for these programmes were only partially utilised. Even the meagre state funds were available with much difficulty.

REFERENCES

1. *Seventh Five Year Plan*, Planning Commission, Paras 11.1 and 10.1
2. Ibid.
3. Ibid., Para 10-34
4. Brian Abel Smith, *Poverty, Development & Health Policy*, W.H.O. 1978, pp. 101.33.
5. Brian Abel Smith, *Poverty, Development & Health Policy*, W.H.O. 1978, pp. 103.33.
6. Based on Moonis Raza's, *Atlas of the Child in India*, Paras 4.19, and 4.22.
7. T.W. Schultz, *Investing in People*, 1981.
8. *National Housing Policy*, Ministry of Urban Development, Government of India, May, 1988.
9. World Development Reports, 1980, 1981, World Bank.
10. Human Development Report, 1993, U.N.D.P.
11. National Family Health Survey, Bihar, 1993.
12. *The Girl Child*, Bihar, UNICEF.
13. *Nutrition Trends in India*, 1993, National Institute of Nutrition, Hyderabad.
14. Abhimanyu Singh, Care for Women and Children in Bihar: Some Issues, *Yojana*, Nov. 1996.

10

Mobilising Resources for Development

In industrialised and modern economy, the capital stock and the flow of investment determines the level of development. Unexploited natural resources and idle man power are of no benefit to the society. The capital stock has to be built up by generating larger savings and utilised for productive investment activities. In a poor and undeveloped economy savings are low and therefore investments are low. This can be made up by borrowing and external aid. Since Bihar is part of federal India, it can negotiate for foreign aid only through the Central Government. Bangladesh, which has about the same per capita income as Bihar, has the benefit of substantial foreign aid, mostly on humanitarian consideration. It gets as much as ten times per capita foreign aid than India, and this has enabled it to prop up its economy. Nepal also gets as much per capita foreign aid. Bihar's share in external aid to India is much less in proportion to its population.

Thus, Bihar can step-up its investment activities only by mobilising resources internally or by obtaining larger share in Central investment or assistance. Bihar's reluctance and inability to tighten its revenue collection machinery and raise additional resources internally has led to serious resource crunch in recent years. Bihar was not able to spend even 50% of its plan outlay, approved by the Planning Commission for the Seventh Plan. In

Eighth Plan also the performance was no betters. This has been so, when Bihar has the lowest per capita plan outlay. The situation is indeed alarming. Resources have to be found to salvage the situation.

Mobilisation of Resources & Better Utilisation of Assets

Our effort to raise additional resource has to come through broadening of tax base so that larger number contribute to State revenue; through lower tax rates for greater incentive to produce; and through efficient tax administration for preventing tax evasion and by reducing cost of collection and making the system simpler for the tax payer. Mobilisation of resources for development should not be looked upon only as an exercise for raising adequate financial resources, but also include efforts to raise productivity, and achieve economy in expenditure. If capital is crucial for development every care must be taken to ensure its most effective and productive utilisation. Our over-all strategy should be to ensure optimum utilisation of assets that are created, thus available irrigation potential should be fully utilised, higher plant load factor in case of generation for power and better utilisation of available capacity in industry, are necessary for higher productivity. The installed capacity of Thermal Power in the country is about 80,000 MW. One per cent increase in P.L.F., which is curently a little above 50% is equivalent to an additional capacity of 1600 M.W. or invastment of nearly Rs.5000 crore at prevailisng cost. Renovation, modernisation and maintenance of the units for attaining higher plant load factor will cost much less and also take less time. In Bihar, P.L.F. since 1990-91 has fallen below 25%. Improvement in P.L.F. will have much greater impact. The same applies to better utilisation of irrigation potential and better utilisation of the fleet available with State Road Transport Corporations. With more passengers and larger mileage coverage by vehicles, the transport service will give greater satisfaction to the public and also generate larger surplus for future investments.

Tax Receipts

The immediate concern of all governments is to find enough money to fulfil the plan and non-plan obligations. Revenue collected by the Central Govenment comes mainly through Customs and Union Excise Duties, which together accounted for 71.4% of the gross revenue receipts of the Center (Rs. 88, 770 crores in 1994-95). The taxes on property and capital, Corporation Tax and Income Tax, are comparatively unimportant sources of revenue. They accounted for 28.4% of the tax receipts. Nearly 25% of the tax revenue collected by the Centre is transferred to the States and this constitutes nearly 30% of the total receipts of the States. Share of Central taxes in the total receipts of Bihar Government during the Seventh Plan period was as high as 45%.

As far as the States are concerned the major sources of revenue are the Sales-Tax, which contributed nearly 40% of the total tax receipts in 1990-91, State Excise Duties, Stamps and Registration Fees, Taxes on Vehicles, Taxes on commodities and services contribute over 60% of total revenue.

There are regional variations, but sales tax is the most important source of revenue for all the States. In Bihar out of the tax revenue of Rs. 906 crore in 89-90, sales-tax contributs Rs. 649 crores (70% of the tax receipts), State Excise Duties Rs. 86 crores, Stamps & Registration fees Rs. 64 crores and taxes on Motor Vehicles Rs.51 crores. Royalty and cess on minerals has emarged as very important source of non-tax revenue to the State of Bihar. The Central Government raised the royalty rates in 1991, but put a ceiling on the rate of cass as directed by the Supreme Court. At present the revenue from mines and minerals is the largest source of revenue after sales-tax for the State.

Tax Burden

The question which is generally asked is whether tax receipts are in keeping with the tax potential. Taxable capacity is a vague concept. It depends not only on Gross Domestic Product (G.D.P.) but also on level of per capita income, share of commerce and industry in G.D.P., and the degree of urbanisation. Moreover, we cannot concentrate on tax potential without bothering about the effects of taxation on the incentives for production. A tax system must be fair and equitable. The rich must bear the major burden of taxation. Since majority of the poor are below the poverty line further taxation on commodities and services will add to their misery. The existing practice is to assess tax burden on the basis of indicators such as per capita tax recipts, percentage of tax receipts to G.D.P. etc. In a poor economy per capita income would be low and a fair assessment of the tax burden can be had by correlating per capita tax receipts with per capita income. The incidence of tax on income and property is on the rich, whereas the incidence of taxes on commodities and services is on both rich and poor alike. This is also supported by the fact that the number of assessees having income above Rs. 1 lakh constitute only 0.2% of the total number and provided nearly 6.5% of the tax receipts in 1987-88. Their share in Income-Tax receipts has been gradually going down over the years; surprisingly the effective rate of income-tax on salary earners and professionals is more then landlords, investors and manufaturers. The declining importance of receipts from taxes on income and property would suggest that our tax structure is becoming regressive. It is not practicable to isolate articles which are consumed by the rich and tax them at higher rates. Many articles which are considered to be items of luxury like Televisions and Refrigerators are becoming articles of necessity and are being brought in increasing number by lower midle class families also.

The share of direct taxes in the total tax revenue of Union, State, Union and Local Bodies has been going down rapidly. It contributed 29.7% of total tax revenue in 1960-61, declined to 21.2% in 1970-71 and slipped further to 16.5% in 1980-81. In 1989-90 it was only 14.4%. Since then the trend has been reversed and it was 28.4% in 1994-95. With bulk of income and property concentrated in the hands of a small privileged class, the declining receipts from direct taxes indicated that this class was not contributing in accordance with their capacity.

Since an individual has to pay taxes to the Centre, State and Local bodies as well, the burden of taxes is the sum total of taxes paid by him to all the three.

The per capita tax receipts for the contry as a whole is 22.4% of the per capita income. Subsides amounted to Rs. 10,862 crores in 1989-90. Nearly 43% of this was on production and distribution of fertilizers and benefited the surplus producer of foodgrains. An equal amount was spent on food and export promotion. The effective tax burden after allowing for repayments by way of subsidies would therefore be about 19.3% of per capita income. This is, however, only a notional figure and does not give the real picture of the distribution of the tax burden among different classes. But the dominant share of taxes on commodities and services does imply the major burden of taxation is on the common man.

Bulk of the tax payments are to the Centre. For the country as a whole the amount of taxes collected by the Centre and the States is in the ratio of 2:1. With centre getting the lion share of taxes, the States' ability to squeeze in more revenue through taxes is severely limited. Thus additional resource mobilisation by the Centre was Rs. 3324 crore in 1990-91 and Rs. 2,589 crore in 1991-92, the aggregate for the all the States was only Rs. 437 crores and Rs. 213 crores respectively. There has been no worth-while additional taxation in Bihar's Budget, since 1985-86.

Total tax revenue for the country as percentage of G.D.P. has risen from 8.9% in 1960-61 to 12% in 1970-71, 14.6% in 1980-81 and was 17.6% in 1989-90. With savings being about 22% of the G.D.P. one wonders whether there is much potentail to raise additional revenue through taxes. Since over 80% of the savings is provided by the household sector, it is apparent that higher receipts from taxes would be possible only at the cost of savings. Since 1976-77, gross domestic savings as percentage of G.D.P. has been more than 22%, it attained the peak in 1978-79 (24.5%) but came down to 22% in 1983-84 and has lately fallen below that level. The table (10.1) below gives the gross rate of savings as percentage of G.D.P. and total tax revenue as percentage of G.D.P. since 1980-81.

It is significant that the sum of two columns "savings" and "taxes" has hovered around 35 to 38% and not crossed 40%. This may be upper limit in the Indian situation with a free market economy. Taxes on income and property directly affects savings. Taxes on commodities and services are tax on consumption. For those living at the margin of subsistance or whose incomes are insufficient, the pressing need of consumption is too strong to dissuade them from postponing expenditure on necessities. Our only hope lies on accelerated growth which would generate more

Table-10.1

Year	*Tax as % of G.D.P.*	*Gross Domestic Savings as % of G.D.P.*	*Total% (1+2)*
1980-81	14.6	21.2	35.8
1981-82	15.1	21.0	36.1
1982-83	15.3	19.1	34.4
1983-84	15.2	18.8	34.0
1984-85	15.5	18.2	33.7
1985-86	16.5	18.9	35.4
1986-87	17.0	19.5	36.5
1987-88	17.1	21.5	38.6
1988-89	17.0	21.9	38.9

income as well as tax revenue. The dilemma being that without more resources we cannot accelerate the growth rate. It is for this reason that while talking about mobilisation of resources we also emphasise better utilisation of assets that are created i.e. obtaining better return per unit of capital. High taxes on narrow base are bad as they encourage avoidance of tax and lead to distortion of tax effort. There is psychological barrier to greater effort, saving and profitable investment when the marginal rates have been more than 50%. Lately this has been reduced to 50% of the additional income above Rs. 1 lakh to provide incentive to high income earners. But a uniform rate of tax of 50% on income above Rs.1 lakh does not appear logical. There is a case for reduction of rates for lower income levels say incomes upto Rs.5 lakh, and raising the rates for income levels above this. From the point of view of growth, we should encourage energetic men with intelligence and initiative to make money, for the country also benefits in the process. Such persons should not be objects of envy.

Tax Effort

In the table (10.2) we have pressented some of the important indicators to have an assessment of the tax effort being made.

Table-10.2

	Centre & State Combined		*Bihar*	
	1983-84	1989-90	1983-84	1989-90
Net national product at current prices Rs. crores.	1,66,550	3,46,994	9,178	17,824
Per capita income	2,180	4,252	1,248	2,122
Total tax receipts Rs. crores	31,525	77,693	442	906
Share in Central taxes.	5,245	13,232	–	1,383
Per capita tax receipts (fig.in bracket indicates % of per capita income).	422 (19.4)	952 (22.4)*	60 (4.8)	108 (5.1)**
Taxes on property & income as % of total tax receipts.	15.6	14.4	12.6	5.6

N.B: ** with State's share in central taxes this becomes 12.82.
* share of states in central taxes is 7.5% of N.N.P.

Combined tax receipts of Centre and States was 22.4% of net national product in 1989-90. Of this 14.9% was realised by the Centre and 7.5% by the States. With State's share in Central taxes, the total revenue receipt of the States swelled to 11.3% of N.N.P. Bihar's own tax effort in comparison yielded a modest 5.08% (compared to 7.5% for all States) of its net domestic product. With State's share in Central taxes it increased to 12.8%, which is higher than the average for all States (11.3%) Bihar's share in Central taxes transferred to the States was 10.5%, almost the same as its share in total population. The State recovered Rs. 523 crores in 1989-90 as non-tax revenue, of which Rs. 452 crores came as royalty and cess on minerals. The distortion in the tax structure of the State is obvious from the fact that only 5.6% of the total receipts is from taxes on income and property. The entire amount comes from land tax and registration and stamp duty. The latter is a distress transaction and is truly speaking not a tax on income or ownership of property. The per capita tax receipts in the States of Bihar is among the lowest in the country. Bihar has the lowest per capita income among the major States and is also the least urbanised and industrially backward. Table 10.3 gives per capita State's own tax revnue for the Eastern States, average of 1987-90 for comparison.

The higher receipt in West Bengal is due to greater industrialisation and commercialisation of the State. The lower receipts in case of Bihar is to be attributed to either lower tax effort or greater leakage in revenue.

Table-10.3

State	*Per Capital State's own tax revenue in rupees (Average of 1987-90)*
Bihar	99
Orissa	149
Uttar Pradesh	164
West Bengal	265

Source - Tenth Finance Commission.

The additional reaource mobilisation during 1985-90 was Rs. 316 crores for West Bengal Rs. 48 crores for Orissa and Rs. 32 crores for Uttar Pradesh. There was no additional resource mobilisation in the State of Bihar. In the case of Orissa and Uttar Pradesh also this was an one time effort in 1985-86.

In case of non-tax revenue, major contribution comes from royalty and cess on minerals. In case of Bihar revenue from cess on minerals was 15 times more than royalty in 1988-89. The Centre was reluctant to raise the royalty rates but the State Government progressively raised the cess in search for more revenue. The value of minerals production in Bihar in 1986-87 was Rs. 1,563 crores. The amount realised as royalty and cess by the State was nearly 25% of this value. This is a high figure considering that total tax and non-tax receipts of the State Governments is less than 10% of the S.D.P. Whereas revenue from mines and minerals was only Rs.42.06 crore in 1980-81, it increased to Rs.663.61 crore in 1988-89 and was more than that from Sales-Tax. Efforts to raise additional resources have been concentrated in the recent past on cess on minerals. When the royalty rates were ultimately revised by the Centre in 1991 and the cess had to be withdrawn as a result of supreme Court's judgement, the State was faced with reduced receipts of nearly 25%. It is doubtful if Bihar and the other States in the Eastern Region can exploit this source as easily any more. It is natural, therefore, for the coal based States to demand that royalty should be related to value of coal.

Black Money and Evasion of Taxes

The growth of black many both from illegal sources and by evasion of tax, has progressively increased during recent times. High rates of taxes provide the inducement for concealment of taxable income. Natioal Institute of Public Finance Policy in a study conducted in 1985, has estimated that black income generation in the country which was Rs.20,500 crores or about 18% of the G.D.P. in 1980-81, increased to Rs.31,700 crores or over 21% of the G.D.P. in 1983-84. The Direct Taxes Enquiry Committee (Wanchoo Committee) had estimated the income on which tax was evaded at Rs.1,400 crore or 5% of the G.D.P. in 1968-69. Inflation and exchange controls have further accelerated black money generation. The beneficiaries are generally from the high income groups. By allowing black income to proliferate and remain outside the tax net, we not only lose valuable resources but also allow such people to become financially powerful and exercise their pernicious influence over the economy and political life as well. Efforts to induce people to declare their black income by exempting then from punitive action has proved to be abortive. It is needless to State that black money on such a large scale threatens to undermine our commitment to establish an egalitarian and socialistic society.

Taxes on commodities and services have also attained very high rates and pushing them further may prove to be futile. With high rates, the temptation for evasion increases and large scale leakage of revenue taxes place in connivance with the tax enforcing authorities. The extent of evasion of taxes in Bihar is highlighted in a study of "Sales Tax System in Bihar" by a team of N.I.P.F.P., which was headed by Dr. R.J. Chelliah. The study observes,"while no reliable estimate of the magnitude of avoidance and evasion of the sales tax are available, the impression one gathered is that these are practised on a large scale. This is corroborated by the results of the commodity flow surveys for potatoes and automobile parts conducted by the study team. The surveys have revealed that in case of automobile parts, tax evasion is up to the extent of 50% of potential revenue."[2] The study further observes,"The proper administration of the Sales-tax requires a well trained and well equipped staff and a sound information system. Owing to the weakness on the staff front and an almost total lack of information system, the realisation of the sales tax in the State is below the optimum and tax delinquency is of a substantial magnitude. This is evident from the fact that the Department gets as much as 98% of the sales-tax revenue from admitted tax and only a very small fraction form the enhanced demand arising from assessments done by the Dapartment."[3] It is reported that thousands of assessment cases are pending for more than 5 years for final orders. Whereas the average receipts from sales tax during 1990-91 to 1992-93 was Rs.555 crores in Bihar; it was Rs.1378 crores in Andhra Pradesh, Rs.709 crores in Madhya Pradesh, Rs.743 crores in Rajasthan. Realisations from sales tax was Rs.1675 crores in U.P.,Rs.1034 crores in West Bengal and Rs.353 crores in Orissa. The lower realisations in Bihar are to be explained by poor tax administration and leakages.

All shops whose sales exceed Rs.1 lakh per annum are supposed to be registered with the Commercial Taxes Deptt. Still the number of registered establishments is only 60,000, which is unbelievably low. The petty shop-keepers operate in perpetual fear of the department officials, who exploit them. If the limit is raised to Rs.5 lakh per annum, shopkeepers would not have any inducement in concealing transactions upto this limit and evading taxes. Even under the existing arrangement 7% of the registared units provide 90% of the tax receipts. The contribution of petty shopkeepers is negligible.

Revenue from State Excise Duties in Bihar was more or less static between 1974-75 to 1982-83. There has been some increase since then. In terms of constant prices the receipts have actually gone down. Excise duties have been raised at regular intervals to squeeze in more revenue. Though higher excise duties have failed to net the desived revenue, they made illicit trading in liquor more lucrative. It is difficult to believe that consumption of liquor is falling. Excise duty on country spirit is more than 5 times the duty on spirit. The big margin has encouraged clandestine sale of spirit through active collusion of excise staff. The saving of duty on truck load of country spirit is about Rs. 3 lakh and on a truck load of I.M.F.L. is about Rs. 4 lakhs. Next to smuggling of hashish and narcotics, clandestine dealing in liquor is the most profitable illegal business. There is evidence to believe that there is flourishing trade in illicit liquour in Bihar. The illegal income to people engaged in such trade is said to be as much as the total excise revenue to the State Govenment. Lately some corrective measures have been taken. Country liquor is now being sold in sachets. There have been recurring incidents of large number of deaths due to consumption of poisonous liquor and even when the offenders have been tracked, they have escaped punishment. The overwhelming influence of liquor kings has prevented strong deterrent action and illicit trading of liquor has continued to thrive. It is not surprising, therefore, that excise revenue has only marginally increased in Bihar through it has increased substantially in the neighbouring States.

The rate of stamp duties and registration fees are also very high and there is large scale evasion through under statement of value of property. Even if the rates are reduced the receipt will not be very much affected as many may be induced to pay the actual amount and avoid the discomfiture and problems arising out of under-valuation of property. Recently the Bihar Government has introduced the system of fixing floor prices for different types of land. This implies that land is properly classified and the floor prices are fixed at regular intervals, so that they reflect the market price correctly. Extra alertness would be required on the part of government staff. The initial experience has been that where prices have been fixed arbitrarily, the buyers have postponed their purchases, placing the seller in predicament. At present the High court has stayed the operation of the system.

The experience in respect of realisation of motor vehicles taxes has been no better. In view of the ever growing number of vehicles, the receipts from motor vehicles taxes are gaining in importance. There is extensive leakage due to partial realisation of road tax dues and plying of vehicles without permits. The transport offices are most affected by corrupt practices and there is genuine suspicion that there is sizeable defalcation of revenue. In Bihar the transport department has no separate cadre for its officers. The deputationists, who are too small in number to cope with the job, only look for their personal gains during their stay. Collections are only about half of the realisable revenue.

From the foregoing discussion of receipts from States' taxes, it is clear that efficiency of tax administration must improve and there should be strict vigilance over revenue collecting departments. This would require reversal of role of the political executives. Corrupt officers bargain with Ministers for lucrative postings in the revenue earning departments. Postings are sold to the highest bidders. The price for postings varies according to the amount of graft they can yield. The officers who hold such posts after paying the "salami" indulge in plunder at the cost of public exchequer and add to the misery of the tax payers. The "salami" is appropriated generally on the excuse of raising funds for political purposes.

Transfer of Resources from the Centre to the States

Transfer of resources from the Centre to the States has become the most important part of State's over all resources, and the States have come to depend heavily on the Centre not only for execution of their plan schemes but for meeting their non-plan liabilities as well. Thus in the Sixth Five Year Plan, the States got central assistance of Rs. 17,567 crores (35% of the States' plan outlay) for executing total plan outlay of Rs. 50,132 crores. During the same period (1979-84) the States received Rs. 20,843 crore (41.5%) by way of transfer of resources from the Centre on the basis of recommendation of the Seventh Finance Commision. During Seventh Plan 1985-90, States were to receive Rs. 29,737 crore as Central assistance and Rs. 39,452 crores as transferred fund on the basis of recommendations of the Eighth Finance Commission (1984-85). During 1985-90, the States received Rs. 123,532 crores as share of Central Taxes, loans and grant from the Centre and Rs. 36,554 crores as Central Assistance for the plan. The share of Central assistance in financing the States' plans (Rs.80,700 crores) was thus 48% and the Centre transferred nearly 1/3rd of its total revenue and capital receipts to the States. The extent of dependence on the Centre can be judged from the fact that the share of resources transferred by the Centre to the State of Bihar increased from 34% of the total receipts in 1965-

66 to 55% in 1985-86. During 1985-90 the resources transferred from the centre to the State constituted 45% of the total.

In case of externally aided schemes, only 70% of the equivalent of external assistance in Rupees was shared with the States. From 93-94 on persistent demand by the States it has been increased to cent per cent. In view of the fact that the extrnally aided schemes, have generous component of staff and equipment and expeneses over the project have to be shared by the States, and since they are subject to stringent accounting rules by the donor agencies, the schemes put much strain on the State revenue. Because of their better resources position, the well to do states are able to attract the externally aided projects. However, to correct regional imbalance, we should encourage lacotion of such projects in backward regions. Apart from the entire external aid being (reimbursed) to the state, the Centre should also help the backward States by providing additional assitance to meet the resource constraints. Else the externally aided schemes should be in the Central Sector. This would help in expeditious preparation and clearance of project reports as well as in their proper location and management.

As we have stated earlier this over-dependence on the Centre for finance is not conducive to the autonomy of the States and does not allow for much flexibility in expenditure. The States also have no urge or incentive to make efforts to raise the additional resources. They have the feeling that the Centre would come to their rescue if there is any resource gap.

It is natural for the States to ask for higher share in central receipts and larger amounts of grants in view of their growing deficits. The Centre is in no better position. Its commitments on revenue account are also larger than its revenue receipts. Any suggestion as to what should be the State's share therefore depends on the priority we attach to the state schemes and our judgement of the ability of the State machinery to execute these schemes satisfactorily

Relief Expenditure

In respect of relief expenditure, the Eighth Finance Commission had recommended that the States will be entitled to draw on the

Centre's contribution after it has exhausted its own share of margin money. This meant that as long as relief expenditure did not exceed the State's share of margin money, Central assistance was not available. There was tendency on the part of State Government to exaggerate reports of expenditure over relief. Moreover the procedure required assessment of the needs and approval of expenditure by a Central Team for release of the Central share. This was time consuming and the Centre's contribution remained uncertain. This situation was rectified by the Nineth Finance Commission with the creation of Central Relief Fund in all the States. The size of C.R.F. was determined by calculating the average amount spent on calamity relief during the last ten years. Thus the size of C.R.F. came to be indirectly linked with the resource capacity of the States. The Tenth Finance recommended for continuation of this practice during 1995-2000. Centre's contribution will be 75%. States' contribution will be 25% Not surprisingly the poor and backward States have pleaded for being exempted from making any contrbutions to the fund. The size of C.R.F. for 1995-2000 for Bihar as recommended by Tenth Finance Commission is only Rs.273.5 crores. Bihar suffers from savere floods frequently. The size of C.R.F. for Gujrat is Rs.735 crores and is more than that of Uttar Pradesh Rs.659 crores. It is open for the States to approach the Centre in case of calamity of rare severity. This places the poorer States at the mercy of the Centre. To get over this problem, National Relief Fund at the Centre has been proposed. This will be operated jointly by the Centre and States, with Centre contributing 75% of the funds. How this will work in practice, and resolve conflicting claims of States, only experience will indicate.

Some Measures to Improve Finances of State Undertakings

The public sector undertakings, barring a few, are making losses and are heavily dependent on budgetary support.The State Undertakings in Bihar are heavily over-staffed and have poor financial discipline. Their accounts are never complete or upto date and fail to check the corrupt practices and wasteful expenditure. Because of pressure from employees' Union as well as interference, the work culture has been badly affected. Most of the undertakings have been reduced to such straits, that they have no work or task to perform, but they are required to meet the ever growing demands of their employees for better remuneration. How to close these non-performing units is going to be our major concern in future. The assets can be transferred but none would accept the employees. It will take long time for all the employees to retire, and there are not enough jobs in government which can absorb them. Golden hand shake affords a solution, but from where is this money going to come. A National Renewal Fund has been created for the purpose in the last budget, but it has not become operative so far. Transfer of assets can release substantial funds, but initial experience has been that such transfer has been much below rated value and involved loss to the government.

We have separately dealt with the subject of organising public enterprises more efficiently. In several cases, the State Undertakings are providing services at less than cost price. Even the accepted principles of costing are not followed. There is generally a long time gap between the rise to cost of inputs and revision of prices of services and goods to cover the cost of this rise. The private sector uses price rise in its advantage, but it is rarely so in the case of State Undertakings. Why should the State Housing Board allot sites on the basis of prices fixed decades ago. The Housing Board has to pay interest on capital. The Housing Board confers this largesse to its allottees free of capital gains tax. The allottees are not surprisingly mostly Ministers, Legislators or those enjoying their patronage.

The high auxiliary consumption of power by generating stations and transmission losses, the two add up to nearly 1/3rd of the power generated, makes rational pricing of power difficult. The inability to check pilferage and the tendency to recover this loss from genuine consumers has resulted in undue increase in per unit price of power. This in turn is bound to have detrimental effect on the otherwise viable development activities. The practice of "averaging" of electricity dues is depriving the State Electricity Board of substantial revenue. The meters installed by S.E.Bs are either of poor quality or are tampered. They remain unattended for long time and during this period bill is submitted on the basis of average consumption during the preceding months. If the load increases, theS.E.B. loses. Otherwise, also, the staff for illegal gratification gives a lower figure as average. This is a pernicious practice which has to be stopped. It cannot be accepted that S.E.Bs are unable to provide and maintain meters in fit condition.

Power is provided at subsidised rates to agriculture, still there is substantial theft in rural areas, in collusion with staff, which is concealed by S.E.Bs by showing them as transmission losses. Such pilferage of power has to be prevented, not only because there is dearth of funds but also in the intersrest of better work discipline. The losses incurred in Rural Electrification have to be met by the Government. When the power generation in some States is so bad that even essential urban and industrial requirements cannot be met, extension of transmission and distribution lines at exorbitant cost to rural areas serves no real purpose. If this is done in fulfilment of the national objective to attain cent per cent rural elecification by the end of the century, then this scheme should be a Central Sector scheme, with the S.E.Bs being fully compensated for the cost incurred over the programme by the Central Government.

Bihar State Road Transport Corporations passenger load factor at 56% and low route coverage per vehicle (176 KMs. per day) is the result of wrong policy, mis-management and corruption. It is surprising that passenger load should be only 56% when it is a common sight to find people travelling on bus stops. The various indices for judging the performance of Road Transport corporations are confusing. A reliable index would be passenger KM per vehicle per annum expressed as a ratio of the desired level of operation. If private bus oprators are allowed to run on the nationalised routes and the State buses are compelled to take care of unremunerative city services, profitability of State transport service is bound to suffer. Since the staff cannot be retrenched, by reducing the fleet of B.S.R.T.C. we may be cutting down the cash loss but we are indirectly committing ourselves to maintain the existing staff without requiring them to render any service. Such a situation will only undermine their capacity to work efficiently when required.

Receipts of Local Bodies

The subject of finance of Local Bodies has not got the attention it deserves. With urbanisation at phenomenal pace, the responsibilities of Local Bodies have become more onerous. At the same time inability and reluctance to raise sufficient resouces to meet the rising cost of services has completely debilitated them. The converging of population in and around cities is natural, for the cities are the centres of growth. We cannot permit our cities to be filthy and unhealthy. The State Government disowns resonsibility for civic services, as the Local Bodies are responsible for these services. Supply of clean drinking water, maintenance of road, street lighting, proper drainage and sewerage facilities are all expensive services. The Local Bodies are becoming more and more dependent on grants and loans from the State Govt. to make their ends meet. Budgetary support to Local Bodies to fulfill their obligations is unavoidable. With large scale migration to cities, the neglect of cities is a serious hazard. It is the responsibility of the State Government as much as that of the Local Bodies to maitain sanitation at hygienically satisfactory levels and safeguard the health of the people.

The holding Tax, Water Tax and Latrine Tax imposed by the Local Bodies in Bihar are very high; they add up to nearly 40% of the assessees annual income from the holdings. It is so high that none can afford to pay it. The result is that the holdings are almost as a rule under-valued and there is large scale evasion of the taxes. In practise the municipal tax law becomes an obnoxious provision which can be used to harass property owners. It is advisable to be realistic and make the municipal taxes rational. Holding tax should be assessed on the valuation of propety, giving due consideration to the size and qulity of construction, its location and the purpose for which it is being utilised, i.e.whether it is being used for commercial or residential purpose. Sizeable rebate should be given for self occupied houses. However, assessment of holding is always problematic. It is worth considering that in case of house occupied by tenants, the tenants also may be authorised to pay the holding tax, the rate of the tax being kept at 10% of the rent being paid by them. With tenants also entitled to pay tax it may be difficult for the house owners to conceal income from house property.

Water supply should be preferably metered, alternatively it should be assessed in proportion to the size of the house and the number of taps in use in the households. Financial assistance to Local Bodies is provided on the basis of 25% grant and 75% loan for water supply schemes. But is has not been possible to recover these loans. Providing piped water supply to households is an expensive service and people should not assume that they can get it free. There is no reason why the Local Bodies should default in realization of water tax. The service tax (latrine tax) should be related to the cost of the service being rendered. Providing sewerage and drainage facilities like piped water supply requires lot of investment. The city dwellers cannot expect the State to pay for these services entirely. The users and beneficiaries must share the cost for which a special development levy may be realised from the beneficiaries. A system of incentive grant should be introduced so that the Local Bodies are not complacent in realising their dues.

The Local Bodies should try to realise the full potential of their available resources, before asking for additional powers to levy new taxes. Their performance in collection of taxes has been very disappointing. Financial control is minimal. Tax revenue is concealed and there is considerable leakage of revenue as well as mis-appropriation of funds. The estimed income from holding, Water and Latrine Tax declined from Rs.193 lacs in 1982-83 to Rs.156 lacs in 1987-88 in Patna, even though the number of holdings increased substantially during the period. The licence fee for Rickshaws was fixed at Rs.14 per annum in 1957 and since then has not been revised. The number of licensed Rickshaws is only 30,000, though the number of Rickshaws which are plying is about 100,000. The licence fee could be very well enchanced to Rs. 10 per month. Rickshaws have to be gradually eliminated from the bigger cities. As an occupation it is degrading. Being a highly personalised mode of transport, they create traffic congestion and encroach on roads through unauthorised parking. It is expensive for the user. Modern life requires quick and cheap means of transport. There are over 1 lac Rickshaw pullers in Patna who are mostly pavement dwellers and create major civic problems for the city.

There are other possible sources of revenue which could be gainfully tapped. Parking of vehicles, carts, stalls, etc. on road sides is threatening to choke the cities. If we are unable to prohibit this, a parking fee may be levied, after demarcating suitable parking sites. Otherwise also this is a lucrative source of illegal income to traffic constables and staff of local bodies. By regularising it we will be saving the people from harassment and freeing the main roads of congestion.

There is a huge influx of population, non-residents who come to the cities for work or business and return after their work is over. This mobile population uses the public hydrants and toilets most. They add to the congestion in traffic and litter which they leave behind needs to be promptly removed. Such daily commuters thus impose a big burden on the cities. A tax of Rupee one per head on all passengers coming to select cities by rail and bus would be a good source of income. Most of these people come to the cities for business and would not grudge paying this small amount. Those travelling to the city on a regular basis, may buy seasonal tickets on which tax may be levied at a lower rate.

Realisation of Water Rate

Water both for irrigation and drinking purposes can be had free only in the State of nature. But pumping of water from under-ground and treating it in filtration tanks, and carrying it over long distances by pipes to households is a costly affair. The maintenance of water works is equally expensive. The Local Bodies have to recover the cost incurred over supplying drinking water or else it will be difficult for the State to meet the growing burden and provide the basic service of supplying safe drinking water to the people. Irrigation schemes also require heavy investment in construction of dams and distribution channels.

It is true, irrigation projects cannot be equated with power projects. They are not revenue earning assets, totally. If beneficiaries are required to pay for maintanance and also amortize for the capital, we will be unable to attain the objective of full potential.The farmers are too poor to pay for the investment in over-heads. According to the norms which have been prescribed, power projects are expected to generate a surplus of 3% over and above 7% return on the capital invested. Power projects are financed largely by loans from Govt. and market borrowing; and due to losses the S.E.Bs. are unable to service these debts. On the other hand, irrigation schemes are financed entirely on budgetary support from the Government with no condition as to any return on the money invested. This has lad to perfunctory control over investments in irrigation schemes, and whether the irrigation schemes give any return or not is of little consequnce. Table 10.4 gives the revenue from irrigation and the expenditure incurred by the Eastern States over maintenance of irrigation for the year 1983-84.

Table - 10.4

State	*Revenue form Irrigation (Rs. in Lakhs)*	*Maintenance Expenditure on Irrigation (Rs. in Lakhs)*
Bihar	729	1901
Orissa	408	861
West Bengal	85	1553
Uttar Pradesh	3941	2565

Apart from U.P. the other States are unable to recover the cost over maintenance of irrigation works and the gap is widening. Receipts from water rate in Bihar continue to be unsatisfactory and the total collections have been less than the expenditure incurred over collecting the amount.

The question arises, do we recover the cost of maintenance of irrigation works from the beneficiaries? The finance Commission has recommended the norm of Rs.100 per hectare of gross irrigated area for maintenance of irrigation works. We have to recover the running cost, otherwise it will be difficult to find resources to maintain irrigation work and utilise them fully. Failure to do so would imply that we are over subsidising irrigation at the cost of other productive avenues for investment. The limitatons of major and medium irrigation schemes have been repeatedly exposed during drought. While computing operational cost we may exclude expenditure over repairs and modernisation but include minimum establishment cost. There are several considerations in fixing the rate for use of water. The economic rate will be one which will enable us to recover the cost of the project, including a minimum return over the capital invested, over a certain period time. This a we have stated may not be socially desirable. From the beneficiaries' point of view, the water rate should be such as to encourage them to use the irrigation facilities. As productivity increases it may be possible to raise the irrigation rate. If water rates are not levied or not realised (both have similar detrimental effects) water would be wastefully utilised.Besides it will be difficult to resist the pressure of influential political leaders to locate irrigation schemes in areas, without considering their cost effectiveness. There is similar pressure for extending distribution systems that do not justify the cost involved. Irrigation schemes have a big impact, in terms of size and aspirations it gives rise to, and have a lot of prestige value for political leaders. Non-levy or non-realisation of water rates will strengthen the tendency for big and influential cultivators to monopolise the use of water (it is easier to realise water rates form the smaller farmers),lending support to the criticism that green revolution widens the gulf between the rich and the poor.

Better Maintenance of Assets

The Eighth Finance Commission rightly observes, "State Government must accept it, as a matter of policy that proper maintenence of capital assets already created in order to preserve them for their full life is equally, if not more important than creating new assets. These capital assets have been created at great cost and they cannot be allowed to be neglected as this would be a waste of the outlays incurred. Under utilisation of assets,i.e. production below capacity due to poor operation and maintenance, also amounts to wasteful investment. Production below capacity is one of the principal reasons for low productivity and high capital output ratio of the Indian economy . With better utilisation of assets productivity will increase, which in turn will generate additional resources for new investments. If there is lack of demand, under-utilisation of capacity is understandable. But low plant load factor of power units, partial utilisation of irrigaton potential and below capacity utilisation of road transport facilities are indicators of serious mis-management.

Though adequate provision for maintenance expenses will add to our problem of finding resources for development, satisfactory maintenance of assets will lead to higher productivity and more than off-set the expenses over maintenance. The results are tangible in the case of revenue earning assets like power, road transport, railways, irrigation works, etc. In the case of non-revenue earning assets like educational institutions, hospitals, ect.,it will result in greater social satisfaction. The yardstick for judging the quality of educational and health services is not the number of institutions or staff that is employed but the quality of service that is rendered, i.e. standard of education and medical treatment. Better maintenance of roads through better cummunication helps in the development process, as bad roads mean greater wear and tear of vehicles, and therefore, higher running cost; it also means that more time will be taken over transport.

Control of Public Expenditure

Control of public expenditure is difficult yet necessary, in order to make the goverment and people conscious of 'saving' and making it thrift minded. Prodigality in expenditure sets a bad example and creates an atmosphere unsuited for development. Control of expenditure, especially imposing checks on wasteful and sterile expenditure should be our main concern. There are limits to borrowings and taxes which can be raised by Government. Ability to raise revenue depends not only on the taxable capacity of the people, but also on the integrity and efficiency of the staff engaged in collection of taxes. People also resist payment of taxes. This goes on increasing with increase in incidence of taxes. The 'leakage' and 'resistance' factors combine to impose a limit beyond which it becomes futile for the Government to impose new taxes or raise the tax rates. Similarly additional borrowings and the consequential rising debt burdens can be serviced only through higher tax revenue generated by higher productivity. But if borrowings are utilised only for the purpose of meeting revenue deficits, a situation may emerge when borrowing will only widen the budgetary gap.

The deterioration in the Central finances is mainly due to sharp rise in non-plan expenditure particularly under interest payments, defence and subsidies. The sharp rise in non-plan expenditure has resulted in pre-emption of resources that might otherwise be available for plan-expenditure and has led to increased borrowing to meet the overall financial requirements[5]. Whereas development expentiture increased from 16.7% of the G.D.P. in 1980-81 to 17.9% of G.D.P. in 1989-90; non-development expenditure increased form 9.3% to 13.4% during the same period. In absolute terms the increase in non-development expanditure was five times compared to only 325% increase in development expenditure. The increase in non-development expenditure has to be checked.

There has been lately tendency on the part of the Government to depend more on market borrowings to cover the gap in revenue. Market borrowing which constituted only 18.8% of the total receipts in the Fifth Plan had increased to 22.2% in the Sixth Plan. Total receipts from market loans (net) was only Rs.3,163 crores in 1980-81, but went upto Rs.6,691 crores in 1985-86. Market borrowings, including bonds issued by public enterprises, provided 23.6% of the reciepts during the Seventh Plan. Since borrowed capital is not always spent on revenue earning assets, it means that debt service burden will increase. Investments from borrowed capital must give a rate of return which is higher than the rate of borrowing on else the buden of interest repayments will increase.

The first report of Nineth Finance Commission rightly states,"one of the major causes for the rise in the net interest burden on the general budget is the poor returns on the major investments of Central and the State Government..... The total borrowing requirements of the Central Government has become large, amounting to nearly 9.4 per cent of G.D.P. This is not conducive for monetary stability. Under the reforms initiated in 1991, it is proposed to bring it down to under 5%.

Expenditure has also gone up because of the mounting liability to maintain assets created in the previous plans. The controversy that maintenance of capital goods should be a part of plan expenditure and not non-plan is misconceived. The real issue is that sufficient funds should be available for maintenance of such assets. The State Governments complain that Finance Commission makes estimates about maintenance cost on the basis of prevailing prices in the base year and does not take into account the escalation of costs and rise in wages, etc. It is true that Finance Commision estimates are based on static costs and prices and therefore, under estimate the actual requirements. But there is also need for close monitoring of maintanace expentiture. There is very little information about utilisation of maintenance funds. Not much planning goes into maintenence, with the result that maintenance is often of sub-standerd quality. There is also substantial leakage of funds in the name of maintenance. The staff for maintenance is generally in excess, who have to be property utilised by transferring them to jobs where they are required. Like plan expenditure, maintenance expenditure also should be closely monitored both at the field and state levels.

Office expenses constitute only a small part of total administrative expenses, but control of such expenditure acts as a trend-setter. Expenditure over the two legislative bodies in Bihar increased from Rs. 2.26 crores in 1980-81 to Rs. 8.61 crores in 1989-90, on council of Ministers from Rs. 0.87 crores to Rs. 3.31 crores, on Secretariat services from Rs. 6.06 crores to Rs. 25.45 crores, on Administration of Justice from Rs. 8.84 crores to Rs. 35.42 crores and on District Administration from Rs. 8.84 crores to Rs. 30 crores, i.e. by nearly 4 times. Maintenance of Rajyapal cost the state Rs. 43.36 lakh. The trend has continued with accelerated pace. With further increase in the number of districts, administrative expenses are bound to shoot up. The above are budgetary figures. Actual expenditure is more. Considerable expenditure on Ministers' telephone, car, office and residence is met by their deprtments. Currently the avarage expenditure over a Minister is nearly Rs.1.5 lakh per month. Expenditure on furnishing of legislators' dwelling units is met out of funds meant for "tools and plants" by the buildings deparment and electricity consumption bills of legislators' flats are paid out of annual/maintenance provision. Strictly speaking such payments ought to be recovered from the legislators, but in practice it has not been possible. Government realises by way of rent less than one-fourth of what it spends on the maintenance of residential buildings owned by it. It is obvious that those who have control over funds are more generous and inconsiderate in its use also. The legislators recently (1993) in an unabashed display of authority appropriated for themselves benefits which cannot be justified on economic or moral grounds. The State Government's commitment to social justice and rescuing the down-trodden appears doubtful. This included motor car advance of Rs. 1.30 lakh @ 2.5% interest, travelling allowance at Rs. 4 per kilometre, two free rail passes for 25,000 kilometres, 85,000 free telephone calls, maximum pension of Rs. 3,000/- per month. When the State is reeling under poverty and paucity of resources, such profligacy on the part of the elected representatives, certainly does not display their concern or accountability to the public. It is not surprising that the Lagislature High Court and the Governor are exempted from the austerity measures imposed from time to time.

Expenditure over Police by Government of India increased by nearly 15 times, between 1970-71 and 1989-90. The combined expenditure of Central and State Governments quadrupeed on Police, from Rs. 1163 crores in 1980-81 to Rs. 4,833 crores in 1989-90. In Bihar also the trend has been the same. Expenditure over police in the State was Rs. 64.6 crores in 1980-81, which increased to Rs.386 crores in 1992-93. In spite of this phenomenal increase in expenditure over police, there has not been much improvement in prevention or detection of crime. Incidence of kidnapping of businessmen for ransom is on the rise. Bank robberies have become frequent. Musclemen and party workers realise tolls from contractors and transport agents. The entrepreneurs are naturally scared. Special attention has to be given to this aspect of crime in order to give confidence to those who want to invest in the State.

Economy drive is only a small part of control of public expenditure. For effective control of public expenditure we require strict financial discipline, including price control, prevention of time over runs in execution of projects, pruning of superfluous staff and avoidance of unproductive schemes. This is easier said than done, but it is necessary for generating savings and achieving higher productivity.

The animal husbandry scam, popularly know as' Gwala Scam' rocked the State in 1996. Nearly Rs.1,000 crores was drawn from the treasuries against fake allotment order for payment of fake bills of the Animal Husbandry Department. The period covered almost a decade, but 80% of the amount was swindled after 1990, i.e. during Janta Dal rule. Even though, excess drawls found mention in official reports, none intervened. The suppliers, the animal husbandry staff, the treasury staff, the Finance Department, the Public Accounts Committee and also those who held the reins in Finance and Vigilance Departments were in a grand unholy alliance to plunder the State exchequer. Even the Chief Minister and Cabinet Ministers were involved. Government staff in many departments went without salaries for years. There was no fund for maintenance of essential services and for execution of vital development work. When the guardians of financial management connive with cheats to loot public funds, they forfeit their authority to occupy such responsible places and any talk of development with such persons at the helm does not make sense.

REFERENCES

1. *Economic Survey*, 1989-90 to 1992-93, Government of India.
2. *Sales-Tax System in Bihar*, p. 82. NIPFP, Somaiya Publication, 1982.
3. *Sales-Tax System in Bihar*, p. 82.
4. *Eighth Finance Commission*, Govt. of India, paragraph 3.115 and 3.116.
5. *Report on Currency and Finance*, 1987-88 p. 3a.
6. *First Report of the Nineth Finance Commission*, July, 1988 (paras 2.19, 2.20, 2.23).
7. *Second Report of the Nineth Finance Commission*, December, 1989.
8. *Report of Chelliah Tax Reforms Committee*, Ministry of Finance.
9. *India Economic Statistics*, Public Finance, Ministry of Finance.
10. R.B.I. *Annual Reports and Reports on Currency and Finance.*
11. *S. Chakravarty Committee Report on Working of the Monetary System*, R.B.I., 1986.
12. *World Development Reports*, World Bank.
13. *Budget and Plan Documents*, Government of Bihar.
14. *Report of the Tenth Finance Commission*, December, 1994.

11

Paucity of Credit

The role of credit as a crucial determinant of develpment is well recognised. To derive maximum advantage from credit we should have knowledge and resourcefulness (entrepreneurhip) to utilise it productively; and there should be the necessary infrastructure to facilitate such deployment of credit. Bihar's economy is heavily dependent on agriculture. But agriculture because of low productivity has not generated enough investible surplus to enable exploitation of other available natural resources. Bihar has, therefore, relied on outside capital for development of its potential. It were ousiders who were pioneers in exploitation of the rich mineral deposits. Tata set-up the first steel plant in the country in Bihar. British companies developed the coalmines. Paucity of capital has been largely responsible for retarded industrialisation and also under-developed agriculture.

Because of the recent changes in economic policy and shift towards privatisation and liberalisation, it will be even more difficult to channelise more public investible funds for development of the backward and laggard States. Private capital flows are, therefore, to play crucial role in investment activities. Banks are the conduit for channelising savings into investment. Since banks are also required to earn profit and their performance is judged by the amount of profit they earn, there is a natural tendency for the banks to lend to those who can borrow at the highest rate of interest. They will also like to lend to people who are credit-worthy and for activities which they consider safe.

Drain of Capital from Bihar:

Because of the agrarian character of the economy, and for reasons stated above Bihar has been treated as source for funds for investment in profitable ventures outside the State. This may appear paradoxical but it is true. The credit deposit ratio in the State has been much lower than the national average. It has been hovering between 30% and 40% for the last two decades. It had declined to 32% in 1995. During 1993-94, deposits in the State grew by nearly Rs. 1678 crores, but outstanding advances grew by only Rs. 183 crores. Of course the latter figure does not include the total investment by the financial institutions. The outstanding advances went down because of higher recoveries during 1993-94. Total investment under State Credit Plan was merely Rs. 388 crores. Investment by Financial Institutions in the State could not have been more than Rs. 100 crores. Thus there was considerable drain of resources. 1993-94 was not an unusual year. Of course the situation has worsened as industrial activities have slackened very much lately.

Large and Medium Industries

Large and medium sized industries will choose their location primarily on the basis of market opportunities available to them. Western India because of the presence of financial institutions and easier access to them: with better marketing and comunication facilities has a definite edge over the rest of the country. Power supply is dependable and the State administration is more reponsive to the needs of industry. Bihar's share in the investment by All India financial institutions (cumulative total upto 1991) was only Rs. 1548 crores or 2.3%. Even Orissa's share was larger, 2.85%. Maharashtra (19.92%) and Gujarat (12.24%) between them accounted for 1/3rd of the total. Share of West Bengal was 5.39% and Uttar Pradesh 9.38%. We do not have information of the investments made in Eastern U.P. After the liberalization of economy in July, 1991 the trend for industries to concentrate in the industrially favourable pockets in Gujarat an Maharashtra has accentuated. Out of the 1296 foreign investment approvals between 1.1.93 to 31.7.94 accounting for an investment of Rs. 11459 crores, Bihar's share was just 5 cases involving an investment of Rs. 52.02 crores. Maharashtra accounted for 202 approvals for investment of Rs. 1900.4 crores; and Gujarat 65 for 1123.87 crores. The other favoured locations were Tamil Nadu, Delhi and Madhya Pradesh. There is not much which can be done in the existing circumstances to tempt major industries in the private sector to backward regions. Strong bid was made by the State Government to induce private sector, Messrs. R.P. Goenka and Tata and others to invest in Bihar; but it was of no avail. The Tata's have recently commissioned a slag-based cement factory and have been deepening their investment in the already existing units, but new ventures are not there.

The Importance of Agriculture & Allied Activities

We are perforce compelled to look upon developoment of agriculture and allied activities as the thrust areas in the immediate future. We should not under estimate the potential of this sector or its capacity to absorb credit for increasing production and employment. Agriculture still provides employment to 70% of the populaion and 87% of the people in Bihar reside in rural areas. Development of agriculture and allied activities and small scale cotttage industries will consederably add to the prosperity of the rural population.

Banks accord preferential treatment to agriculture, small scale industries and trade and services meant to benefit the agricultural and rural sectors. For this priority sector 'NABARD' under direction from R.B.I. prepares credit plan every year for each branch, district and the State. NABARD has prepared a large number of schemes for inclusion in the priority sector and provides refinance facilities to cooperative and commercial banks to encourage lending for such activities. The Government sponsored programmes for which subsidy is provided by the State/ Union Government are also important part of the credit plan.

Weak Infrastructure

Poor credit flow is linked to the stage of development. It is argued that since 'infrastructure' is not developed there are limited applications for credit. This is a specious argument. Low credit flow and poor development are indicators of a depressed and stagnant economy, but credit flow also contrubutes to development. The Centre for Monitoring Indian Economy has compiled indices for assessing the status of infrastructure development.Bihar's index at 98 is almost at par with the national average. It is better than that of Rajasthan and Orissa, who absorb much more credit than Bihar. As has been pointed out credit flow in the priority sector in Bihar is confined to government sponsored programmes and is totally of the nature of directed credit. Credit flow for other activities is negligible. It is due to the co-operative and State financial institutions in the State being; 'sick', and also because commercial banks are not interested and do not want to be involved. This change in attitude of commercial banks has to be brought about by appropriate policy decisions at the centre. The investment in large and medium industries are matters of national policy and favourable economic factors. Bihar has distinct advantage in respect of coal and iron are deposits and major investments have taken place in coal mining and Steel Plants. But Bihar, unlike Uttar Pradesh, which does not have any locational advantage, has not been able to attract industries in other sectors. 'Development' lately has not been a priority issue with the State Government. Other issues have taken precedence. Apart from accusing the Central Government of step motherly treatment, no cogent efforts have been made to create conditions conducive for industrial growth.

Shortage of power is no doubt a major hurdle. It must be also realised that inadequacy of demand for power in the State has been held against the State for proposals seeking strengthening of generation capacity for power. Thus the State finds itself in a helpless predicament; industries are discouraged from coming to the State because of lack of power, and on the other hand proposals for strengthening the power base are shelved as there is lack of demand for power.

Inadequate Credit Disbursements

Implementation of the Credit Plan in Bihar has been very unsatisfactory. Disbursement under the credit plan was Rs. 525 crores in 1988-89, Rs. 485 crores in 1989-90, Rs. 402 crores in 1990-91, Rs. 329 crores in 1991-92, Rs. 289 crores in 1992-93, Rs. 388 crores in 1993-94, and Rs. 401 crores in 1994-95. The fluctuations have been primarily due to variations in lending by Commercial Banks. In 1992-93 the total lending by Commercial Banks and regional rural banks under the priority sector was Rs. 211.16 crores out of which nearly Rs. 150 crores was for I.R.D.P. Thus 72% of total financing was for I.R.D.P. In 1993-94 out of the total lending of Rs. 296 crores by commercial banks and R.R. Bs, Rs. 150 crores was under I.R.D.P. Government sponsored programmes include the subsidized programmes. Since 1993-94, Prime Minister Rojgar Yojna is an important constituent of this. The State Government is also closely involved in disbursement of crop loans, Crop loans or Production Credit account for nearly Rs. 100 crores every year. Financing of schemes, which are not Govt. sponsored programmes is nominal. Great stress is laid on schematic lending by NABARD for diversifying and strengthening the rural economy, but except for farm mechanisation it has been of no consequence. The total lending for schemes of minor irrigation, land development, dairy, poulty, horticulture, fisheries and cottage industries was merely Rs. 1.95 crores in 1991-92. In 1989-90 it was Rs. 1.39 crores and in 190-91 Rs. 6.19 crores. In 1992-93 too it was less than Rs. 2 crores.

The banks to avoid embarrassment, reduced the size of the credit plan for the state. In 1993-94 it was kept at Rs. 696 crores only, which is indeed very low consedering the size and needs of the State. The reason which was given for this low outlay was past achievement, which was attributed primarily to poor absorption capacity of the State. Considering the size of the economy and the undisputed potential of the State, this is a cynical judgement and denies solution to the problem. It is difficult to conceive that in a population of 9 crores, there are not even 5 lakh persons who can not borrow on an average more than Rs. 25,000 and put it to proper use. The credit plan of Karnataka is around Rs. 1,500 crores, that of Andhra Pradesh nearly Rs. 4,000 crores, and of Uttar Pradesh over Rs. 3,000 crores.

Task force Recommendations for Improving Credit Flow

The low C.D. Ratio of Bihar has been a matter of much concern for more than a decade now. Several high level committees were appointed by R.B.I. to suggest measures for improving the C.D. ratio and bringing it on par with the national average. This issue was again raised before the Regional Consultative Commmittee in November, 1992 at Patna presided over by the

Union Finance Minister, Sri Manmohan Singh. The Task Force which was consitituted for the purpose by R.B.I. was asked to expedite its report. The Task Force submitted its report in January, 1993. The recommendations were accepted by R.B.I. and Government of India. When the Task Force was constituted, the C.D. ratio for the State was 40%, whereas the national average was 60%. The task force recommended that in the first phase lending should be stepped up in a phased manner to reach C.D. ratio of 50% by end of 1996-97. It identified thrust areas and activities for profitable investment. It assumed that deposit would grow by 15%, and it will be posssible to recover 50% of the dues, and suggested incremental credit deposit ratio at 60%. On these hypotheses it projected an investment of Rs. 9,160 crores between 1993-97. This included Rs. 5,480 crores in priority sector, Rs. 2,480 crores in large and medium industries and Rs. 1,200 crores in trade and commerce. These are realistic and practical recommendations. For agriculture and allied activities an investment of Rs. 3,200 crores was envisaged. With 104 lakh hectares of cropped area, the recommendations amount to an investment of Rs. 1231 per acre of cropped area over a period of four years, a modest amount. But to achieve this much effort will be required by banks. They will have to adopt a positive approach to reassure the cultivators that their credit needs will be promptly met.

Crop Financing

The Sen Committe estimated the upper most requirement of credit at Rs. 900 crores, taking into consideration the area under cultivation and the minimum requirement of credit per acre. He thus arrived at an estimate, which was far in excess of the prevailing absorption of credit. The total gross cropped area in the State is 104 lakh hectares. NABARD has prescribed the norm of Rs. 5,000/- per hectare for crop financing. Thus the total requirement of credit for the State would be about Rs. 5,200 crores. But the maximum amount of lending in the State was Rs. 215.5 crores in 1987-88; of which cooperatives contributed Rs. 203.5 crores. Between 1989-90 to 1991-92 it was less than Rs. 100 crores. In 1992-93 it was Rs. 116 crores. In 1993-94 it was Rs. 104.3 crores. It was only marginally better in 1995-96, Rs. 117.36 crores. Certainly the demand for credit is not based on simple arithmetic but depends upon availability of credit, the willingness of farmers to take risk for investment in inputs; the availability of inputs and the returns from farm produce. Access to credit is a major determinant. Thus share-croppers do not have access to credit. The coverage by Banks and Co- operative in not cent per cent. The administrative and financial capacity of banks to process the applications is also a limiting factor.

It is difficult to concede that the demand for agricultural credit in the State is only Rs. 100 to 150 crores. On an average not more than 1.5 lakh farmers get the benefit of crop finance, whereas the number of holdings in the State is 112 lakhs. The total number of members of cooperatives is nearly 60 lakhs. Per hectare value of agriculture output in Bihar was estimated at Rs. 3,470 per hectare (average for the year 1982-83 to 1984-85). Since then because of increase in price of agricultural produce, the value has doubled and we can put it at Rs. 7,000/- per hectare. Even if we treat 1/3rd of this value as investment by agriculturist on different inputs; seeds, fertilizers, pesticides, irrigation etc., it means that for the present level of agricultural production, capital of Rs. 2,330 per hecatre is deployed, i.e. a total of nearly (102.6 lakh × 2,330) or Rs. 2391.6 crores is deployed, in agriculture. This is a very rough estimate. Credit deployment at existing level can be reasonably estimated to be around Rs. 2,000 crores. If the organized rural credit system is not able to deliver this amount, the farmers manage to obtain it from private sources, probably at prohibitive rates. They are compelled to borrow from foodgrain dealers, who exploit them later by buying their produce at depressed prices. The share croppers are compelled to borrow from their landlords, lending themselves to further exploitation. If farmers can not afford to borrow money or are unable to obtain credit, they are compelled to cut down their expenses over the inputs by not using them in the desired proportion. This results in uncertain yield and the cultivators are unable to reap the advantage of the inputs in full. There can be little doubt that non-availability of credit from prescribed channels is imposing a heavy burden on the cultivators and is acting as a brake to the agricultural development of the State.

Poor financing in the State is explained by large number of defaulters, who are, therefore ineligible. There is another pertinent factor, though 75% of the land is cultivated by share croppers, they are not entitled to crop loan. There is clear directive from R.B.I. that banks should not obtain collateral security by way of mortgage of land on third party guarantee for crop loans upto Rs. 15,000 and terms loans upto Rs. 15,000 where moveable assets are created. Only primary security by way of hypothecation of crops/moveable assets should be taken. In actual practice the banks insist on certificate from government functionaries regarding cultivating possession of the crop by the share croppers. This is not forthcoming in view of the law on the subject and political situation in the State.

Share cropping has been banned by law in the State. However, it is common practice for landless agericultural labourers or those with tiny holdings to obtain land on oral lease for cultivation. In view of this any action by administration which creates evidence in favour of the share cropper is suspected. The banks may seriously consider, whether it is possible for them to finance crop raised by share croppers on the basis of joint guarantees furnished by them. Their proof of residence can be provided by Mukhias of the village concerned.

To elicit the co-operation of banks, the Panchayats in West Bengal have not only taken over the responsibility of obtaining applications from the farmers and processing them with the help of banks, but also assist the banks in recovering the dues. Unless such collaboration takes place it will be difficult to overcome the hesitation and inertia of bankers to augment the flow of credit.

Cooperative Institutions have Become Sick

The Central Co-operative Banks provide short term credit (crop loan) and the Land Development Banks provide medium and long term credit for agriculture and allied activities. Both these institutions because of mounting overdues are becoming ineligible for refinance from NABARD. The two cooperative institutions are superseded at present. They both need to be revamped and democratic working of these institutions has to be restored. The lending operations of L.D.B. are virtually at a standstill. NABARD have lowered the eligibility condition to 20% recovery instead of 40% to maintain the credit flows. But such relaxation is given only towards the end of the year and it fails to provide much relief. Both these vital institutions for financing of agriculture have been brought to the present impasse because of irresponsible management, bad loans and lately by loan waivers granted under A.R.D.R. scheme in 1991. In case of Bihar the claim for nearly Rs. 450 crores was settled by Government of India after a lapse of 4 years. Settlement could be reached only in 1995. Flow of credit was choked during the period. The State Cooperative Bank deducted interest amounting to nearly Rs. 100 crores, from the claims of C.C. Banks. This has crippled the C.C. Banks. On top of this Nabard deducted 5% from the total claims at the source, further adding to the burden.

Schematic Lendings

The potential for dairy development, fisheries, fruits and vegetable production in the State is well recognised. But due to lack of co-ordination between Government functionaries and Bank officials and also due to apathy, such schemes have made little headway. The numerous mans and chaurs of North Bihar are ideal for fisheries. Orissa has made commedable progress in this respect. Bihar has a very large population of milch cattle and buffaloes and as far as fruit production is concerned, it ranks next only to Uttar Pradesh in the Country. In spite of this, the major cities in the State depend on supply of fish and eggs from Andhra Pradesh, Bihar depend on supply of dairy products from outside the State. It is surprising that fruits like guava and mangoes are also brought from outside. There is unsatisfied demand for these products within the State. There is no reason, why Bihar with proper incentives and encouragement should not make better utilization of the opportunities in fisheries, dairy and horticulture. Bihar enjoys virtual monopoly in production of makhana and lichies. The "maldah" mangoes of the State are rated among the best in the country. North Bihar grows high quality bananas and plantains. Panapplis can be grown in Purnea and Kishanganj district. There are abundant opportunities for fruit processing industries and agro-products. The Eighth Plan has proposed an investment of Rs. 1,000 crores for development of horticulture. It is necessary that the State is able to take advantage of this programme for which financial institutions must provide unstinted support.

Small Scale Industries

The small scale industries constitute a very important segment of the priority sector. Unfortunately nearly 70% of the S.S. I. units are sick and closed. Inspection of the major industrial estates indicates that only a few units are successful. Large number of units are patiently pursuing their applications for working capital with commerial banks and financial institutions to resume their production. But their optimism is not shared by the banks. It is unfortunate that units located in Bokaro and Adityapur Industrial Estate are not able to take advantage of orders preferentially alloted to them as ancillaries. The Bihar State Financial Corporation has run into difficulties because of overdues and at present is not eligible for refinance from I.D.B.I. In the circumstances, commercial banks have the added responsibility of meeting the credit needs of Small Scale Industries. In fact the Task Force made strong recommendation for this. The Nayak Committee recommended that aliments should be detected in time and adequate credit support should be provided to prevent sickness among. Small Scale Industries. Though R.B.I. accepted the recommendations in letter and spirit, the State Level Committee set-up to enquire into such cases has not been able to provide significant assistance to sick and closed units. Also, just because sickness exists, it does not mean that the banks should penalise or discriminate against the healthy units by hesitating to provide adequate finance to them. Small Scale Industries are facing severe constraint in obtaining finance. The number of pending applications from Small Scale Industries for bank credit run into thousands. Large industry has access to capital market, institutional finance, Euro issues and banks which bend backwards to lend to them; the small firms have no recourse to equity. In fact the S.S.I. entrepreneurs are often required to give personal guarantees to avail money from financial institutions and banks.

For promotion of Khadi and village industries, it is proposed to invest Rs. 5,500 crores (including Rs. 3,600 crores as loans from financial insitutions) in 1995-96 and 1996-97 for the whole country. Eleven Blocks in Bihar have been selected for intensive development and it is sought to provide employment to 1000 persons in each block. Besides 4 districts Saharsa, Madhubani, Khagaria and Godda have been selected under self-employment programme. The programme envisages creation of additional 10,000 jobs in each of these four districts. To encourage Khadi and village industries, interest subsidy is provided to applicants. Only 4% interest charge is paid by borrowers, the balance amount is subsidised by KVIC. Till November, 1994 K.V.I.C. & K.V.I.B. issued Interest Subsidy Eligibility Certificates for loans amounting to nearly Rs. 18.35 crores, but banks had sanctioned only Rs. 5.04 crores as loans under the project. There is abnormal delay in sanction of such schemes ranging from 6 months to 2,1/2 years, when it should not take more than 8 to 9 weeks. The banks have been generally lukewarm to the programme.

Recently Government of India has enlarged the scope of the schemes for sef-employment of educated un-employed youth (S.E.E.U.Y.). The maximum amount of loans was only Rs. 35,000. Now under Prime Minister's Rojgar Yojna the maximum amount has been raised to Rs. 1 lakh, including the subsidy amount of Rs. 75,00. Under S.E.E.U.Y. the target for the state was 10,000 per year. But achievement was not more than 30% and the average amount of lending was also around Rs. 20,000. The initial experience with P.M.R.Y. is no different. The target for 1993-94 was 3,377 but only 1352 were benefited; in 1994-95, the target was 22,150, but disbursement had taken place only in 8023 cases. Non-achievement of the target implies that the unemployed in the State are being deprived of the opportunities for employment under the scheme. If P.M.R.Y. target is fully achieved it will mean investment of Rs. 210 crores.

It does not makes sense that new applicants below the poverty line should be denied assistance, because of bad financing in past. It is true that recoveries are the backbone of sound credit system. The State Government has to extend strong support for recoveries. But banks must realise that the initiative must come from them. There are large number of bad debts, which were incurred by laxity of bank staff to exercise proper vigil.

Neglect of Priority Sector Programmes

Priority sector lending is not getting priority attention. It is implemented only in so far as it covers directed outlay; i.e. financing of schemes directed by Government of India. Banking is a central subject. Since banks do their business in the State, it is expected that the States' needs will be taken into consideration. The posting of ombudsman by Government of India in each State to probe into grievances of the borrowing public is a welcome step. The R.B.I. is supposed to oversee the implementation of these programmes, but they consider these activities residual. No action is taken against banks who have failed to achieve their targets under the credit plan. Similarly no bank official is taken to task for his failure to achieve the target assigned to him under I.R.D.P., P.M.R.Y. and under the credit plan. There is only formal participation of the State administration in formulating credit plan. The activities to be funded are hardly known to the borrowers with the result that there is no response. The credit plan itself is made available after half the year is over. The returns prescribed for monthly and quarterly monitoring, (L.B.R.- I & II) relating to achievement and recoveries are not compiled. The result is that the credit plans remain only on paper, and achievement is confined to programmes in which the State Government is directly involved.

Ensuring Minimum Levels of Performance for Thrust Activities:

In view of what has been said above it is necessary that priority should be emphasised for priority sector lending. Some minimum physical and financial targets should be prescribed for different activities and joint effort should be made by the State Government and banks to attain them. Any shortfall should be viewed seriously.

If people are assured that credit will be availabe for genuine production activities, they will consider the options for using it. Unnecessary documentation, cumbersome procedure, delay and burden some levies by way of stamp duties or registration fees makes borrowing from commercial banks and financial insitutions unattractive and people are discouraged from approaching them. There is a strong case for withdrawing stamp duty on loans for priority sector and self employment schemes upto Rs. 2 lakhs. Trust is mutual. In the prevailing climate, Banks do not have faith in the capability of small borrowers. The borrowers too are hesitant to approach the Banks. For most of them it is not worth while to approach the banks Corruption has made matters worse. J.B. Say, a classical economist of the last century asserted that supply creates it own demand. Even bankers feel that timely and adequate availability of credit is more important than the rate of interest at which it is available. Easy access to credit is re-assuring to borrowers. In an age of liberalization the system of dispensation of credit certainly needs to be made more simple and liberal.

Since the banks are public undertakings of Government of India, appraisals of the State Government about banks is not needed. Government of India should evolve a proper forum, where State can place it problems and views in regard to credit deployment in the State. The State Level Bankers Committe fails to perform this role. It has become ritualistic in character. No representative of Government of India has ever attended the meeting of S.L.B.Cs in Bihar. Majority of the meetings are presided over by General Manager of the Convenor Bank. Same issues are raised again and again and problems remain as they are.

Table. 11.1. Banking Profile of Bihar at a Glance as on March, 1996

1. Total Number of Banks operating in the State

Bank Group

(a) State Bank and its associates	3
(b) Scheduled Commercial Banks	45
(i) Nationalised Banks	20
(ii) Private Sector Banks	3
(iii) Regional Rural Banks	22

2. **Branch Network**

Bank Group	*Rural*	*Semi-Urban*	*Urban*	*Total*
State Bank Group	523	255	150	928
Nationalised Bank	1415	340	363	2118
Private Sector Banks	. -	-	6	6
Regional Rural Banks	1743	114	30	1887
Total:	3681	709	549	4989

3. Commercial Banks having more than 100 brances in the State:

State Bank of India	918

Punjab National Bank	439
Bank of India	386
Central Bank of India	371
United Commercial Bank	201
Allahabad Bank	225
United Bank of India	110
State Cooperaative Bank	14
Central Cooperative Bank (34)	483
No. of PACS and LAMPS	7057

Table.11.2. Business of Banks in Bihar

(Rs. in Crores)

	Commercial Banks		*R.R.B.S*		*C.D.*
	Deposits	*Advances*	*Deposits*	*Advances*	*Ratio*
31. 3. 1994	12,047	4,114	1,099	557	38.5
31. 3. 1995	14,073	4,407	1,313	609	34.2
31. 3. 1996	16,506	5,216	1,601	641	34.2

Deposits with State Cooperative Bank (31. 3. 1996) — Rs. 366 Crores

Deposites with C.C.B.s (31. 3. 1994) — Rs. 342 Crores.

Credit Flow to the State under Priority Sector

(Rs. in Crores)

Years	*Agriculture*	*S.S.I.*	*O.P.S.*	*Total*
1988-89	308	73	143	524
1989-90	260.7	88.1	136.23	485.03
1990-91	213.81	75.84	112.64	402.29
1991-92	223.89	42.05	73.06	340.00
1992-93	184.2	33.1	57.7	275.0
1993-94	-	-	-	388.4
1994-95	-	-	-	401.3

Investment by All India Financial Institutions (Term Loans in Rs. Crores)

1986-87	137.00
1987-88	207.00
1988-89	179.9
1989-90	224.6
1990-91	122.8

Table. 11.3. Bank Operation in Bihar and All India

			December- 1991	
			Bihar	*All India*
A.	(a)	Total No. of branches	4870 (8)	60597
	(b)	Population served by a branch	15000	11000
B.	(a)	Aggregate Deposite (Rs. Crores)	9562 (4)	60597
	(b)	Gross Bank Credit (Rs. Crores)	3824 (3)	133745
	(c)	Credit Deposit Ratio (%)	40	61
		C.D. Ratio in rural Centres	52	59
		C.D. Ratio in sem- Centres	33	47
		C.D. Ratio in Urban Centres	36	66
C.	**Per Branch**			
	(a)	Aggregate Deposits (Rs. Lakh)	196	362
	(b)	Gross Bank Credit (Rs. Lakh)	79	221
	(c)	Business Mix (Rs. Lakh)	275	583

Note: Figures in brackets indicate percentage to all India.

REFERENCES

1. Report of the Task Force on C.D. Ratio in Bihar, Jan, 1993.
2. Report of the Task Force on Augmenting Rural Credit in Bihar, NABARD, 1993.
3. Refinance Assistance for Non-Form sector, NABARD, July, 1992.

12

Strengthening the Planning and Implementation Machinery

Formulating the Plan. The Need for Decentralization

The Choice of schemes, allocation of resources between different schemes, the organisation and agency for executing the plan, the procedure adopted for effective monitoring and appraosal of plan schemes, all have important bearing on achievements under the plan.

The allocation of resources is determined by the plan priorities. The priorities are decided at the highest level. The Planning Commission prepares the draft in light of the projected perspective, prevailing needs and experience accquired in execution of the earlier plans. The 'draft' is placed before the National Development council where the State Governments express their view points. But this is only a formal get-toghether. The draft Seventh or Eighth Plan prepared by the Planning Commision did not undergo any substantial change in the National Development Council. There is nothing wrong in an expert and an Apex Body like the Planning Commission, headed by the Prime Minister, suggesting the plan priorities. Our plan is mainly prepared by the Central Government and the State Plans have to be fitted into the national scheme of things. After providing for the on-going schemes and the centrally sponsored schemes, only limited resources are available to the State Governments to be spent at their discretion. As far as states are concerned, size of the Plan is determined by the resources provided by the Centre and their own internal resources. The centre contributes nearly 50% of the resources and naturally dictates the priorities of the State Plans as well. The Working Groups set up by the Planning Commision see to it that the priorities suggested by the State Governments are in conformity with the National Plan.

The State Governments have enough discretion in the choice of individual schemes. But there is no organised and rational system for processing the selection of schemes. Political and regional pressures determine the choice rather than conscious decisions based on the study of comparative costs, cost benefit analysis or maximum social benefit from the scheme. Neither the perspective plan nor the Five Year Plan serve as reference. There are wide deviations from them. The cost benefit estimates are manipulated to suit the requirements. Though there is much talk of productivity, employment potential, reducing time lags, forward and backward linkages, in practice we tend to lose sight of these criteria. New schemes are taken up without considering avalialbility of additional resources, whereas on-going schemes are starved for funds and allowed to linger. It is needless to say that unproductive schemes apart from being a waste of scarce resources, impose a heavy burden by way of idle staff and unutilised capacity. Feasibility and project reports exaggerate the benefits from schemes. Over estimates of costs of projects, for which no check is built into the system gives enough margin to the contractors and middlemen, who use this money as grease money to bargain for more lucractive contracts and orders. The contractors have vested interests in approval of higher estimates by delaying execution of projects and pressing for revision of estimates. In selection of projects, comparative study of the available alternatives is also essential. This is not possible in absence of detailed study of the alternatives, for which competent planning personnel having adequate technical knowledge are required. Apart from the Planning Commission and the Planning Bodies of a few State Governments, planning machinery in most of the states is woefully indequate.

The size of the Plan has lately acquired political significance. A large plan is considered to be evidence of Government's commitment to meet the people's needs, prestige of the ruling party and its influence with the Centre. The Chief Ministers, therefore, insist that the annual plans for their State Government should be larger in size than in the preceding years and comparable to the bigger States. This is possible only on the basis of inflated anticiapted receipts, when matching resources cannot be found. The result is that the administration finds itself helpless in implementing such a plan and the plan loses its sanctity. This has been the case of Bihar's plans during the last decade. The situation has become really serious since 1990. It has been difficult to provide for even 50% of the outlay. The plan not only lays down the priorities of expenditure but is also based on the underlying assumption that resources for achieving the targets laid down in the plan would be available when required. If the resources are not there, it implies that large number of schemes will have to be dropped. Since this is seldom done on careful consideration and scrutiny of the projects involved, the over all implementation of the plan becomes distorted as uniform cut is applied indiscriminately on all plan outlays. Establishment cost cannot be pruned. Programmes having higher dosage of central assistance find favour. Capital outlays are postponed, for such postponement, does not hurt anyone. Crucial infrastructure development schemes suffer. Bihar has been the worst example of this.

Centralization is basic to planning. Decision making is concentrated in a central authority. Decentralization proposals are therefore largely corrective measures to make the planning process more realistic, with wider participation but without parting with effective control. The Seventh Plan sought to introduce popular participation through Planning at the District Level and the switch over to District Planning is expected to be achieved throughout the country by the end of the century. The main stumbling block is the lack of exsperienced staff conversant with the planning mechanism at the District and Block Levels. Planning involves compilation of statistics and data relating to resource availability and identification of potential areas and activities of growth. Planning also involves the ability to identify local needs and problems, determine their priorities and formulate feasible schemes for development of the area, on the basis of realistic assessment of resources, within a given time framework. Though there has been much talk of decentralised planning or planning from below; planning up till now has been largely on the basis of directions given from above. In the socialist countries committed to the ideology of planning, the individual units, such as, factories, farms and co-operatives formulate own their plans which are integrated into the plans for different sectors and areas. It is a continous process and the system has been well established.

Popular participation is necessary for effective execution of poverty all eviation programmes, for proper identification of beneficiaries, for prevention of leakages and for mobilising popular support and for ensuring due share to the weak and deprived sections. With delegation of authority to Panchayats, there will be proper surveillance over execution of schemes in the field and useful feedback to Government. As long as execution of beneficiary oriented programmes or even area development programmes is in the hands of the bureaucracy, which is controlled by a central organisation from a distance, and which depends upon intermediaries in the field, full benefits from development programmes would not flow to the poor. The 73rd amendment to the Constitution has established Panchayats as the third ties of democratically constituted executive bodies closest to the people. Direct allocation of funds for J.R.Y. to Panchayats is a bold step and has placed considerable initiative with the Panchayats. Though decentralised bodies like zila Parishads, District Planning and Development Councils, Block Commettees and Panchayats have been created in Bihar, they have little or no executive powers. The real executive power continues to be vested in the State Government, and decentralisation so far has been tantamount to administrative delegation. This lack of confidence in the popularly elected bodies has prevented effective popular participation in the planning process at the district and lower levels and has led to somewhat strained relationship between official and non-officials.

Even the legislators and parliamentarisns view the Panchayats with suspicion as growth of parallel authority. M.P.s and legislators of several states have been given a 'quota' for taking up development schemes in their constituencies. In case of M.P.s this is a substantial amount of Rs. 1 Crore per annum. Choice of such schemes is entirely their discretion. In respect of several other schemes also (i.e. choice of location of hand tubewells) decision is to be taken by legislators. When concerned M.P.s and legislators are fully represented in the District and Block level Planning and Executive bodies, granting them discretionary authority amounts to undermining the status of such elected bodies. Thus the attempt to decentralise planning and delegate planning functions to ground level functionaries has met with limited success. Apart from a few States like West Bengal, Gujrat, Maharashtra and Karnataka it has not taken roots. In Bihar elections to Panchayats have not been held for over two decades.

Distortions in Execution

Huge disbursement by government servants has thrown up temptations to make money. Complaints of corruption are on the increase. Corruption is a serious malady and must be curbed or else the objectives of planning would be defeated. Planning would be reduced to a convenient device for diverting public resources to influential politicians, unscrupulous contractors and corrupt officials. It will create a new class of "Zamindars", in political rulers, bureaucrats and other privileged classes. There are certain schemes which easily lend themselves to abuse. Schemes based on 100% subsidy fail to involve the beneficiaries and the assets are generally retransferred to well to do classes for pecuniary gain. Claims for subsidies are seldom processed in time and the distributing agencies also extract a share.

The bureaucracy suffers from the inherent defect of being extremely parochial in safeguarding its own interests at the cost of the general interests of the public. Thus the bureaucracy continupusly grows in size, for that adds to its importance and increases it bargaining power with government, and also improves the prospects of promotion for its members by enabling them to move up the heirarchy. The great increase in the number of police personnel, and employees in the State government and public sector undertakings since the inception of planning without corresponding improvement in the quality of services to the public calls for rethinking on the role of the bureaucracy. If any organization becomes too big, its major attention is taken by internal squabbles and problems. Political leadership is not fully conversant with the complications of administration and industrial management rendering control over bureaucracy difficult.

Subsidies are becoming increasingly important in the planning process. The effect of subsidy is not confined to its direct effect of encouraging use of the product or conferring benefits to the recipients. It has indirect effects by changing the inter-relationship between prices of different goods and related inputs. If the subsidies encourage production, the purpose is well served. But if the subsidies are given to suppliers of certain commodities, it does not necessarily reach the producers and it fails to act as an incentive to production. Similarly, the procedure for disbursement of subsidy should be simple, so that, the claimants of subsidy are not harassed and they actually receive the benefit. Else, the subsidy will be sopped up by the middlemen with no benefit to producers and no impact on production. Subsidies to the weaker sections are justified for there is no way to motivate such depeived people. Schemes for promoting non-conventional sources of energy are similarly justified for preserving the non-renewable and irretrievable sources of energy. The direct and indirect benefits from subsidies should ordinarily be able to cover up the costs or else the subsidies will result in misallocation of resources, except when it is with the avowed purpose of meeting any pressing social objective. To what extent we should subsidies is, therefore, quite important. It should not be more than what is necessary to ensure reasonable return on investment and enable the infant ventures to stand on its legs.

Entrepreneurs left to themselves would make capital investment decisions on the basis of market prospects and returns expected from the investment. Grants and subsidies to promote industries or other economic activities, however, are not based on pure economic considerations. The various industries and trades can survice and run successfully only if they are economically viable. This should be our ultimate goal. Else the heavy grants and subsidies may create a situation in which it may be profitable to set up an industry rather than run it for public benefit. The high incidence of sick small scale industries in the States is to a large extent the consequence of such a policy. The bureaucratic machinery which prepares the schemes for disbursement of grant and subsidies ensures that it has a tight control over the relaese of funds and it is not averse to exploiting the situation to its own advantage. High rates of subsidy confer advantage and benefits on certain groups which have strong political lobby, bringing more economic strength and power to them. Such unearned income creates vested interest in continuance of such irrational system of subsidies.

The engagement of consultants out even for small and tiny projects on payment of fees, far in excess of the real service being rendered by them, is also the result of a system, which tries to build a facade of feasibility and success on the basis of such expert reports. Except for heavy industries, power projects, major irrigation schemes, mining projects etc. requiring very specialised know-how, feasibility and project reports should be prepared by the executing departments or the public sector undertakings themselves. Responsibility for failure or erroneous reports can be fixed in such cases. This would reduce the incidence of non-viable projects. Shelter of an expert report is a good device to escape responsibility for wrong decisions. The quality of consultancy services avilable in most of the States is also not of requisite standards and it is difficult to establish effective rapport with agencies located outside the State.

Monitoring Plan Implementation. The Need for Proper Appraisal

In monitoring plan schemes there is preponderant stress on expenditure. Further such monitoring will be useful only when the reporting agency is objective and faithful in reporting its performance. Physical targets are seldom adhered to. Allocation of funds takes time, and some times fresh release of funds depends on utilisation of previous allocations. Performance of executing agents too is judged on the basis of expenditure. The result is that exaggerated expenditure reports are given out of fear of incurring displeasure of the government. This also programmes in which lump-sum transfer of funds is involved like subsidies, grants, payments of share capital, equity share etc. Thus, mere stress on expenditure alone may be counter productive. Monitoring of financial outlays overlooks cost and time over-runs, which drastically reduce the output-capital ratio. Monitoring, therefore, should be also with a view to ensure completion of plan schemes within minimum time and cost. This would involve examination of projects in greater detail and identifying the "indicators" of performance, which have to be closely watched. Responsibility should be fixed for slippage of projects and the causes carefully analysed. Similarly the factors responsible for cost over-runs should be identified and timely corrective action should be taken to prevent further erosion of funds.

Targetting is a convenient practice for performance evaluation. But this places exaggerated emphasis on quantitative achievement and overlooks qualitative performance. For irrigation schemes, under the 20- Point Programme, the additional potential which is created is the basis for quantification and monitoring. But this overlooks the fundamental fact, the area that is actually irrigated. Creation of potential are rough estimates, and there is no check against overstimates, for there is a big gap between the potential created and potential utilised. Non-monitoring of actual irrigated area has resulted, in poor management and maintenance of irrigation works that have been constructed at heavy cost. There are strong reasons to believe that irrigated area in Bihar has been decreasing during the last few years. Nearly 3/4th of State Tube Wells in Bihar at present are non-functional and those which are in working order do not irrigate more than 10% of their command area on average. The monitoring of these projects on the basis of additional potential created conceals this failure, and on the contrary may convey a favourable impression.

Similarly on the basis of "number of villages electrified" performance of rural electrication programme can be rated as very good; but if we take into consideration the number of connections provided,i.e. the number of households which have benefited from village electrification, we find that not more than 4 households per village on an average in Bihar have availed electricity. This raises doubts regarding the economic efficiency of the programme. There could be several reasons for this. There may be unauthorised connections which are not officially reported. It may be because supply of power is not regular and dependable. When we focus attention only on the number of villages electrified, we ovelock the main causes and therefore fail to take appropriate corrective measures. The true test of economic progress is the returns, the flow of income, goods and services directly and indirectly from the project. If quantification focusses attention on construction activity, the emphasis shifts to asset creation. Monitoring should ensure better qualitative performance as well.

Monitoring, however, is not an end in itself. It presumes that there is an efficient reporting system which gives details of the progress and other relevant informations on a regular basis so that decision taking is facilitated. Such data-processing system is in a rudimentary stage in most of the States. On the other hand, because of too much emphasis on monitoring and because of multiple supervisory levels, the field functionaries, especially at the block level, complain that they are not able to find enough time for extension work and for implementation and supervision of schemes in their charge.

With the introduction of Twenty Point Programme (TPP), the core programes of the Government are being monitored on a monthly basis from district to the national level. This has activated the implementation machinery, given it a direction and also imparted a national perspective. With T.P.P., processing of reports and communication links have greatly improved. The table at the end of the chapter gives the physical achievements under T.P.P. in Bihar from 1985-1992. The statement highlights the achievements and failures. The major achievements are in respect of S.S.I. units (over 70,000 registration), I.R.D.P., under which nearly 32.5 lakh persons have benefited, drinking water, plantation and Indira Awas, under which 125, 779 dwelling units have been constructed. The failures are in respect of Family Planning Programme, opening of health centres and housing for low income group and economically weak. There are complaints that the registration of S.S.I. units are on paper only as it has had little (in fact employment in manufacturing was lower in 1991 compared to 1981) impact on employment or production; and that the dwellings under Indira Awas Yojna are sub-standard and have remained largely unoccupied. In absence of strong evaluation organization it has not been possible to probe into these complaints and weaknesses of the programmes or sort-out the difficulties being faced in respect of the programmes, where progress has been poor. Timely intervention is necessary for better qualitative performance.

We are in an age in a which production technology and management systems are rapidly changing. Surplus labour and high costs are generally the result of obsolete technology. We are witnessing a shift from labour intensive industries to capital and knowledge intensive industries. The shrinkage in manufacturing jobs is a phenomenon which is clearly discernible in developed economies. The less developed countries as they adopt modern technology will also come up against this problem. To cope with the problem of obsolescence, labour should be encouraged to acquire new skills with changing needs.

In order to ensure economic efficiency, i.e. to ensure proper utilization of scarce resources, proper formulation and appraisal of schemes has to be institutionalised as a check against arbitrary decisions. Formulation and appraisal of plan projects is being done by the Project Appraisal Division of the Planning Commission at the Centre. Some of the State Governments have set up Planning Boards on the pattern of Planning Commission to look after the function. But most of these Planning Boards are working unsatisfactorily. In Bihar it has become defunct. The result is that formulation and appraisal of projects and schemes is very unsatisfactory.

The Planning Commission rightly observes: "Projects are poorly formulated because of inadequate field investigation, lack of adequate data, inadequate analysis or attention to environment and rehabilitation (including land acquisition) aspects. Time and cost over -runs are inherently built into poorly formulated project, which run into problems, many of which could have been foreseen and avoided" (Eighth Plan pp 469). There has been tendency to justify projects on the basis of vague social benefit returns over costs. In view of acute scarcity of resources, it is suicidal to ignore the economic and commercial viability of projects.

The main purpose of appraisal is to provide an objective assessment of the investment proposal. The project is considered viable when it gives reasonable rate of return in financial and economic terms over and above the sacrifices which have to be made in executing it. The tools applied for appraisal are generally cost-benefit analysis, and where this is not possible cost effective analysis. The indicators used for financial/economic analysis include internal rate of return, net present value, unit cost of production, domestic resources cost, etc.

We must have system of evaluation of schemes and projects on a continuous basis, so that, unproductive schemes are identified timely. Evaluation studies at present are for specific purpose and for the important projects only, and the findings are available long after the projects have been completed. Though such studies have much educative value it is too late to adopt corrective measures on the basis of such studies. There must be the authority and option to close unproductive schemes and divert resources to productive schemes. This will prevent idle staff from being retained on schemes that have no utility. Unless we have this flexibility the drag of unproductive schemes will be a major hurdle for future plans. This approach is not possible in respect of projects having long gestation periods, like major irrigation schemes, power projects, etc. We have to be very selective in such cases. The choice in respect of these projects should be made after careful appraisal of project reports, especially in respect of the returns from the investment, its forward and backward linkages and its impact on environment, so that, the risk of taking a wrong decision is minimized. Politics should not dominate the economic issues in such basic sectors involving huge capital investments.

The Executing Agency

The responsibility for executing the plan schemes primarily lies with the I.A.S. and the State Civil Services. The suitability of a generalist administrative service to execute development programmes covering wide variety of programmes is doubted by some. But there is no other service which is as well organized. Both the I.A.S. and the State Service have the advantage of working in field and have intimate knowledge of local conditions, human problems and aspirations of the people. However, their approach to problems is over cautious, and also detached. Because of the hang-over of the past, when bureaucracy happened to be the masters, they have a superior stance and a big brother aproach.

In development programmes the executing agents should act as friends and guardians. The official agency has to be some sort of a 'salesman' for the development programmes. He has to be more venturesome in his approach and also committed to the development programmes. This approach involves departure from the present attitude. The transformation is difficult. Training can make up for lack of knowledge of planning methodology, but cannot bring about change in attitude, in the executing machinery. For this, a suitable system has to be evolved. Unfortunately this has not kept pace with our plans. The Socialist countries have party functionaries for execution of plans and they are dedicated to the programmes. In West Bengal the party functionaries have been playing a major role in implementing government programmes. We talk of associating voluntary organizations and participation by grassroot organizations. But as the situation exists there is no alternative to the administrative services, who by and large enjoy the confidence of the people and who have performed their new role of development quite satisfactorily. However, conditions have to be created to make the administrative services more responsive and accountable in their new role.

It is often questioned whether the administrative organisation, which we have inherited from the British with its conservative attitude of non-involvement and non-interference in people's affairs is helpful to development programmes. Development is not a routine administrative matter to be achieved on the basis of rules, however well formulated. There has to be some measures of flexibility to take care of the changing situation. Administration today is called upon to perform multifarious duties of miscellaneous nature at State, District, Block and Village levels. The casual, routine and ad-hoc handling of sensitive development subjects can lead to unsatisfactory results and cause much frustration. Development Programmes are meant for the people. People's satisfaction, response and reactions and the linkages of the programmes have to be fully considered. The administration of development programmes does not culminate with disbursement of funds. There must be follow up action to check the progress of implementation and also appraisal of performance of the projects so that corrective action is initiated in time for improving effectiveness of programmes and eliminating the constraints and leakages that may be diluting the impact of the programmes. All this requires knowledge of the fundamentals and specialised administration committed to the tasks of development. The approach of general administration is generally rigid, whereas an exploratory approach is required to meet the needs of a developing situation.

Delegation of authority has to be commensurate with the capabilities at different levels of operation, and for this purpose programmes should be devised to develop the capabilities of the functionaries at the lower levels. One of the main shortcomings of present day administration in the country is that it has become top heavy. Those in regular employment in order to secure quick promotions, put pressure for creation of more and more supervisory jobs. In the name of economy creation of jobs at lower levels is shelved. There is proliferation of jobs at the Secretariat and district levels, but there is shortage of staff in the field. The vacancies at the Block level are carried over for years. If we want the delivery services to improve, we must ensure adequate number of properly trained and equipped staff at the Block and Village levels. It is the field staff which constitutes the cutting edge of the administration and delivers the services. It is their capability which largely contributes to the successful implementation of the programmes.

It is our experince that the lower echelons of administration are not motivated by considerations of national interest or public welfare but by their own personal gains. The lethargic, inefficient and dishonest workers are protected by their strong unions and the knowledge that the offenders can be rarely punished makes them indifferent to their work. How to make lower echelons conscious of their crucial role and motivate them to perform their duty faithfully and hoenstly will be a major task for the government in future.

Government has a critical role in development activities. The public sector outlay constitute nearly 54.4% of the total developmental outlay during 1992-97. Total expenditure of the Union and State Governments is nearly 1/3rd of the G.D.P. It is clear that development outlays and pattern of Government expenditure sets the pace for the rest of the economy. It is necessary to maintain high level of performance in the public sector. The choice of intersectoral outlays, choice of technology and the choice of agency for execution of development programmes by the public sector have, therefore, far reaching implications.

Concentration of Development Functions With the Union Government

The Plan has Central component and the States' component. The share of the States and U.T.s in the Eighth Plan outlay is 43%. The total Central assistance for the State's plans aggregating Rs.179983 crores is Rs.78,500 crores or 53.6% of their total outlay. Thus the Central Plan is not only larger in size than the aggregate of all the States' plans, but it has also a strong grip over the states' plans through its control over States' resources. The Central Government is channelising substantial funds through the centrally sponsored schemes to the States on a matching basis. Besides the Centre meets cent per cent cost over the Central sector schemes meant to benefit the States. Thus the Central Government plays a commanding role in allocating the resources, in deciding the priorities and in selecting the schemes. It is extremely difficult for a Central Government howsoever, competent, to formulate a plan and oversee its implementation over a vast country of the size of India with a population of nearly 900 millions and with such diverse conditions and problems. Planning in India so far has been very much centralised. But as the coverage and size of succeeding plans increase, planning is becoming more complicated and it may be advisable for the Central Government to confine itself to subjects of national importance or subjects which are of inter-state importance and leave detailed planning and execution of schemes to the States.

The Planning Commission appointed an Expert Commettee in 1984, to examine the scope and role of centrally sponsored schemes. The findings are significant. The National Development Council had recommended that the total monetary value of centrally sponsored schemes should be limited to between one-seventh and one-sixth of the total Central assistance to the States during the Sixth Plan (1980-85). The total amount of central assistance actually provided to the States was Rs. 17,567 crores or 35% of the total for the States' plans during the Sixth Plan (Rs. 50,132 crores). The total amount transfered to the States, during the same period, under the centrally sponsored schemes was Rs. 9,319 crores, i.e. it was as much as 53% of the total central assistance compared to the recommended ceiling of 15%. In 1985-86 assistance for Central and centrally sponsored plan schemes was Rs. 2,848 crores, i.e. 43.6% of the Central assistance for States and

Union Teritories. In 1986-87 Budget the share was 49.6% the amount being Rs. 3,208 crores. Since most of the schemes are financed on a matching basis, it means that an equal amount has to be provided by the States. This means that out of total central assistance provided to the States, a little more than half the amount has to be spent over centrally sponsored schemes, thereby drastically limiting their discretion to select their own schemes based on local potential and needs. Whereas the more developed and well to do State are able to provide the matching grants and claim central share, the poor States because of constraint of resources are hard pressed to provide the matching share and are generally the losers. The Expert Committee was of the view that relatively backward States like Bihar, Orissa, Rajasthan and Uttar Pradesh have received less per capita assistance through Centrally sponsored schemes than what they would have received had the resources been transferred on the basis of normal Gadgil formula.

During the Sixth Plan (1980-85), Bihar received a total Rs. 1415 crores as normal central assistance and Rs. 592 crores as assistance thruogh the medium of centrally sponsored schemes. Whereas Bihar's share in Central assistance was 8.05% it was only 6.35% in total assistance received through centrally sponsored schemes. The State had to contribute Rs. 466 croes over centrally sponsored schemes, which meant it had only Rs. 949 crores of the central assistance available for its own projects and schemes. The aggregate expenditure over Central sector/Centrally sponsored schemes during the same period was Rs. 1058 crores. In other words more was spent over Central sector and Centrally sponsored schemes than was provided as assistance to the State for execution of schemes taken up on its own initiative.

The central assistance through centrally sponsored schemes for Bihar was projected at Rs. 708 crores out of the total Rs. 2290 crores of central assistance during Seventh Plan (1985-90). In the first two years of plan more than what was projected had come through centrally sponsored schemes. In 1985-86, against the central assistance of Rs. 410.60 crores, Rs.203 crores was received through centrally sponsored schemes and in 1986-87 against the total central assistance of Rs. 447.25 crores. Rs.208 crores was received for centrally sponsored schemes. The proportion of centrally sponsored schemes has been nearly 50% of the central assistance.

The higher weightage to centrally sponsored schemes has far reaching consequences. The Expert Committee referred to some of these in its report. The inter-state distribution of funds is not based on any rational criteria. These schemes are initiated without prior consulation with the State Governments and they are drawn on a uniform basis without taking into consideration the varying conditions of the States. The result of all this is that the States' participation in the formulation of centrally sponsored schemes is partial and ineffective. The centrally sponsored schemes create financial problems for the States, as many of them are formulated during the middle of the plan, and the States find it difficult to arrange funds for such schemes. Though the cost of establishment set up for the centrally sponsored schemes is met from central resources fully or partly during the plan period, the burden of establishment is transferred to the States on completion of the plan. On the other hand, even after the Central Govt. has creased to finance such schemes, very few schemes could be closed by the States. Thus a lasting liability is created for the States.

The Central Government Ministeries take the plea that the centrally sponsored schemes are designed to achieve the national goals and ensure minimum standards in priority areas. It is conveniently ignored that the States' plans are prepared under the guidance and in accordance with the priorities and norms prescribed by the Planning Commission and with its approval. The apprehension, therefore, is mistaken. The argument that due to constraint of resources, the State Government may divert resources from the priority areas and there may be shortfall in achievement of targets and that it is possible to monitor progress of schemes effectively through centrally sponsored schemes is a specious argument. The problem of constraint of resources will be always there. The Central Government Ministeries do not have the personnel to supervise or monitor the progress of each scheme. Such monitoring or supervision at present is being done through periodical meetings at Delhi or at the State Headquarters. Apart from updating information it does not serve much purpose. It would be advisable for the Central Government to abstain from participation in implementation or execution of development programmes, and make the State Governments fully responsible for the execution. As it is, the Central Government does not assume responsibility, their role is only advisory, for the programmes are executed through the State Government functionaries. Involvement of Central Government only detracts from the responsibility of the State Governments. Emphasis is more on release and utilisation of funds. The implementing agency is not much concerned with the impact of the programmes, the attitude being whether the programmes are acceptable or not they have to be implemented and somehow utilise the outlay.

The Central sector schemes should be confined to nationally sensitive areas and sectors, including those which have strategic significance or where scientific survey and research is involved, which is beyond the competence of States. It can also cover projects of inter-state character or schemes designed for the development of backward areas or for weaker sections. Thus the central sector schemes should be an effective tool in correcting regional imbalance in growth and for assisting backward communities to come up to the level of the rest of the country.

Poverty eradication programmes, health and family welfare schemes and agricultural development constitute the bulk of the centrally sponsored schemes. They are State subjects and the States are fully capable of implementing them. They do not require much expertise and can be conveniently handed over to the States. In actual practice the Ministries utilise these schemes as means to extend their authority. But it reduces the State Administration to a subordinate role. This does not help in implementation of programmes. The Central and State Government machineries are equal partners in executing the national plan. The Central Government's task of rendering advice and providing the guidelines are quite onerous. It has the advantage of having national perspective and drawing upon the experience of the whole country. The details of implementation can be better left to the States, because of their proximately and exposure to local conditions and consequently their greater awareness and knowledge of local needs and problems. The senior officers in the States are also drawn from the I.A.S Cadre and there is no reason to doubt their ability or sincerity. Most of the States have strengthened their planning organisation and have acquired considerable experience of planning. They are quite capable of innovative schemes. By making them fully responsible for execution of schemes we would enable them to be selfreliant and also tone up their planning and implentation machineries. If the Centre is convinced that any scheme should be taken up under the central sector, it should fund it cent per cent. Such a stipulation would prevent proliferation of centrally sponsored schemes and would also free the States from any financial obligation. It need not be emphasised that State Government officials should devote maximum time to supervision and implementation of programmes. If too much attention is taken by co-ordination and review meetings, not much attention will be given to execution. This is the natural consequences of having multiple layers of supervision. Emphasis on review, meetings and progress reports is the consequence of decision making authority being remote from field and its inability to give time to details and physically supervise the schemes. With Centre's shadow looming large, the senior officials of the State Government are reduced to the role of post office.

Role of Public Sector Undertaking

Under the Industrial Policy Resolution of 1956, the public sector was responsible for setting up strategic industries, such as steel, coal petroleum, arms and ammunition and heavy industries; and for providing basic public services such as power, rail transport, communications, civil aviation etc. In the case of State Public Enterprises, there has been no dominating guiding philosophy. These are either public utilities, welfare bodies, manufacturing enterprises, trading and marketing organisations, or development corporations set up with the avowed purpose of promoting industrial development. The public enterprises were considered necessary for preventing concentration of economic power and growth of monopolies. At the same time because of their commanding position they are expected to serve as an effective instrument for promoting galitarian society and achieving balanced regional and sectoral development. Compared to government departments, they have greater freedom and flexibility in taking investment decisions. Market forces left to themselves do not take care of the externalities, especially the negative effects, e.g., damage caused by pollution to environment. The State owned enterproses cannot ignore these negative effects.

Most of the major public sector undertakings under the State Governments have no worthwhile planning organisation. Their plans are at the most a statement of the tasks assigned to them by the government. With larger and larger amounts being spent on development the Stakes have gone up. Planning assigns key role to the public sector so that the areas and activities which are neglected by private sector, but are vital to the economy are adequately developed. The public sector is also supposed to generate resources for development and prevent concentration of economic power. The poor performance of Public Sector undertakings is naturally, cause for concern and calls for rethinking on our policy of channelising development programmes mainly through government undertakings. The rate of return on investment in public Sector undertakings on average is just 2%. The Public Sector accounts for 1/4th of the total production and 3/4th of the total employment in the organised sector, and consumes over half of the capital investment.

Lack of motivation and cost consciousness, surplus staff and labour indiscipline are the major drawbacks in government undertakings. Because of the huge investment in public Sector Undertakings, people expect that they will justify their existence through better services and positive contribution of resources for development of the country. Social control of the economy is a laudable objective but it should not impose more than justifiable burden on the people, else the Public Sector Undertakings will turn out to be State protected cartels for cornering privileges for their own empoyees and patrons. Shri Vasant Sathe, Ex-Union Minister for Steel and Energy, while impressing his anguish over the poor performance of Public Sector Undertakings bemoaned, "In the name of socialism all we have achieved is a stagnant, high cost, inefficient, non-competitive irresponsible and unaccountable system of production".

In July, 1991, the New Economic Policy was adopted. It has reduced the number of State controlled industries from 17 to 8. These are industries which have to be kept under Stage control for strategic and security reasons. The emphasis in the New Economic Policy is on liberalisation of the economy through deregulation, greater reliance on market forces, greater competitiveness of manufacturing units and export promotion.

One of the measures envisaged in the N.E.P. is to sell share of Public Undertakings in the capital market. It will serve dual purpose, raise resources for future investment and enable greater private participation. Between 1991-92 to 1995-96 total amount of over Rs.10,000 crores had been disinvested to public sector financial institutions, mutual funds and general public.

Nearly Rs.102,000 crores had been invested in public sector undertakings till 1991. The Central Public Sector Undertakings, 236 in number accounted for 2/3rd of the total investment and the State Public Sector Undertakings 827 in number accounted for the balance. If we deduct the investment made in the State Electricity Boards and the State Road Transport Corporations the amount invested in the remaining State Public Sector Undertakings was only Rs. 5,164 crores. The Central Undertakings are much larger than the State Undertakings. The net profit of central public undertakings in 1990-91, was just 2.3% of the capital invested. If we exclude the petroleum product units, there was no profit. The S.E.Bs made a loss of Rs.4,169 crores and the S.R.T.Cs. lost Rs.362 crores in 1991-92.

In Bihar there were 48 public undertakings on 31. 3. 89. A sum of Rs.3,402 crores had been invested in them. Investment in power units account for Rs. 2,432 crores. The total accumulated loss incurred by them was Rs .639 crores. The losses incurred by units other than B.S.E.B. and B.S.R.T.C. amounted to Rs.224 crores. The State undertakings employed 90,580 persons and the total establishment cost in 1988-89 was Rs. 222 crores. The operational fleet of B.S.R.T.C. was only 750 (1990) and the service rendered by it is was of not much consequence.

The heavy losses being incurred by the Public Undertakings, the poor rate of return on the capital invested, and their dependence on budgetary support, only for future expansion but also for meeting their running expenses has put much strain on State finances. This implies that scare resources are being utilised unproductivly and the investment primarily benefits those who are employed in or associated with public sector undertakings. If the services rendered by public sector undertakings were good and cheap, they would have made positive contribution to social welfare, but the cost of goods and services being provided by the public sector undertakings are high, compared to similar goods produced in the private sector in the domestic market, Data-relating to performance of public enterpeises are incomplete and not available on a regular basis. Accounts are four to five years behind schedule. This lack of transparency makes their proper evaluation difficult. Inspite of the repeated assertions by the Government, that losing public sector undertakings, excepting those in the core sector, would be closed, there has been further proliferation by Government in large industrial ventures through joint ventures.

The public sector undertakings attribute their poor performance to restrictions on their autonomy, their operation as extensions of the administrative departments rather than on sound management principles, decision making being concentrated in top echelons of Government dominated by red tapism; uneconomic decisions regarding investment outlays and marketing of products at unremunerative prices. Much has been written on these issues and there is no point in repeating them.

The over dependence of public sector undertakings on budgetary support naturally implies loss of autonomy. This applies more to the State Undertakings than Central Undertakings. During Sixth Plan 1980-85, 56% of the developmental outlay of Central Public Enterprises was provided by the Central Government and only 28% came from their own internal resources. In case of State enterprises only 3.5% of their developmental outlay was financed by their internal resources. Even if the budgetary support is by way of loans, it is seldom repaid. Cash losses of losing units, too are met by Government to keep the Enterprises running and enable payment of salaries to employees. All this has led to very lax standards of financial management in public sector undertakings. There is no well planned conscious effort on the part of public sector undertakings to reduce their losses or to cut down their expenses. The total budgetary support to central public undertakings during Seventh Plan was Rs.38,515 crores or, nearly 30% of the central plan outlay. Subsidisation of public enterprises by Government may be justified in case of public utilities, but in other cases it implies diversion of resources from more productive uses.

The Ninth Finance Commission classified investments into three categories namely promotional, financial and commercial and have worked out dividends at zero, 3% and 5% respectively. These indicators are recommended as minimum acceptable levels of efficiency. But with market borrowing rate around 17%, the recommended rates are certainly not viable. The servicing cost of loans is estimated at 4%. For efficient running of state undertakings the rate of return on financial enterprises should be atleast 10% and for commercial enterprises 17%.

Management is unable to resist the pressure of vested interests and the coterie that stands to gain from such inefficient operation. Unions keep pressing for enhancement of their benefits. No benefit granted to them in the past, howsoever, illogical or unjustified can be with drawn. The Bihar State Electricity Board Employees' Union claims benefits on part with the State Government employees, but they are not prepared to surrender the benefits which they enjoy in addition to those of the State Government employees. The public sector undertakings are the biggest employers. No political party or leader can afford to antagonise the workers' unions. The unions constitute excellent source for raising funds, for extending one's influence and for building up leadership. The bullying and nagging approach adopted by the unions not only breeds indiscipline and affects operational efficiency but also demoralises the management. No union can compel their fellow workers to observe work discipline or work for higher productivity. Bonus is claimed by even the losing concerns. All principles of sound management lose their relevance and the only way to survive is to compromise. The situation can be tackled, but it requires more than the tinkering, the Government or management is prepared to do.

The workers in organised industry are better paid and enjoy more privileges. They are also well protected against depreciation in value of their real wages, through built in provision for dearness allowance with escalation of prices. The per capita income of an employee in public sector undertaking (State Undertakings are guided by the pay scales in Central Undertakings, some paying even more) is several times more than his counterpart in private sector. The frustration and discouragement as a result of this, to the energetic and enterprising class of workers, who are not employed in organised industries, can be well imagined. It is not surprising that public sector employees resist direct recruitment claiming promotion to all levels and reservation for their own wards. The number of employees at the lower grades is generally in excess (Pairvi and Sifarish play dominant role in public undertakings). If the demands of low grade employees are conceded, entry of suitable, qualified and trained personnel at higher levels, requiring greater technical knowledge and skill would be restricted. Inspite of large number of vacancies in the grade of Assistant Engineers, Junior Engineers, Bihar S.E.B. has not been recruiting Engineers through open competition on regular basis. Adhoc appointments are made in large numbers, which are subsequently regularised. These appointments are largely backdoor appointments to oblige the wards of influential politicians and officers. This is the experience with most of the public sector undertakings. It is necessary that public sector undertakings play the role of model employer, recognising merit and providing equal opportunities to all. This is necessary if they are to function as efficient commercial organisations. If they function as preserves for the privileged, catering primarily to the needs of its employees or those who control it, then its performance is bound to suffer.

Disciplinary action except for proven acts of corruption is seldom taken. Punishment for bad work is rare. Punitive action is vociferously resisted by workers' unions. When there is no fear of punishment for bad work, when incentive bonus is granted as matter of right, it would be really extraordinary to expect improvement in efficiency. When the work culture undergoes such degeneration, infecting even the top ranks, the mode and standards of management also undergo transformation. The whole system operates at substandard level. Frequent changes in top management only give more strength to the workers' Unions as they come to realise that by non-cooperation they can dethrone the "Head of Office" earlier. The employees in public sector undertakings should realise that the public by keeping them in employment, inspite of their heavy losses, are making much sacrifice. They should not exploit people's helplessness too far. They are ultimately accountable to public. The political and trade union leadership should not forget the long-term interests of public welfare and national development in their short-sighted zeal for short-term personal gains.

The coverage of public sector undertaking has become very extensive. Earlier bureaucracy exercised mostly regulatory functions. But, through public sector undertakings, the Government and bureaucracy can now dispense greater favour to their friends and kith and kin. They provide large employment opportunities, they provide lucrative order for supply of materials and contracts for contruction etc. and they have a lot of funds at their disposal, whose expenditure is not subject to strict accounting and audit for scrutiny as in the case of Government.

The policy implications are clear. There should be no more proliferation of public sector undertakings. The existing units should be revamped and strengthened. The public sector enterprises should be located preferably in the core sector and concentrate on building up a strong infrastructure or manufacture of basic and intermediate goods, leaving consumer goods to private sector, as the private sector has more experience and skill in marketing. Bihar's ventures in manufacturing of glazed tiles, ceramics, pottery, television, bicycle, scooter, pharmaceuticals, etc. in public sector have proved to be disastrous. It has resulted in unnecessary drain of public money. The factories deprived people of their valuable agricultural land, by giving them hope of jobs, which did not materialise. It appears surprising that BHEL which manufactures sophisticated and heavy equipments for power plants should diversify its production to include minor electrical gadgets of common use. Production of consumer goods by public sector which does not require much skill, is not necessary. It would only lead to diversion of scare resources from the capital starved basic and intermediate goods sector. To quote Keynes "The important thing for Governments is not to do things which individuals are doing already, and to do them a little better or a little worse; but to do those things which at present are not done at all".

In case of many public sector units, production is planned without adequately investigating the marketability of the products. The result is that the manufacturing units face rough weather from inception and soon become sick. The success of a manufacturing unit ultimately depends on the acceptability of its product in the market and its ability to compete with units manufacturing similar products.

The giant public sector units are both the producers and major consumers of goods. It is not possible for the S.E.Bs and S.R.T.Cs to raise the price of their services without approval of the Government, and Government is generally very wary of raising prices as it hurts the public and makes the Government un-popular. The result is that these services are generally priced lower than the cost prices. In case of Central Government Undertakings, the principal customers are the State Governments, Public Sector Undertakings and Private Industries. Price in the case of central Government Undertakings is raised to cover the higher costs and to cover higher wages, without considering the financial constraints it may create for the State Governments or any regard to public reaction as it is the State Governments, who have to directly face the consequences of public discontent.

The Central Government undertakings have the support and backing of the Central Government in pressing their claims on State enterprises. The State Governments, on the other hand, are reluctant to come out openly in support of their units, for it may sour their relationship with the Central Government. Thus S.E.Bs are pressurised to clear their dues with Coal India Ltd., ignoring their claims of short and sub-standard supplies. On the other hand, S.E.Bs claim for securilty deposit for providing power connection to new mining industries are sought to be waived on the ground that it will create financial constraints for Coal India. Similarly, BHEL is able to dictate terms to the S.E.Bs because of the support it gets from the Central Government. Whereas NTPC is allowed to negotaite with foreign manufacturers/suppliers for installation of its power stations, the same freedom is not available to S.E.Bs.

Most of the public sector undertakings enjoy monopoly rights. They are able to meet their higher cost of production through upward revision of administered prices, as in case of coal, oil, steel, cement, fertilizers, etc. The practise of covering the gap in resources by the Central Government through periodical upward revision of Administered prices has become a regular feature. It is viewed by some as being undemocratic as it is imposed without the approval of the parliament, though is affects the public just as additional imposts by way of taxes etc. Thus, additional resource mobilisation through revision of administered prices was Rs.2,767 crores in 1988-89, compared to only Rs. 548 crores by way of budgetary resources. Such a practise a obviates the necessity of reducing cost through improvement in operational efficiency. The economy is forced to adjust to higher costs with resultant inflationary pressures.

The public sector undertakings like Coal India, SAIL, DVC, etc. though they operate within jurisdiction of the State, they pose as emissaries of the Central Government. They generally give low priority to problems of the region, which are treated as primary concern of the State Government. On the other hand, because of their superior position, they expect concessions which cannot be normally extended. The main area of operation of the two principal Central Government. Undertakings, Coal India and SAIL, is Eastern India. They have as much stake in the growth of this region as the States Governments of this region. Only through the growth and prosserity of the region, which they serve and in which their main operations are carried, their real objective of regional development and balanced growth can be attained.

Privatisation of Government ventures is not the remedy for losses being incurred by public sector undertakings, as is being sought under the garb of joint ventures or assisted industries programmes. The private sector seldom utilises its own capital for investment and it has always relied on borrowed capital from financial institutions. Financial constraint in the past has acted as a spur to private sector to make the best use of the available resources. It has compelled the private sector to be enterprising and more venturesome in exploring the market and in achieving higher productivity. In joint ventures, Government undertakes to share the capital investments and also provides suitable land sites free of cost besides providing a secured market. The collaboration does not necessarily ensure the pudence of private management. The guarantee of Government funds offers security, and lax control leads to reckless and avoidable expenditure. Bihar's experience with joint sector undertakings has not been very happy. The management press for more support and concessions as their trouble deepens. Sick industries which are not economically viable cannot be revived. The pressure of revival through takeover by Government may be only a covert attempt by the private investors to salvage their own capital invested in the industry. In this they find support of the employees's unions also, for the Government take-over implies protection of their jobs.

To summarise public sector has a crucial role in promoting industrialisation and preventing concentration of economic power. If they are not able to give sufficient return on the investments made in them, it is the public who have to suffer ultimately in meeting the losses. The public sector should confine its operation to infrastructure building activities and in providing the basic and intermediate goods and services, which require heavy capital investment and expensive thechnology. It should abstain from competing with private sector production and marketing of consumer goods. Though Government should help private sector in mobilising financial resources for viable projects. It should not get involved to such an extent as to diminish their accountability or business acumen.

Table. 12.1. Physical Achievekent Under Different Items of 20-Point Programme in Bihar. Target and Achievement During VIIth Plan (1985-90) & for 1990-91 & 1991-92

Point	Items	Units	1985-90		1990-91		1991-92	
			Target	Achievement	Target	Achivement	Target	Achievement
	2	3	4	5	6	7	8	9
01A	I.R.D.P.	NOS.	2364753	2508937	350469	415814	331578	324884
01B	N.R.E.P	LAKH MAN		1588.27				
	R.L.E.G.P.	DO		1239.30				
	JAWAHAR ROJGAR YOJNA	DO		907.31	1125.89	1130.05	923.20	803.51
01C	S.S.I. UNITS SETUP	NOS.	45100	52633	9942	12162	9942	6859
05A	DISTRIBUTION OF SURPLUS LAND.	ACRES	85930	65546	9000	12395	8000	11153
06	BOUNDED LABOUR REHABILATION.	NOS.	1889	1954	27	27	31	30
07A	DRINKING WATER SOLVED (VLG)	NOS.	27174	25696	7000	7091	6007	1404
08A	COMMUNITY HEALTH CENTRE TO BE OPENED.	NOS.	40	54	10	10	–	NIL
08B	PRIMARY HEALTH CENTRE TO BE OPENED	NOS.	1452	1000	191	493	–	NIL
08C	HEALTH SUB CENTRE TO BE OPENED.	NOS.	6550	5695	750	0	–	NIL
08D	IMMUN. OF CHILDREN (DPT. POLIO, BCG)	NOS.	7591600	6825901	2731236	2201869	2758526	114191

	2	3	4	5	6	7	8	9
09A	F.P. STERLISATION	NOS.	2857000	2059773	55000	257951	500000	147310
09B	E.UIVALEN TO STERILISATION	NOS.	825894	501941	184917	58557	162778	33159
09C	I.C.D.S. BLOCKS (COMULTIVE)	NOS.	150	142	181	172	211	211
09D	ANGANBAIDS (COMULTNE	NOS.	15138	15620	18845	14401	22977	18122
11A	SC. FAMILIES ASSISTED	NOS.	1372415	1361525	250000	237322	300000	175501
11B	ST. FAMILIES ASSISTED	NOS.	619050	724615	125000	122768	115000	122323
14A	HOUSE SITES ALLOTTED	NOS.	119000	125007	17299	16381	17289	20550
14B	CONSTRUCTION ASSISTANCE PROVIDED	NOS.	-	-	-	-	-	-
14C	INDIRA AWAS YOJNA	NOS.	47552	84074	16346	21155	16346	20550
14D	EWS HOUSES PROVIDED	NOS.	50000	51037	483	427	660	24
14E	LIG. HOUSES	NOS.	1739	2509	886	478	1300	NIL
15	SLUM IMPROVEMENT	NOS.	209800	193923	25000	25001	25000	41873
16	TREE PLANTATION TO BE COVERED.	NOS. HECT.	14000	13243	2150	1170	700	837
18	FAIR PRICE SHOPES OPENED	NOS.	300	1206	150	419	126	331
19 A	VILLAGES ELECTRIFIED	NOS.	14642	12798	2500	528	450	517
19 B	PUMPSETS ENERGISED	NOS.	82000	58219	10000	5514	5000	2712
19 C	IMPROVED CHHULAHAS	NOS.	260000	303378	120000	75391	120000	136562
18 D	BIO-GAS PLANTS INSTALED.	NOS.	27800	27438	5000	3189	4000	417

SOURCE: (DEPARTMENT OF INSTITUTIONAL FINANCE & PROGRAMME IMPLEMENTATION- BIHAR)

13

Evolving the Strategy for Development

Development is associated with change for the better. It is a dynamic concept. The strategy will differ with the situation. In 1950s, the absence of strong infrastructure to sustain the development process, compelled us to give greater emphasis to heavy industries (The Mahalanobis Model). But with international pressure for relaxation of controls and globalisation of economy, we have to rely on market forces and promote competitiveness. It implies more forcibly than ever before that we develop the human skills and aim at optimal utilisation of available resources.

Planning as a Strategy for Growth and Development

Planning is perceived in different ways by people belonging to different specialisations and vocations. Thus statisticians and econometricians view it primarily as an exercise correlating factors of production to achieve the desired objectives; the capital-output ratio and the input-output tables become the basic tools for analysing the growth process. For the economists it is essentially deciding the priorities correctly and finding resources to achieve the objectives. For the politicians and public servants it assumes the task of building up an organisation to have better control over the working of the economy and extending the sphere of public expenditure. Whereas for the private entrepreneurs it is exploring possibilities for extracting greater profit; and for the individual households it is primarily an exercise in thriftiness. The free market capitalist economy has faith in an invisible hand which guides individual actions towards general welfare. The centralised planned economy does not see such a linkage. Public expenditure has to be strictly controleed for greater welfare. The critical factor is, therefore, how wisely this control is exercised by political leadership.

Planning for development in the Less-Developed Countries also aims at evenly distributing the benefits of development amongst different sections and regions of the country. The Socialistic Pattern of Society, and with it reduction in the distribution of income and wealth has come to be accepted as a major goal of development. Development by itself, does not ensure that the benefits of development programmes would be evenly shared or would even percolate to the poorest. The benefits accure to those areas where the development projects are located; and benefits those who are either employed on those projects or who are linked with those projects. Due to the immensity of the task and scarcity of resources, it is not possible to launch a comprehensive plan for development, catering to the needs of all parts of the country and to protect the interests of all sections of the population. The well-to-do and influential sections in the society, who can seize the opportunities for making money offered by the development programmes are naturally the major beneficiaries. The propertied classes can take advantage of higher technical education for specialised jobs. The educated, because of greater skill and better knowledge and understanding stand to benefit more from development programmes. No one will grudge this, if it was the result of the enterprise and energy of the beneficiaries, but if it is due to the inequities of the system, that is patronage or favoured treatment accorded to the chosen few, it will naturally cause resentment. The Scheduled Castes and Scheduled Tribes enjoy constitutional protection and thereby enjoy advantages over others, but there are also large number of people who are weak and deprived and also deserve protection of the Government.

Similarly, neglect of some areas because of their inability to bring pressure on the appropriate centres of authority will perpetuate undeveloped backward regions. It is well known that urban areas have benefited more from development than rural areas and that development tends to be concentrated around the metropolitan cities. On the other hand, backward regions have continued to suffer, and over a period the regional disparities have got accentuated. Bihar's slide down the path of development compared to the rest of the country demonstrates this trind. Hill areas and deserts, because of their poor resource endowments are being accorded special assistance. But there are areas which inspite of their rich potential are poorly developed. They are also heavily populated and as such deserve more attention. The return to investment in such areas is also likely to be much more.

Over emphasis on some sectors and neglect of others may also create imbalances. Thus, between 1970-71 to 1984-85, production in the primary sector had increased by only 30%, compared to 75% growth in the secondary sector, 105% in community and personnel services. In absolute terms also the increase in plan outlay over community and personnel services was more than the increase in agriculture, though the number of those engaged in the above services is only a small fraction of those obtaining livelihood from agriculture. One may derive satisfaction from the fact that such a structural shift in favour of the services sector is a sign of development, but it only highlights the distortion in the system and the poor plight of those engaged in agriculture. Within the agricultural sector also, the benefits have gone largely to the land owners. The agricultural labourers have benefited little.

The quantitative indices of development adopted by statisticians such as Gross National Product and per capita G.N.P. conceal the real State of well being. The qualitative aspects, such as, extent of literacy, coverage of health services, longevity of life, state of environment and security to life and property contribute considerably to well being but are not capable of being quantified. Many African countries have higher per capita G.N.P. than India but are far behind on the basis of the above socio-economic indicators, and they cannot be described as more developed than India. Other things remaining the same, a country with higher literacy, better health services, cleaner environment and less incidence of poverty than others is better off than others. Besides, pursuit of development aimed at only increasing production and ignoring the qualitative aspects may prove to be self defeating, as it may lead to social distress and involve far greater investment at a later date to rectify the ill-effects.

A growth rate of 1% or less per annum in per capita income will not have visible impact during the lifetime of an individual. Such a growth rate will hardly satisfy the people. An economy with zero-growth rate or growth rate below 0.5% per annum is almost stagnant. There are areas which have shown negative growth rate. A backaward region may be described as one whose growth rate is either negative or stagnant or whose growth is sluggish and has lagged far behind the rest of the Country. We do not have sufficient data about growth rates of different regions and sub-regions constituting a State, but the existence of such stagnant and backward regions is a serious problem and constitutes a major hurdle in the over-all growth of the country. Only through planning at the regional or ground levels, we can hope to tackle the problems of such backward areas effectively.

Obviously low level of investment cannot catapult an economy into the higher orbits of development. It is generally suggested that adequate level of investment provides the solution to the problems of low production and poverty. Amount of investment is no doubt important but far more important is how this money is spent, this includes not only the activities on which the money is spent but also the manner in which the money is spent. Planning has, therefore, been rightly described as prudent allocation of resources to achieve the desired objectives. On the face of it, it may appear to be a truism but in practice it calls for a very clear understanding of the needs and problems, the priorities, behaviour of the economy and a firm commitment to the objectives. Our priority must reflect the aspirations of the people correctly. We cannot afford to fritter away scarce resources cver programmes which are not productive and beneficial to the people. Apart from infructuous expenditure it builds up pressures within the economiy to divert funds to the 'soft avenues' where the emphasis is on expenditure rather than on results. These include disbursement of loans, grants and subsidies on programmes, more for political gains than for fulfilment of economic objectives. It must be realized that resources are very scarce in a poor country and we are pressed for time also. We cannot afford to take things easy as our problems accentuate with time.

Planning has long term objectives. We have to deal with problems that have to be tackled over a projected period. Most of the programmes have a gestation period. It is for this reason that socialist countries are better organised for 'planning'. In socialist countries there is firm commitment to objectives and little fear of incurring unpopularity. The strong governments can tackle the vested interests more effectively.

Planning has to operate within given parameters. There are settled objectives which it must fulfil. It has to be guided by certain principles and 'tests' for selection of programmes and projects. Else the system would come to be dominated by pressure lobbies there will be avbitrary decisions and investment will not have the desired effect. We should not be too rigid in approach, but in the name of flexibility we should not bend the system so much that disciplined action becomes impossible. Planning is essentially enforcement of discipline.

Planning thus involves commitment to adhere to the priorities that are decided. There is the genuine risk of planning being converted into a tool for serving the ends and whims of those who are in power, for enhancing their economic strength, or simply for their glorification, rather than catering to the basic needs of the common man, that is providing them with clothing, food and shelter. Planning requires that we allocate the resources on the priority items and prevent its diversion to unproductive items, which give more profit to middlemen, and allows unnecessary expansion of bureaucracy and through all this adds to the clout of those who wield power. The distinct identity of plan schemes as capital or assets creation programmes has to be preserved. The pressure to do away with the distinction between plan and non-plan schemes is only a disguised attempt to relax control over expenditure. The reluctance of Bihar Govenment to control non-plan expenditure, even though it reduced the ability of the government to invest over essential capital outlay necessary for development, confirms our worst apprehensions.

If the self-seekers combine to bend the system to subserve their own needs, the very objectives of planning are at stake. In such an eventuality, planning becomes a sham exercise. The impressive paraphernalia and procedures evolved for planning become non-functional because of the large scale leakages and outlays do not give the expected results. Though financial targets are achieved, physical achievements are not commensurate with the expenditure that is incurred. The wasteful expenditure only adds to the inflationary pressure and to the hardship of the common man. The benefits are cornered by the influential sectons. The bureaucracy is a willing partner for it too finds an opportunity to aggrandise itself.

The Special Nature of Development Problems

Development, as has been stated earlier, involves change for the better. This means that there must be an innovative approach and willingness to venture with new technology and programmes. The technological improvement induces change not only by enhancing the production capacity, but also in the attitudes and life-style of people. People must have the 'urge' to better their lives through acquisition of property and income, which will give them better command over goods and services which they desire. This will act as a strong motive for hard and careful work. The psychological conditions necessary for modernisation, of which industrialisation is an important part, are individualism, competitive spirit, strong work ethics and rationalism. Our educational system should inculate these values. The invention of the printing press, steam engine, electricity, jet plane, micro-chips, brought about revolutionary changes in the production processes and gave big thrust to development. Thus apprehensions of stagnation have been belied by human ingenuity, which has thrown open new and unexplored vistas for technological advance and human welfare. When we say this we have material welfare in mind, for attaining materials welfare has become the prime objective of economic development. Similarly, advances in medical sciences have enabled people to enjoy life more than before. The developing countries cannot afford investment in expensive research to evolve new technologies. But the latest technology evolved by the developed countries does find its way to the developing countries, though after some time lag. To take advantage of the changes, we must be receptive and open to such modernising influences, otherwise we may be faced with serious drag on development schemes because of technological obsolescence. The criteria for choice of programmes/projects for development should be net increase in welfare of the population. There should be careful weighing of the benefits and sacrifices that have to be made in accepting a project. A programme for development cannot be judged in isolation, i.e. on the basis of simple cost-benefit analysis.

Protecting the Environment and Displaced

Though the positive aspects of change are taken into account in cost-benefit analysis, not much weightage is given to the negative aspects, especially the damage caused to environment and the losses inflicted on inhabitants of the area. Opening of factories or starting of mining operations results in displacement of local inhabitants and also deprivation of their means of livelihood. It is necesssary that we compensate such losses, or else the negative effects may snowball into major resisting force. Coal India has acquired vast areas in Chotanagpur under the Coal Area Bearings Act. The compensation is a pittance, and the demand for jobs by the displaced is much more than what can be absorbed. The gigantic problem of rehabilitation lingers on for years causing much resentment among the displaced persons.

The pollution by way of industrial waste, noise and influx of population introduces health hazards for which adequate protective measures are hardly taken. One of the duties assigned to D.V.C. (Damodar Valley Corporation) is to prevent pollution of any water source under its control and to prevent discharge into such water of affluents which are harmful to public health or agrarian life. But there is heavy pollution of River Damodar, principal source of drinking water in the areas fed by it, by dumping huge quantities of coal-ash by the Thermal Power Stations at Bokaro in the river. The ash emitted by the Thermal Power Stations renders vast agricultural area adjoining the Power Stations unfit for cultivation. Similarly, the discharge of toxic waste products by the Refinery at Barauni in the Ganga, and by the Bata's Tannery and McDowell's Distillery at Hathidah, a few miles upstream, has led to large scale destruction of fish and loss of income to the large community of fishermen in the area. These unforeseen environmental and ecological damages are generally ignored in the choice of schemes for development. What value should be attached to beautiful and healthy surroundings; or to education and eliminataion of illiteracy; or to health measures to prevent disease for better health and capacity for work and output and greater longevity of life; or to elimination of poverty and greater economic equality for greater social harmony; are all relevant issues which form an integral part of the planning process. Their value cannot be ascertained in quantitative terms. Planning for development thus implies that we take a comprehensive view of proposals, as opposed to taking a narrow and sectarian view. It involves consideration not only of the direct benefits and costs but also of the indirect social (including the invisible) benefits and costs. It requires knowledge and understanding as well as appreciation of public needs and problems. This is possible only with intimate knowledge of the region, its people and the public programmes.

The impact on environment of development schemes is difficult to assess in monetary terms, but has far reaching effects on the quality of life as well as productivity. Earlier environmental issues did not bother us, but with more and more industrialization, rapid urbanisation and increasing use of fuel consuming vehicles, the ill effects of atmospheric and water pollution are posing serious threat to health and cannot be ignored. Pure air, fresh and safe water and abundance of green forest are the most vital and life sustaining resources of the earth. There are no incentives to use them sparingly as people have free access to them. There is a tendency to over use and despoil them. The destruction of forests has meant extinction of many rare species of birds, animals and plants, apart from the adverse efects on climate and the resultant soil erosion, leading to loss of soil and fertility. Pollution of water has direct effect on the health of users apart from its lethal effect on aquatic life. The pollution of Ganges has led to the multimillion Ganga action plan to cleanse the river. Prevention of pollution and protection of environment involve heavy cost and will certainly impose an additional and sometimes heavy burden on the developing countries. In such situation educative measures for protecting the environment become important. People have to be made conscious of the need to preserve their environment. Preventive measures for protecting the environment have to be built into development projects as far as possible.

Development involves structural adjustment to meet the changing situation. This not only requires a venturesome, innovative and enterprising government, but also a population which is receptive to change Ill-informed and ignorant masses are easily gullible and can be mobilised to resist even well conceived and well meaning programmes for development as has happened in the case of Koel Karo Hydro Electric Project in South Chotanagpur. This Hydro Electric Project is an excellent project of great potential and would go a long way in meeting the acute power shortage in the region and thereby help in the industrial development of Chotanagpur. Work on the project has not been possible due to organised resistance by Adivasi leaders and all efforts during the last decade to convince the people of the merits of the project has fallen on deaf ears. This highlights the fact that development does not mean the same thing to all people. It may benefit some and create disadvantage for others. It is necessary that the losers from development projects are compensated for the disadvantages they suffer, by the gainers from the projects. Else, it may create an imbalance, with the influential sections, pocketing all the advantages and becoming richer in the process, with all the disadvantages being loaded on to the weaker sections. If the project cost is financed by transferring the burden to the general public, the beneficiaries form the project will be left with windfall gains. Thus, because of execution of development project, there is tremendous appreciation in value of land in the vicinity of the project, there is also a boom in construction activities, building of more roads, houses, contracts for supply of materials in greater quantities, and hiring of transport agents for moving these goods. The middlemen engaged in these trades, therefore, obtain what may be described as unearned profit. It would be fair and quite appropriate to tax such gainers. Due to the growing political influence of this class of middlemen, they are not subjected to additional taxation. On the other hand, the hardships and losses suffered by the weaker section continue to increase and they are hardly compensated. It should be similarly possible, to realise compensation from those who damage the environment. A fair and just society cannot ignore this redistributive aspects of development process. The development programmes should contribute to reduction in poverty. It should not enable privileged people to grow rich, purely due to fortuitous circumstances, at the cost of the general public.

Approach

The factors influencing growth and development, can be

identified mainly as human skill, capital investment, technological efficiency and social response. Technical and professional institutions, which can impart quality education and also provide training in activities relevant for the growing sectors can fill up the gaps in human skills required for development. Capital investment depends upon the available physical (natural) resources, savings of the community, investment opportunities, cost of raising resources and the returns from investment. Technological efficiency reflects the community's attainments in respect of scientific and technological knowledge of production processes as well as the management skill of the community in organising production activities. It is generally assumed that the society would respond to development efforts. But the degree and the manner in which different communities respond to development efforts varies very much. Social response, i.e. motivations of the population is thus an important factor. Society's homogeneity, adhesiveness its discipline and resilience in responding to changing and new situations is crucial. This would include society's ability to throw up leaders, persons who can face challenges and take bold decisions, a strong public opinion to safeguard public interest and the ability to identify and accept programmes which are of greater benefit to common welfare.

Of the factors mentioned above, only capital investment and technological efficiency are such, which can be so to say arranged. Low rate of interests, foreign aid on concessional terms as well as imported technical know-how have expedited growth of several developing countries which have opened up their economy. But for development to take place on a sustained basis, we must ensure a system that motivates the people to put forth their best effort. Higher savings for sustaining the tempo of growth has to be generated internally through greater productivity and restriction on consumption. Labour should be disciplined and committed to work. They should be reasonable in their demands, otherwise it will be difficulat to generate the surplus for future development activities. The value of these basic human values should not be understimated. If people become self reliant, are conscious of their duty and fair in their dealings with fellow beings, there would be immediate upsurge of development.

There is no common strategy for development. There are no

readymade prescriptions to the different problems of development. Our strategy has to be based on study and analysis of the nature of the problems that have to be tackled, the abstacles that hinder production activities and the objectives which we set for development. The programmes, therefore, would depend on the resource endowments (both materials and human), the level of infrastructure development, the needs of the people and the special features of the area which are holding back growth. The complexities of the task and the paucity of resources, naturally calls for prioritization. It is not a sound approach to provide a bit for everything and spread resources thinly. We must be able to identify the production activities in which the region has distinet comparative advantage over others and provide incentives for maximising production. With 162 lakh cattle and 46 lakh buffaloes, Bihar has nearly 10% of the bovine population in the country. But this immense potential for diary is only partly utilized. The extensive Chaurs and Mans in north Bihar are ideal fisheries and provide potential for agua-culture. Only 3% of the cropped area in the State is covered by horticultural crops. The climate and soil of the State is ideally suited for growth of mango, litchi, betel, guava, pine-apple, water melon, etc. These are commercially profitable and can substantially add to the income of farmers. Very little has been done to develop agro-products and food processing industries. Our biggest advantage lies in the availability of cheap and abundant human labour. Our biggest achievements will flow from mobilisation of this idle man power and enlisting their voluntary support in building up cummunity assets. This can be had only through mutual trust and understanding at the lowest level.

Proper execution of the plan is as important as its formulation. A plan should not be only well conceived but capable of efficent execution as well. The programmes should be acceptable to the people and capable of being executed with available human, material and other procurable resources. We require a competent organisation to translate policies into action as well as appropriate institutions for involving people and harnessing their energies to the task of development. The common man is central to the plan, and unless he is involved; the end result may not be satisactory. The executing agency has, therefore, a very crucial role. It should not only understand and appreciate the objectives and the spirit of the plan but it should also actively promote the plan by educating the people about the new schemes and by enlisting people's participation for successful implementation of the plan. A high degree of commitment therefore, is required from the executing machinery.

The Option

The identification of the process of development with statistical indices such as raising the level of savings to about 20% of the G.D.P., occupational shift from agriculture to industry etc., are over simplifications which may not apply in practice. In India the rate of savings has been above 20% for the last decade but growth rate has not picked up. Our stage of take off has been very prolonged. Inefficient use of resources has neutralised the effect of higher savings. How we spend money is more important than how much money is spent. We fail to realise this obvious truth when we plan for development.

The conflicts in development strategy are quite marked. Higher growth rate is said to be in conflict with reduction in disparities of incomes, though there is a growing view that contrary to common impression, more equal distribution of income helps development by generating higher savings. With income concentrated in the hands of a small section of population, there would be emphasis on production of luxury aticles which are required for elite consumption, e.g., motor cars, air-conditioners etc., but with income more evenly distributed there would be greater stress on producing articles of mass consumption.

For achieving higher growth rates, consumption has to be restricted. High growth rate based on industrialisation requires high degree of mechanisation, and capital intensification implies fewer jobs and less resources for social services. On athe other hand, larger allocation for social services and human resources development would mean less resources for building up physical assets and lower growth rate in the immediate future.

Self sufficiency is given high priority by the erstwhile colonies. The fear of foreign domination has led them to encourage import substitution. This had often led to sheltering of high cost industries and lower growth rate, but the sacrifice is considered worthwhile because of the freedom it confers to pursue independent economic policies.

We generally judge development in quantitative terms, viz. increase in per capita income. Per capita income is a notional figure which gives the average of all incomes. It does not give us any idea of the distribution of income or incidence of poverty. It is the elimination of poverty and hunger, which is our biggest challenge. Our obsession with level of per capita income is the result or our concern with 'status' which is conferred by higher per capita income in all comparisons of well being.

The existence of illiteracy, squalor and disease, insecurity to life and property, unhealthy surroundings due to pollution of environment are also important factors which affect the well being of the population. Other things remaining the same, people with higher longevity of life and higher literacy are certainnly better off. People who enjoy better protction of life and property feel more sucure and live peacefully and enjoy more than those who live under constant threat of being deprived of their possessions. The rural poor who live in cleaner surroundings in their own homes are better off than the urban poor, who have been separated from their families and live on the pavements or in congested and filthy shanties.

Development cannot ignore the aforementioned basic issues. How do we reconcile these conflicting objectives? A possible solution would be to assign suitable weights to different objectives. This involves value judgements and requires assignment of values to different states of well being, which are neither quantifiable or comparable. In the circumstances, per capita income becomes the only rough and ready means to measure growth, and as explained above it gives much weightage to human possessions which have a money-value. The policy implication is that though we may strive for improvement of material well being of the population, we should also actively promote the creation of the other conditions that have a positive contribution on the real well being of the population.

Existence of wide-spread poverty and hunger, largescale unemployment, illiteracy and disease is an affront to a modern welfare state, and need to be tackled on an urgent and top priority basis. But when population is also growing at a rapidly pace, these problems are magnified and become intractable. We have to keep population under control if development is to have its desired impact.

Allocation of Resources

In allocating resources we rarely try to achieve the ideal situation. Since we have several objectives in view and there are non-economic considerations also, we only try to make a convenient compromise. The need to accommodate various considerations becomes an excuse for not adhering to any criteria in allocation of resources. From the purely economic point of view, resources should be invested in those sectors where the incremental output capital ratio (the umber of units of output which can be obtained by investment of an additional unit of capita) is the highest. Capital is more scarce in an underdeveloped and backward economy and requires to be carefully rationed. We should wind up non-productive schemes and divert funds to productive schemes, Without such flexibility and resilience we would be unable to attain higher productivity. Generally speaking, we should try to invest in those projects or programmes where the margin of benefits over costs is largest. The various inputs have alternative uses and the use which gives the maximum benefit to the community is most advantageous.

The capital output ratio criteria does not take into account the element of time. The scarcity of consumer goods and low consumption levels makes it necessary that projects/programmes of shorter gestation periods are preferred. The capital output ratio also does not take into account the indirect and invisible benefits or costs of a project. Thus the capital output ratio ignores the damage to environment through pollution of air, rivers and streams due to discharge of toxic effluents by industries, which pose serious health hazard to the population. Similarly feelling of trees may bring in revenue, but large scale destruction may adversely affect the econogical balance. The capital outpit ratio criterion would assign low priority to roads, education, supply of clean drinking water etc., but these have significant influence on development. Low priority will be also assigned to human resources development. The impact of human resources development programme is realized after considerable time lag and the benefits are not directly correlated to investments. The social product criteria takes into account the indirect effects and is based on an assessment of the project's direct, indirect and secondaary consequences, which are reckoned on the basis of 'shadow' or 'accounting' prices which are supposed to reflect the true value of the factors of production. Thus investment projects should be chosen not on the basis of partial productivity analysis dictated by individual industrial capital/output ratio but also in the context of an overall development programme that takes account of external economies, indirect repercussions and long term objectives.

Since finding jobs for the large number of unemployed and alleviation of poverty is also a major objective, the capital-labour ratio also assumes significance. Labour intensive methods are to be preferred over capital intensive methods. It is in this context that we talk of appropriate technology. A technology which is appropriate in a capital rich developed country with near full employment may be inappropriate for a capital scarce less developed country with large scale unemployment. Apart from shortage of capital, the less developed contries are also faced with shortage of skilled labour and managerial ability to run big enterprises using upto-date sophisticated technology. Opting for appropriate technology, however, should not imply adoption of obsolete or inefficient technology.

There are other considerations which are also relevant in deciding how resources can be best allocated. Investment should be preferably in projects which make use of indigenous resources and raw materials that are produced locally. For the country as a whole, this implies that we should prefer technologies requiring skills which can be easily adopted by the local labour. We should prefer small scale units, if possible, without reducing efficiency very much, for they are easier to manage and can be dispersed geographically.

Because of shortage of energy, energy saving technology is to be preferred. In India, we consume twice as much electrical power to produce a ton of steel than in the Western European Countries. Cement and paper industries in India are also high energy consumers. Such obsolete and inefficient technology apart from reducing our international competitiveness, increases the cost of goods and is a burden to the population. We should encourage industries that produce goods for mass consumption in preference to industries producing luxuries. The former will help to alleviate poverty. The latter by encouraging conspicuous consumption will divert capital for production of non-essentials and will have the effect of eroding savings.

High budgetary deficit, is a result of reckless public spending; adverse balance of payments is due to indigenous goods being non-competitive in international markets; negative rate of interest is due to galloping inflation exceeding the market rate of interest. These are all distress singles. There is a limit to taxation, as high taxes adversely affect production. Taxes can have unhealthy side effects and if they are very high, people try to evade it. Spending spree necessarily creates demand for foreign exchange and import controls can only provide temporary relief. Negative rates of interest results in flight of deposits from banks, making inflation even more unmanageable. The above dilemma describes the difficult and helpless situation in which many developing countries have landed themselves as a result of short sighted and bad economic management. The rehabilitation process, through strict monetary control, foreign borrowing and strict control over public expenditure has been always arduous. It is therefore, necassary to be alert and promote competitiveness, by creating favourable market conditions.

Needless to say a development plan must secure intra as well as inter-sectoral balances. Otherwise imbalances, such as excess capacity, glut of certain products or serious shortages of essential commodities may appear, which may obstruct growth. For example, if we provide for large additions in the number of deep tubewels without assuring availability of power, the tubewells may remain idle. If we plan for larger coverage of high yielding varieties and do not arrange for additional supply of fertilizers in the same proportion, not only our plan for higher agricultural production will be frustrated, but there will be black market in fertilizers, resulting in higher cost of production. Similarly if the number of motor vehicles go on increasing rapidly (the number of vehicles in the country is increasing currently at the rate of one lakh per annum), and we do not plan for better paving and widening of roads, we would be only adding to the operational cost of vehicles and congestion of traffic with its attendant problems. Mutually supporting investment in different sectors of production will help to create demand for each other's products and sustain the growth process. Public outlay has the effect of increasing wage income and consequently demand for goods and services on which wages are spent, mainly food articles, clothes etc. A mismatch between financial outlay and wage goods will therefore result in inflationary pressure which is an indication of the development process becoming distorted.

Planning is thus a complicated exercise. We require a lot of information. The planning organisation in many of the States is not adequately equipped to perform these tasks compentently. The input-output tables have not been worked out for different branches of production at the State level. The estimates of capital output ratios are rough estimates and based on presumptions. There have been few evaluation studies to verify these estimates. In actual practice, therefore, the allocation decisions are taken on the basis of pre-conceived notions about utility or profitability of different production activities. In actual practise, political consideration to give weightage to certain communities or professions for political support also assert a dominant influence in selection and location of schemes. We should be concerned not only with overt acts of corruption for which punitive action can be taken under the law but also with the growing incidence of deliberate acts of public representatives for personal advantage, involving wasteful expenditure of public money in contravention of basic principles. Wrong choice and location of schemes, non-realisation of public dues, conferment of benefits without realization of cost, etc. impose a heavy burden on the economy. The only check against such arbitrary conduct is a strong and educated public opinion. If the people who benefit from development projects do not compensate those who make the sacrifces, development would become a process of exploitation. People are justified in asking for development projects, but they would be exploiting the situation if they put pressure for more and more concessions in the name of displacement. When they go to the extreme of demanding exclusion of others from the benefits of the projects, employment, etc., they subvert the programme into one of local gain at the cost of public welfare. This domestication of development projects is a serious detriment to planned development.

It should be realised that decisions are made in real world and not in tae world of theoretical abstraction. Ignoring the real issues will only make the advice of the economist irrelevent. The economist should attempt to offer the decision maker a clear, objective analysis of the implications of alternative policies from the economic point of view, even though political factors are involved. Thus when the social value of a good exceeds its efficiency value, the good is described a merit good and preference can be given to it. For example we place higher social value on self dependence and with this objective give premium to some economic activities. Programmes meant to enhance the military strength, even though not justified on economic considerations have to be accomodated for strategic reasons. Similarly with a view to reduce our dependence on oil imports we may place a premium price on projects meant for locating petroleum deposits. Likewise we may choose to attach extra value to basic needs of people in target income groups. On the other hand, if the social value of a good is less than its efficiency value they are to be treated as demerits goods and their production should be discouraged. Production of alcoholic drinks, luxury goods such as high grade cosmetics, fancy cars etc. constitute unnecessary drain and diversion of resources. These 'normative issues' are an integral part of project appraisal and decision making in the real world.

The working arrangement requires that on-going projects are fully funded. The externally aided projects are also to be fully funded. Matching funds have to be provided for centrally sponsored schemes. The earmarked outlays are not allowed to be diverted. Similarly shortfall in funds meant for Minimum Needs Programmes and the Tribal Sub-Plan and Special Component Plan (plan for welfare of Scheduled Castes) is not permitted. The Tribal Sub-Plan and Special Component Plan are prepared separately and have to be religiously implemented. Over and above the plan, there is the 20-Point Programme which suggests that it constitutes the hard core. The above working arrangement would suggest that considerations other than purely economic reasoning have important influences in deciding the contents of the plan.

The State plans are supposed to take care of the regional problems, but their capacity to provide resources for fulfilling the regional needs is severely constrained as they are required to provide for on going schemes and centrally sponsored schemes on priority basis as stated above.

Importance of Balanced Regional Development

Planning for development has both time and spatial dimensions. The 'time' factor is very much in focus. The plans are five year plans, embodying programmes and schemes which have to be executed during the period. The investments vitally affect different aspects of our life, different sections of the population and different regions. In macro planning our primary concern is with aggregates. Planning from below is easier said than done; and though serious attempts have been made it has not taken roots as yet. The spatial aspect of planning has been fully recognised by our plans. The Third Plan asserted, 'whatever the present shortcomings, the aim must be that over a reasonable period all regions in the country should realise their potential for economic development and should obtain levels of living not far removed from those of the nation as a whole. Further, "A plan should be conceived not merely in broad national terms but should take into account the possibilities of development of resources in different regions of the country so as to spread the benefits of development without slowing down growth itself". The planning organisations at the ground level are too weak and lack the expertise and experience for proper planning. The critics of the planning process point to the fact that rich have become richer, and whereas some areas have prospered, large areas have continued to languish. It has now come to be realised that benefits of developmnet do not percolate to the poor or percolate too slowly to have any tangible impact. Similarly the linkage between growth centres and the hinterland are too weak to have impact in the short run. The big push theory or inducing development through setting up of major industries that have a strong developmental pull on the area is a fanciful theory which will take a long time to have significant impact. To the common man the giant industrial units offer no consolation, unless it is accompanied by improvement in his own living standard. In a democracy committed to socialism, improvement in the living standard of the people and reduction in inequalities in the distribution of income and wealth, as well as regional disparities are issues of vital importance.

In the introductory chapter reference was made to the phenomenon of circular and cumulative causation, i.e. there are several factors which can be responsible for retarded growth and they are mutually reinforcing. When economic factors are operating favourably there is an upsurge of economic activity. As production is subject to increasing returns, production costs will fall with increase in production. The region experiencing rapid growth will be able to increase its competitive advantage over the region which lags behind and thereby increase their incomes also.

The growth centre thus operates to the disadvantage of the dependent regions. As the growing regions offer investment opportunities and higher returns on investment; capital, labour and entrepreneurship will tend to migrate together to the developed centres. Faster growth rate leads to faster productivity growth. The backward regions will suffer as a result of competition and their growth will be further retarded. The above phenomenon is described as the backwash effect. The hypothesis is that once a region obtains a growth advantage it will tend to sustain it at the expense of other regions. Success breeds success and failure breeds failure.

It cannot be denied that major investment anywhere in the economy does exercise pull on the other areas, by creating demand for raw materials and goods and services. This demand is not met equally by all regions and therefore, the beneficial impact is unevenly distrubuted. There is also diffusion of knowledge and technology from the developed centres to less developed areas. These beneficial spread effects are, however, too weak compared to the stronger backwash effects.

As has been mentioned spread effects of industrial growth in major centres merely trickle down to backward regions and it is not enugh to offset the backwash effects. The result is that backward regions languish. This situation will continue for a long time, before negative economic forces emerge to offset the positive effects of expansion. Thus growing congestion, environmental degradation, higher costs of living, labour unrest will force industries to shift elsewhere. This will take a very long time to occur. The new centress will be chosen on the basis of advantages as assessed by the entrepreneurs in the situation prvailing at that time. Bihar's turn may come or it may have to wait longer. The moot question is whether Government, with certain growth and welfare objectives, can afford this process to take its natural course and to allow the people to suffer in the interegnum.

In spite of being rich in mineral deposits and availability of fertile land for cultivation, because of backwash effects, production is inadequate and Bihar is becoming increasingly dependant on supply not only of manufactured goods but also food, fruits and dairy products from outside the State. Agricultural labourers unable to find regular employment migrate to Punjab in large numbers, where by their hard work they contrubute to higher productivity.

Bihar seems to have been trapped in a vicious circle; created by over-population, landlessness, lack of employment opportunities, illiteracy, low productivity, poor health and paucity of resources to invest in infrastructure vital for development process, especially, power. Illiteracy has led to lack of motivation and disinterestedness among the general people to improve their lot. Low productivity and unemployment has contributed to poverty, which in turn has led to poor health. Further poverty has created a situation in which the economy is unable to generate enough resources internally for development and there is total dependence on the Centre for resources for development.

If we are really serious about development of the backward areas, Central Government has to intervene in a big way by providing incentives for investment in such areas and taking over responsibility for providing the necessary infrastructure support. We have already identified the thrust activities for Bihar; agriculture and allied activities, mineral based industries, competitive small scale industries. For this not only greater flow of funds has to take place but it is also to be ensured that the assistance is actually utillised. Lately our experience has been that the various bodies and institutions which are required to execute the development programmes have become corrupt and incompetent and in several cases defunct; they are, therefore, unable to perform the tasks assigned to them. The State Electricity Board is not able to pay for the power it receives. The State Finance Corporation is sick. So is the State Khadi Board. The rural credit disbursing agencies are also in poor health. These institutions have to be revamped. The corrupt and inefficient have to be ruthlessly weeded out to make the system operational. They have also to be freed from the control of corrupt politicians. Little attention has been given to these aspects and the maladies have been treated as fait accomplee, whereas the success and impact of greater flow of funds depends very much on our commitment to strengthen these executing agencies. It is a folly to shelter the inefficient. There is no dearth of competent people who can replace them. A system which encourages incompetent and corrupt to thrive at the cost of public institutions, without fail would lead to ruin and disaster.

In deciding the inter-sectoral allocations, we may not be guided by the economic and efficiency criteria, but within a sector the efficiency criterion has to be adhered to, else we will end up with lower productivity. We have investigated the policies in respect of the major sectors, which are critical for the developmental process. These are Power, Irrigation, Industries and Human Resources Development (Health and Education). Agriculture, in its present stage of development in India, is the most important sector in terms of its contribution to national product and also to total employment. Agricultural development is very much linked with development of power and irrrigation, as this will ensure the key input, water for irrigation for raising agricultural production. Growth of industries would help relieve the pressure of population on agriculture. Central to all development process are the human beings themselves and through education and better health we have to prepare the population for the critical and onerous tasks that lie ahead.

REFERENCES

1. G.M. Meier, *Leading Issues in Economic Development.*
2. Hia Myint, *The Economics of the Developing Countries*, 1980.
3. John Robinson, *Aspects of Development and Underdevelopment*, Cambridge University Press, 1979.
4. P. Bauer, *Dissent on Development.*
5. P. Bauer, Chapter-14 on Investment Fetish in *Equality, The Third World and Economic Delusion*, Wiedenfeld and Nicholson, 1981.
6. *World Development Reports* 1979, 1991, 1992, World Bank.
7. A.P. Thrilwall, *Growth and Development* - Fifth Edition, ELBS.
8. Todaro, Michael P., *Econ. Dev. in the Third World*, Orient & Longman.
9. UNIDO, 1978, *Guide to Practical Project Appraisal*, Oxford & IBH.

14

In Retrospect

We have tried to analyse the various causes of under development and backwardness. As we probe deeper into the subject we realise the complexity and immensity of the problem. It is as much due to penury of resources, as due to indolence and lack of enterprise on part of the people concerned. Wrong policies and indifferent execution of programmes meant to alleviate poverty and overcome backwardness can make matters worse. Regional planning should be as much the concern of the Union Government as the State Governments. As the Centre has decisive role in laying down the objectives and strategies for planned development, and since it controls most of the investible resources, it is Centre's keenness for balanced regional growth that really matters. If we adopt the poverty criterion for identifying the backward regions, we are faced with the appalling truth that but for a few pockets of prosperity around the major metropolis, the entire country may have to be treated as backward. Most of the rural regions describe themselves as backwards and compete for concessional assistance. The result is that regions which can lobby and put political pressure on Government succeed in being classified as backward and obtain concessional financial assistance. The genuinely backward regions who have no 'voice' are neglected. Thus the demand for Jharkhand State has made the Central Government and the State Government more responsive to the needs of tribals and the areas inhabited by them, though North Bihar by any criterion is equally poor and continues in poverty. The over-populated, flood ravaged North Bihar with higher incidence of unemployment, landlessness and illiteracy, prima facie has equally strong claim to concessional assistance.

Poverty is as much an absolute concept as a relative concept. We cannot insolate ourselves and judge progress purely on domestic scales. China has resolved to double its per capita income between 1985-2000. This will, no doubt, involve harsh decisions like restraints on consumption, restricting the size of the family and restrictions on individual's choice of occupation, etc. In India even if the targeted growth rate of 5 per cent annum is achieved, the per capita income at the end of the century would be only 50 per cent more than its present level and in real terms much less. Though poverty is sought to be reduced in the country by the end of the century to only 5 per cent of the total population, the fact remains that this would be only for statistical purposes, and by international standards, major chunk of the population would be without modern amenities of life and basic necessities for decent human existence. Poverty will continue to be pervasive in the backward regions. The plan documents strongly espouse the cause for eradication of poverty but it is not matched by similar commitment to promote balanced regional growth.

The national strategy to break vicious circle of poverty does not distinguish between developed regions and backward regions. Poverty is not evenly distributed. Agricultural labour, which constitutes upto 40 per cent of rural population in Bihar, has found more dependable source of employment in Punjab. Punjab's agriculture has come to depend heavily on cheep migratory labour from Eastern India. This migration, however, has not alleviated the poverty of the seasonal migrants, as the net wages are only marginally higher than those available at home. The rural employment programmes have failed to arrest the flow of migration.

Even the highly educated and skilled seek employment opportunities in the industrially developed centres, as Bihar offers limited opportunities. The State is denuded of talent and those who remain behind suffer the consequences of nepotism and decadent system.

For the international community, India is a poverty stricken and less developed region. Bihar with a per capita income equal to that of Bangladesh is even poorer. The difference is one of degree rather than kind. The main hurdle appears to be paucity of resources required for exploiting the available potential and lack of enterprising persons to take the lead in development activities. Bangladesh is an independent sovereign country and can bank on foreign assistance. Bihar has to depend on indigenous resources and on the assistance to be found within the Indian Union. With all the States competing for scarce resources, it becomes very difficult for the less developed States to procure central assistance.

Bihar is the strongest citadel of Mandalism in the country. It is because of unemployed youth being disappointed in their search for livelihood, which the stagnant economy is unable to provide "Reservation" raised hopes, howsoever elusive and the backward caste leaders shrewdly used it for rallying the backward castes under their banner. It is another matter that such jobs in a stagnant economy would be few and will be grabbed by the creamy layer and by the resourceful among backwards. Only through accelerated growth rate more jobs would be available.

Caste allegiance, religious fanaticism, communal loyalties, regional chauvinism and linguistic affinities create a confused situation in which real issues are suppressed. The political parties for their narrow and selfish interests fan up regionalism, casteism and communalism. In the process they cause irrepairable damage to the society by generating feelings of hatred among fellow men and frustration and despair among those who want establish themselves on the basis of ability and hard work. Only unanimity of interests can generate the driving force for development.

Corruption at the decision making level has emerged as the greatest threat to development. Such a Coterie only pays lip service to the welfare of the people, their main objective is to strengthen and enrich themselves by exploiting the weak. The anti-corruption machinery is drawn from the bureaucracy and totally subordinated to the political executive. They dare not expose their political masters, whose bounty they enjoy. They select only such public servants who can fulfill their evil designs. When people at top become corrupt no effective control can be exercised over corruption at lower levels. The entire administration becomes exploitative. The poor farmers have to pay illegal subscriptions for getting water for their fields or permits for fertilizers and seeds. They have to pay commissions to get loans. A class of professional intermediaries 'Brokers' has emerged, who charge speed money for getting work done in government offices. The officers demand their share as they have to make payments for being in a particular post. The Ministers demand money with impunity in the name of raising funds for party or elections. The contractors, who have to pay, do it by doing sub-standard work or enhancing the estimates. The businessmen similarly sell goods in black market. Development is the casualty and the poor people suffer.

The upheavals in 1967, 1977 and 1989 have occurred at regular intervals in a cycle. But the change of Governments which we witnessed did not bring about any qualitative change. The approach, motivations and style of functioning remained the same. The policies and programmes, apart from cosmetic changes remained the same. The governments which emerged, continued to follow populist programmes with little concern for strengthening the economy or attending to the urgent problems facing the people. On each occasion people were seeking a viable alternative. The disillusionment which followed each time is not a happy augury for democracy in the country in future. The new set of rulers were as avaricions as their predecessors. They lacked the character and capacity to come to grips with challenges of development. Instead they blamed the 'centre' for step motherly treatment to cover up their own failure.

The situation becomes really grave when the legislators exert their influence to obtain contracts for public works. If those who have to keep vigil over public expenditure, themselves become the agencies for government spending, there would be no control over improper expenditure. It is not surprising, therefore, that our programmes suffer major distortions in the process of implementation. The corrupt elements in the bureaucracy aid and abet this process for their own selfish gains. In a backward economy, these negative influences operate with impunity, rendering the development process meaningless.

Economics is subordinate to politics in a democratic set up. Present system of elections has enabled large number of muscle men and persons with criminal antecedents to be elected to legislature. They are averse to reason and impatient of rules and regulations. Programmes are drawn mainly to garner wider political support rather than to strengthen people economically. Development is irrelevant to such leadership. The prevalent emotion in backward regions is of servility towards persons, whose decisions determine the course of events. Chronic poverty and ignorance reduces society to impotence in the face of hunger, natural calamities and exploitation. Any plan of action or strategy for development can succeed only with enlightened persons, who are committed to such programme and zealous of development. So people will have to bury their differences and shed their prejudies and combine in electing a government, which is genuinely concerned about eradication of poverty. The media, too, has a crucial role in enforcing/moral and social accountability in persons who wield executive authority.

In essence the strategy for development has to be very pragmatic and cater to the specific needs of the people and area. We have conflicting options. We must concentrate on the activities and thrust areas. We have to aim at greater well being. The strategy must decide on an appropriate technology which gives priority to the use of indigenous resources and local skills, and which is resource and energy saving. With limited resources and pressing demands, the major problems, which are thwarting our development efforts, should be identified and checked effectively. The strategy for development, therefore, must simultaneously aim at checking over-population, eradicating illiteracy and reducing poverty. The critical sectors are power, irrigation for agricultural development and industries for creating employment opportunities outside agriculture. Once the priorities have been decided on social, considerations, investment decisions have to be guided by the efficiency criterion i.e., selection of schemes which give higher return per unit of investment. Efficient execution of plan schemes depends not only on well conceived policy decisions in respect of investment outlays and our ability to raise efficient resources for the purpose; but also on the capacity of the organization to execute the programmes honestly and efficiently and also on the sincerity and commitment of leadership to development goals.

Index